RECOGNISING ACHIEVEMENT

A2 Media Studies for OCR

Jacqueline Bennett, Tanya Jones and Julian McDougall

Edited by Richard Harvey

Hodder & Stoughton
A MEMBER OF THE HODDER HEADLINE GROUP

The authors and publishers would like to thank the following for permission to reproduce copyright illustrative material:

Time Out for the cover on page 133; *Private Eye* for the cover on page 108; *Men's Health*, Rodale Publishing UK Ltd © 2002 for the cover on page 200 and in the colour plate section; © News International Newspapers Limited 2002 for the front pages of *The Times* and the *Sun* on page 44; the *Guardian* and Popperfoto for the front page on page 44; Moviestore Collection Ltd for the images from *Band of Brothers* on page 9 and in the colour plate section; the Ronald Grant Archive for the following images: Pierce Brosnan on page 14 and in the colour plate section, *Little Man Tate* on page 89 and in the colour plate section, Gurinder Chadha on page 91 and in the colour plate section, *Bhaji on the Beach* on page 91 and in the colour plate section, Sally Potter on page 92 and in the colour plate section, *Orlando* on page 92 and in the colour plate section, *East is East* on page 170 and in the colour plate section and *Asoka* poster on page 182 and in the colour plate section; Advertising Archives for the following images: *Economic Disaster* poster on page 111 and in the colour plate section and *New Labour New Danger* poster on page 114 and in the colour plate section and *Labour* poster on page 113; ActionPlus for the images of David Beckham on page 126 and a snowboarder on page 127; The Kobal Collection/Warner Bros/Mountain, Peter for the image from *Harry Potter and the Philosopher's Stone* on page 185 and in the colour plate section; © BMG UK and Ireland Limited for pages from the Westlife website (www.westlife.com) on page 58 and in the colour plate section; Channel Four Television for the image from *Brasseye* on page 109; 2DTV for the image from *2DTV* on page 109; BBC Picture Archives for the images of the *Tweenies* on page 118 and in the colour plate section and *Blue Peter* presenters on page 118 and in the colour plate section; Granada plc for the image from *Night and Day* on page 152 and in the colour plate section; © Languevin Jacques/CORBIS for the image of September 11th on page 156 and in the colour plate section; © Rufus F. Folkks/CORBIS for the image of Jodie Foster on page 89 and in the colour plate section; © 1998 Aardman Animations Ltd for the image of the set from *Morph* from *Cracking Animation: The Aardman Book of 3-D Animation* on page 79; © travisonline.com owned by Independiente Ltd for pages from the website on page 58 and in the colour plate section; the Conservative Party for the poster on page 112 and in the colour plate section; the Liberal Democrat Party for the poster on page 112 and in the colour plate section; © DC Thomson & Co for the *Beano* covers on page 37; © DC Comics for the *Superman* covers on pages 37 and 38 (*Superman*, *Action Comics* and *The Adventures of Superman* are trademarks of DC Comics. All Rights Reserved).

The authors and publishers would like to thank the following for permission to reproduce copyright material:

© BBC for an extract from the website on page 9; Bernard Crick and the *Guardian* for the article on pages 22–23; *Rolling Stone* for the article on pages 98–99; Richard Wray and the *Guardian* for the article on page 103; *Daily Mail* for the article on page 121; Danny Leigh and the *Guardian* for the article on pages 136–138; Sue MacGregor for the extract on page 159.

Every effort has been made to obtain necessary permission with reference to copyright material. The publishers apologise if inadvertently any sources remain unacknowledged and will be glad to make the necessary arrangements to correct any ommissions at the earliest opportunity.

Orders: please contact Bookpoint Ltd, 130 Milton Park, Abingdon, Oxon OX14 4SB. Telephone: (44) 01235 827720. Fax: (44) 01235 400343. Lines are open from 9.00 – 6.00, Monday to Saturday, with a 24 hour message answering service. Email address: orders@ bookpoint.co.uk

British Library Cataloguing in Publication Data
A catalogue record for this title is available from the British Library

ISBN 0 340 847778

302.23
BEN

First Published 2002
Impression number   10 9 8 7 6 5 4
Year   2007 2006 2005 2004 2003

Artwork by Chartwell Illustrators
Typeset by Fakenham Photosetting Limited, Fakenham, Norfolk
Printed in Great Britain for Hodder & Stoughton Educational, a division of Hodder Headline, 338 Euston Road, London NW1 3BH by Martins The Printers, Berwick-upon-Tweed

Contents

Introduction

You will now have completed the work for your Advanced Subsidiary GCE and in doing so you will have studied a range of media texts and topics, as well as the construction and deconstruction of media products. These studies have been within the context of the key conceptual areas of Media Forms and Conventions, Media Institutions, Media Audiences and Media Representations.

This book builds on the work you have done at AS Level and although it is freestanding you will benefit from using it in conjunction with its complementary publication, *AS Media Studies for OCR*.

Although the content and structure of this book is targeted specifically at the OCR Specification, it covers all the key concepts and relates well to the A2 Specifications currently available from other awarding bodies.

You are given full and detailed guidance to enable you to engage in more advanced skill levels that relate to A2 and assistance in developing investigative techniques when undertaking independent research and analysis. In addition, help is provided to develop a range of critical arguments in response to a variety of issues and debates. Advice is given to apply contemporary theories to media texts and their contexts.

This book follows the pattern of the OCR Units, the first being the Advanced Practical Production. In Section 1 you are given advice and practical hints progressing from the development of a basic idea through to completion. You are offered full guidance to refine your technical skills and devise your own production brief. You will also develop your Critical Evaluation skills and be able to assess the process and outcome of your own media production. You are shown how to work through the problems and difficulties you may encounter when trying to reach your final goal. All the key concepts are fully addressed. Furthermore, the Bibliography and Websites Section at the end of the book has specialist references dedicated to each medium. A case study is offered to give more detailed reference for exploring the making of a product within each medium. Basic advice is given on the production of a Production Log but more detailed guidance is given in Section 4 which is dedicated to Writing Skills.

Section 2 gives detailed preparation for an innovative form of assessment at A Level. The Critical Research Study offers you the opportunity to develop your own individual research skills and identify and explore your own specific topic with certain parameters. This could be a daunting task, but you are guided through all the stages from choosing a suitable topic, through research methodology to applying critical theory. There are carefully chosen case study examples for set areas of study.

Section 3 on Media Issues and Debates draws together key concepts that you have studied throughout the course. Advice is given for approaches to individual topics for the examination areas of Broadcast, Film and Print. Preparatory activities are suggested and each topic has a practice examination as well as an extension activity.

Section 4 on Writing Skills is a self-contained section which guides you through the problems you may encounter when presenting written work for assessment. Guidance for each unit is given, including the written elements of the Advanced Practical Production unit, from early note-taking to the finished Critical Evaluation. Remember, however, that the Production Log does not have to be submitted in its entirety for external moderation. It is primarily for teacher/centre assessment. Assistance for the Critical Research Study takes you through finding resources, note-taking, creating your own critical response and presenting your findings. The section on Media Issues and Debates provides advice on overall structure, including paragraphing and language. Specific examples are given for each selection of the topic areas, covering sample examination questions and essay plans.

The glossary is substantial and takes account of the terms and concepts that you will encounter while studying A2 Media Studies.

You will find that although the book can be used as a whole-class textbook, the advice and guidance given also make it a perfect self-help text. This book is all you need to guide you safely through to the final A2 assessments.

Section 1
Advanced Practical Production

Introduction

At AS Level, practical **production** required the creation of a media text from a set brief. At A2 the choice of which text to create is open. There are no set briefs. However, the requirements for the project are rather different and more demanding. They are also intended to be more interesting.

The most important point to remember, when beginning to prepare for A2 production, is that you are not allowed to work in the same medium as you did at AS Level. As part of your evaluation for A2, you are asked to identify which of the designated AS briefs you completed and to state that you are not working in the same medium. This is done to ensure that you get practical experience with at least two mediums during your course and to give you a chance to demonstrate and translate your skills across media. Remember that you are allowed to use the same medium for delivery if the textual intention is different. For example, you may choose to be assessed on film for A2, having done television at AS Level (both submitted on video) or choose a magazine at A2, having done print advertising at AS Level (both submitted on paper).

You should be aware that the work is expected to be realised to a far higher standard at A2 with a highly competent use of the necessary technology. Several times throughout this section we reiterate that you should be competent with the equipment before you start this project. You will be marked down if your work suffers because of your technical skills. However, you will not be penalised in any way for technical limitations that are outside your control, such as degrading tape quality due to being recorded from VHS to computer and then back again. Nevertheless, you could lose marks if this process has been repeated several times unnecessarily, resulting in significant distortion.

The A2 Specification stipulates that the purpose of this unit '*is to assess the origination and construction of a media text, demonstrating technical skills and conceptual understanding (Assessment Objective 8). Candidates should also demonstrate critical evaluation of the process and outcome of their own media production (Assessment Objective 9)*'.

Here, the key differences from AS are that the work is expected to be realised to a high standard both technically (an extension of AS standards) and conceptually. This was not so significant at AS; provided there was an element of conceptual understanding, the intention was to demonstrate application of fundamental media skills.

At A2 the choice of brief is intentionally open so that candidates can demonstrate significant research and ownership of their chosen text. This text must not be created in isolation, but in direct relation to the chosen **genre** and medium, with explicit address to **audience** and institution. In other words, all the factors that are part of professional practice are required at this level.

Thus, the Critical Evaluation is significantly different from AS and this is reflected in the higher proportion of marks allocated and the requirement to produce 3000 words. For each of the topic areas discussed below, some comments have been made about the content of the four different sections of the evaluation, directly related to the medium and task discussed. However, in Section 4 of this book, there is far more information about how to structure your writing tasks for A2 and how to approach an evaluation. You should make sure you read Section 4 in conjunction with this section.

You are free to choose your own topic area for A2, using one of the specified mediums: film, television, print, radio, ICT/new media and cross media. It is unlikely that you will find a media text that does not employ one of these mediums so your choice is completely open. You must remember that it is central to this unit to show synoptic knowledge and understanding of key conceptual areas and their related issues and debates. Therefore, it may be sensible for your whole class to work within one topic area or related area. This will allow for shared knowledge and understanding and the opportunity for detailed analysis of relevant texts and exploration of key concepts in relation to this area.

As at AS Level, the permitted maximum group number is four, to ensure equal and comparable work distribution among group members. There is no minimum group size so you could work on your own, but A2 projects are fairly substantial conceptually and individual work may be excessively demanding. Each group member must produce an individual evaluation (although the research and preparation can be shared) and it should be obvious that the evaluations have been completed individually. Your group can duplicate **storyboards** and other planning sheets or deconstruction examples for the appendix of your evaluations, as long as you have all been involved in them.

It is important that you write about your particular role and responsibilities within the group as part of your evaluation. You must highlight your individual contribution and reflect upon your individual learning and group practice in the evaluation. Again, you will find more comments about this in Section 4 of the book.

When your project is marked, it is marked out of 120 and the breakdown is as follows:

- Planning – 30 marks
- Construction – 60 marks
- Critical Evaluation – 30 marks

As you can see, half of the marks are awarded for planning and evaluation at A2 to reflect the importance placed on conceptual learning and construction, not just technical competence.

Planning

Marks will be awarded for time and equipment being organised properly and the production schedule being sustained (this means that the project basically runs to time, not that marks could be deducted for each missed print deadline or delayed shoot). It is a requirement that you submit a storyboard or equivalent documentation for all time-based work and evidence of drafting for print-based work. If this evidence is excluded from your evaluation, you cannot be credited with the marks for planning – no matter how much thought has gone into your project. Your teacher will write about how you have planned and organised your time and what planning documentation you have used, so make sure that you provide the evidence to support the work you undertake. It is not permitted at A2 to submit a storyboard as a realised project in its own right, only as supporting documentation for planning evidence.

Notice as well that you are required to define a specific target audience and to test your project on that audience for asssessment in the evaluation. You should identify this audience and plan how you will test your artefact during the planning process. Remember to allow time between completion of the artefact and your final submission date to test market your artefact properly and to analyse the feedback you receive.

Construction

You are expected to be technically competent at this level and this is fundamental for your construction marks. Work that is not technically secure will not be very successful at A2 Level, despite its potential. You are expected to use and/or subvert established forms and conventions to make meaning and to make this meaning clear to your target audience as required. You must ensure that your artefact is a credible media product, realised to a high standard and evidencing awareness and understanding of the relevant conceptual areas for your chosen medium and task.

Do not send in your master copy of your work for assessment. You should always retain the master copy and submit a copy instead. If the work is mislaid or lost during transit, for example, and you do not retain a copy, you may find you cannot submit. Allowances cannot be made for work lost in this way, except by express permission from the Board in exceptional circumstances. As at AS Level, you may find that your work is not returned by the Board for some reason and so, unless you have your master copy, your work could be lost to you.

Critical Evaluation

As already indicated, the approach to the Critical Evaluation is discussed in detail in Section 4 of this book. Suggestions about possible content are made in Section 4 for the various examples offered during this section. You should provide your planning evidence as appendices to your evaluation and it is important that you word process this evaluation and present it clearly. It is usually worth numbering the pages because 3000 words can involve a substantial amount of pages. Make sure you have your name on each page in case your work becomes separated.

Before you begin

It is worth reading this section of the book in conjunction with *AS Media Studies for OCR*. Because you worked in a different medium at AS Level, you should look at the relevant section for the medium you are working in now to identify and reflect upon the relevant technical competencies and to refresh your memory about the technical standards expected. It is recommended that you read all of the material in this chapter and not just that related to your chosen medium, since there may be useful information in other sections which will help you with your work.

PART ONE
Film Production

Film remains the cornerstone of media production and analysis and it is a global industry. As a medium, film is the oldest form of moving image media and thus, arguably, far more mature and sophisticated in nature than television. Television also tends to be a more realist form whereas film runs the gamut from archetypal Hollywood realist traditions, through **art-house** and more complex texts to **avant-garde** and experimental texts that may be considered too obscure for the majority of television audiences. As a medium for production work, therefore, film offers a vast range of possibilities. In this section we will consider two possible productions but you should bear in mind the range of opportunities available, and reflect carefully upon **form**, style and genre before you begin.

Audience and institution

You may have studied some aspects of film institution in detail elsewhere in your course. Remember to consider the type of institution that would produce your film and how this will affect and influence the production.

If a film is to be produced by a Hollywood studio, the studio is unlikely to invest substantial amounts of money unless a clear audience is identified. The genre, stars and format of the film will be directly related to the audience expectations. Hollywood studios do not always take 'risks' with new films or with divergent approaches. Investors do not usually wish to invest in speculative ventures but prefer tried and tested formats.

However, many art-house and avant-garde films are produced as aesthetic projects with substantially less focus on audience and institution. This is one of the reasons that such films are frequently perceived as 'non-commercial'. The director, cast and crew are able to focus on the film itself, without having to compromise for commercial purposes. At times, this can lead to accusations of 'self-indulgence' and to films that become too obscure to communicate to an audience on any level. If you decide to create an experimental or avant-garde piece, be careful not to allow this to happen to your film. For the purposes of A2 Media Studies, you must produce a mass media text that is credible in a commercial market.

This does not mean that you cannot work experimentally, but you should be aware of the inherent dangers.

Production facilities

It is important not to attempt a production in this medium unless you are competent with the equipment. If you want a particular effect, it can often be added during **editing** or **post-production**. If you are working with non-linear editing equipment you can add 'film noise' effects, for example, in most editing or post-production software, as well as the range of filters, effects, distortions and so forth which might be used in less conventional film formats. The use of a **fish-eye lens** to distort a picture and intensify the focus on the middle of the picture, for instance, can be added fairly easily in post-production if you do not have access to a fish-eye lens for your camera.

You may be fortunate enough to have access to a range of production equipment, ranging from 16 mm film (still favoured by many directors and taught at many film schools), through conventional video equipment to high-end production equipment. You are likely to have access to conventional video equipment, which is more than adequate for this production module. If you have access to other equipment, it may be more suitable for your project – especially if you are working with more avant-garde intentions. However, you should only consider using this if you have previous experience with such equipment.

Remember that although the rules for AS and A2 production stipulate that you may not work in the same medium twice, the exception is that you may choose to use video to present television work and film work, since they are substantially different products but are presented using the same technology. Nevertheless, if you have access to non-linear film and editing equipment, you may decide to work with a 16:9 screen size to reflect film rather than television. Make sure you do not distort your work by rendering out to a different screen size.

Case Study

Use of visual effects to create a particular effect in post-production

Cinesite, a post-production house based in Soho, London, has spent the last 18 months working on the ground-breaking digital effects that make **Band of Brothers** look so stunning. Collaborating closely with Visual Effects Supervisor **Angus Bickerton**, the **Cinesite** team have produced most of the breathtaking sequences in the series, including the astonishing parachute-drop at D-Day, which features 300 computer-generated parachutists.

Cinesite, which is currently working on **Harry Potter and the Sorcerer's Stone** and whose past credits include **Tomb Raider, Mission: Impossible 2, Entrapment** and **The World Is Not Enough**, is also responsible for one of the most dazzling sequences in the whole 10-hour series: the march of the German POWs out of Germany with Allied troops moving in the opposite direction on either side of them.

The company is also behind the natural de-saturated look of the drama. The directors of **Band of Brothers** were keen to convey visually the tone and intensity of how the Second World War might have felt and how viewers might expect footage from that period to look. Colourist **Luke Rainey** spent weeks researching original Second World War footage in order to get the look absolutely right.

See figure 1.

Co-executive producer **Tony To**, oversaw the striking de-saturated look that characterises the show. "Why did **Saving Private Ryan** work so well? And for us, it was because we remember the Second World War in black and white from movies like **The Longest Day**, but reality was, and is, lived in colour. So, trying to bridge that gap, we arrived at this half-way point between colour and black and white which is this de-saturated look that we use.'"

Ken Dailey, digital effects supervisor at **Cinesite**, sums up the philosophy of the SFX team: "I get immense satisfaction out of producing a digital effects shot that is completely seamless."

See figure 2.

Although this focuses on an example from television, the principles of colour and **style** that Spielberg sought for this production are a good example of the use of colour and film stock to produce the deliberately grainy de-saturated effect which was integral to the intention of Band of Brothers. Without these effects, the series would have appeared too contemporary and 'made for TV'. It would have lost the documentary feel and intensity of action which made it so successful.

Information taken from http://www.bbc.co.uk/bandofbrothers/features/visual_effects.shtml
Look at this website for some photographic examples of how special effects were used in the series.

Technical quality of final production

Remember that you are assessed on your skills with filming, editing and post-production work. Your work is marked for technical competence in relation to these skills. If poor **framing**, wobbly shots and awkward **jump cuts** mar your work then this will be deemed unsuccessful against the specified technical criteria for A2 Level work. If, however, the final quality of your video is not as strong as you would like due to the equipment available to you (for example, if your rushes are uploaded to a computer over an ordinary VHS cable, edited and then exported back to VHS using domestic video equipment) this will not impact on your assessment.

This is an important point with sound as well. Good quality live sound for your film work is difficult to achieve without professional equipment but there are some things you can do to improve the sound quality. Whenever possible avoid using the built-in microphones on the video camera but use the 'mic in' socket for a better microphone. Set up a simple boom mike (tie the microphone onto a broom handle if you need to) and point it at the action while keeping it out of shot or use radio mikes attached to your actors if you can. There is more information about sound quality when recording in *AS Media Studies for OCR* if you want to look back.

It is also worth remembering at this point that you do not lose marks for the quality of the acting. You are being assessed on your film production skills and cannot be assessed on the acting. You will however be judged on composition, costume and framing so you do need to think carefully about these elements.

Case Study

A film trailer

One good option for film production at A2 Level is a film trailer. A film trailer is a marketing device for a new release with certain clearly defined conventions. It provides plenty of opportunities to produce something dynamic and visually gripping that is designed to really 'sell' a film.

There are basically two types of film trailer – **teaser trailers**, which are usually about 1 minute or 1.5 minutes long and full trailers, which are usually 2 minutes long. A teaser trailer is released some time before the actual release of the film, whereas a full trailer is released fairly close to the film première to heighten interest and excitement. Film distribution companies usually produce a range of trailers for different placements and different audiences. The trailer shown at the multiplex will probably differ from the trailer shown on the front of a video release and may be different to the trailer used on television. Most distribution companies produce different trailers for different international markets and may use varying trailers on mirror websites for different countries. If the film is marketed on the back of other genre films, there may even be more versions of the trailer cut to match these different audiences.

Preliminary tasks

There are two primary decisions that you need to make at the very beginning of your film trailer project. You need to decide what film genre you will be working within and then to consider whether you will be producing a teaser trailer or a full trailer. Your identification of the target audience, **ideology**, genre codes and conventions to use, likely institution and placement will follow from these decisions.

A single teaser trailer would be appropriate as an individual project but for a group project a series of teasers or a full trailer would be sufficiently substantial.

Questions to ask

- What genre is the trailer?
- What sort of trailer will it be?
- Where will it be shown?
- What is the target audience for this trailer?
- How does this relate to the target audience for the film itself?
- What key genre elements will be employed?
- What will be the key point for the trailer?
- What ideology will the trailer establish?
- What studio/film company will you assign the film to?
- What will be the marketing points for the film (e.g. stars, director, themes, etc.)

Identifying the film

Having identified the context for the film and the relevant constructs, you should think about the film itself. You do not need to complete a detailed screenplay – a 500-word plot synopsis and some basic institutional information such as that identified above will enable you to create and target your trailer effectively. You should plan:

- A title
- A 500-word plot synopsis
- Detailed statement of genre and target audience
- Institutional information, i.e. name of studio, distribution company and release dates
- Star names (if relevant) with justification
- Themes and ideologies employed in the film
- Context for distribution of trailer (e.g. Will it be shown at the multiplex prior to similar films or is it to be shown in a different context? Is it a national or international trailer?)

Many British films have different titles when they are marketed in the US, for example, *Harry Potter and the Philosopher's Stone* (2001) was renamed *Harry Potter and the Sorcerer's Stone* for American audiences.

ACTIVITIES

Either by using one of the websites recommended on p.258, by linking directly to the websites for various film releases, or by looking at the trailers of films from the intros to videos, identify a range of four recent releases within your chosen genre and deconstruct the trailers in relation to the questions below.

Analysis

- Identify the institution for each of these trailers and the institutional codes employed by the institution
- What are the key selling points of each trailer?
- How does each trailer establish the genre, mood and expectations of the film?
- Which of these trailers is more or less successful for you? Can you identify which elements are more or less successful?
- Research the demographics of the target audience for each trailer. Do they match the target audience for the films?
- How is the audience explicitly targeted in each trailer?
- Is there an identifiable format across these trailers? Does this apply for other trailers? Is it successful?
- Why are trailers constructed this way?

DISCUSSION

When researching film production to prepare for the Critical Evaluation for your artefact, it can help to undertake some more theoretical research in advance.

- Are trailers a good way to market films?
- Why are trailers so popular?
- Do successful trailers depend on enigma codes?
- What influence does the institution have on the style and format of a trailer?
- To what extent must a trailer conform to audience expectations if it is to be successful?
- Why was the marketing campaign for *The Blair Witch Project* (1999) so successful?
- How many trailers are in a typical marketing package at a cinema? Are there institutional controls on these packages? Who decides which films to advertise and where?

Case Study

Constructing the trailer

Planning

Having identified the institutional context, film and target audience for your trailer, you can begin to plan the trailer itself. You will need to complete a detailed storyboard for the trailer, part of which could be included as an appendix to your Critical Evaluation, and provide evidence of comparative study of commercial trailers and theoretical grounding for your trailer. You should make sure you justify each of these decisions in the evaluation.

You will need to decide:
- Where in the trailer you wish the title of the film to appear
- How the title should appear – font, colour, position, duration, effects etc.
- What the opening and closing screen of the trailer should be
- What the soundtrack will be – for example, will it involve a voice-over (Male/female? Age? Accent?) and dialogue for 'extracts' from the film or will it be mostly musical?
- If you are using 'extracts' from the film for the trailer that you will need to script, storyboard and film first to incorporate during editing
- What special effects or graphics are required
- Where the institutional information such as the name of the distribution company and release dates will appear
- Ways in which the trailer targets the audience
- How the trailer matches audience expectations and relates to the film itself

Recommended for your Production Log
- Storyboard, shooting script and continuity sheets
- Annotated deconstruction of contemporary trailers
- Drafts for graphics, fonts etc. and sample screens from trailer
- Logging sheets and notes for example if working with a non-linear system
- Production Log and individual accountability information
- Personal schedules and project timeline

It is the producer's responsibility to ensure that all the necessary equipment is ready and that material is edited on time. This does not mean that the producer does all of these jobs, just that they supervise them.

Titles

You will probably need to use a titling programme to overlay the necessary institutional information for your trailer. If you are working with a linear system, you will probably have access to a titler, which will allow a degree of creative freedom when constructing the titles. However, if you are restrained in titling you can indicate this in your evaluation. If effective use is made of the available technology, this will be rewarded more highly than work that does not make creative and appropriate use of opportunities, but you must show evidence for this in your evaluation.

Still images

Still images can be an effective device in a trailer – they can be shown on their own or as part of a larger montage to highlight key points in the film or to signal a star presence, for example. They are used cautiously in many genres, but where used effectively, a series of still images with a powerful soundtrack can successfully establish expectations and excitement for a film.

Action sequences

One of the most common devices in trailers is the use of brief clips from the film, interspersed with the voice-over.

These clips can be very short to create **enigma**, or they can be longer with interaction between characters which creates **disequilibrium** only restored and resolved by the film itself. It is sometimes said that the most effective trailers give enigmatic moments from a powerful construct and plot to attract the audience but that less successful trailers reveal too much of the plot and show how the disequilibrium will be resolved in the film, making it almost unnecessary to see the film.

Sample trailer decisions

If you were creating a trailer for a new James Bond movie, for example, you might decide to follow the traditional format for a Bond trailer, but using original images and constructed graphics.

This is a useful example because there are certain key images and sounds which an audience would expect to see in a trailer for a new Bond film; thus the trailer has to be sufficiently formulaic to satisfy audience expectations. Each new actor playing Bond causes disruption in the audience and it is interesting to note that the formula is becoming more rigid and is almost a genre in itself in order to ensure a degree of continuity. The Bond genre has become so precisely defined throughout the globe, it is unlikely that you would wish to tamper with the formula without a very good reason.

There are plenty of ways to demonstrate ownership of the trailer. You could construct your own title overlays and import these into your editing programme at the appropriate points. You should set up still images of many of the set-piece graphics of a Bond trailer such as the MCU (medium close up) with the gun. Use an actor dressed appropriately – some of the most successful examples have commented upon the genre and ideology by employing a female Bond.

In this instance, try hard not to use any found material, for example, material copied from existing trailers, since you cannot be given credit for found material. The exception is probably the Bond theme, which appears at some point in all Bond trailers and movies. Consider where it appears in the trailers and why.

Again, you are unlikely to be able to recreate one of the standard Bond 'set pieces' of destruction, but an effective substitute can be made with some simple shots and some manipulation. For example, some shots taken from a moving car with a gun appearing in the viewfinder, used when editing with sound effects of bullets being fired or maybe with the footage speeded up to suggest that the car was moving very fast. You may be able to use a non-linear editing suite to merge some live-action shooting with separate shots of fires and merge these layers to create the trailer.

This is a typical shot from a recent Bond trailer, using many of the codes and conventions typical of Bond films. It would not be difficult to set up and shoot a similar image – it could be manipulated in a graphics programme if necessary. See figure 3.

Case Study

Extract from a new film release

Planning

If you choose to produce an extract from a film, you should anticipate producing up to a maximum of five minutes of film. You will need to decide what to include in your extract, what text it is taken from and to consider why this is an appropriate extract to use. You probably will not want to use a section too close to the beginning of the film because the extract may become an opening sequence, with focus on titles and graphics and so forth rather than on **narrative**. You are not allowed to produce the opening sequence of a thriller as this is one of the set briefs for the AS Level. The difference between producing an opening sequence or title sequence and an extract is the focus on narrative.

Film drama is based around conflict. As you know from your study of narrative theory, there are various ways of identifying and analysing this conflict but the basis is still conflict – whether explored through opposition, myth, enigma or disequilibrium.

When planning an extract it is worth beginning with a focus on the key conflict or resolution that you want to feature. Having decided on your complete narrative, you will need to identify what happens in your extract. You might choose to create an original narrative and produce a storyboard for a pivotal moment within it or you might want to create a scene 'that never was' for an existing text.

You may wish to produce a conventional Hollywood action/adventure film, a horror film or a British gangster movie. You may have the knowledge and competence (or interest) to produce a more stylised film extract – perhaps an extract from a new **Bollywood** production or a **post-modern** extravaganza such as *Moulin Rouge* (2001). You might wish to produce a complete short film, using and exploring the philosophies of the Dogma 95 group.

Questions to ask before you begin
- What is the key event in this extract?
- How does it relate to the primary narrative?
- Who is your target audience?
- What devices will you employ to ensure you target this audience directly?
- What will happen in the extract?
- What **mise-en-scène** will you use?
- What locations will you use?
- What actors and additional crew will you need?
- What will be the opening and closing screens of your extract?
- How will you introduce the extract?
- How long will your extract be?
- What genre will you work in?
- If you are working from an existing film, how do you justify this new scene?
- If you are creating an extract from a new film, which institution do you envisage producing the film?
- What ideology will you be promoting in the extract?

Possible prompts
If you have not seen any of the work of the Dogma 95 group, you may be aware of their influence on directors and hence on films. Directors who choose to work within the Dogma 95 directives are asked to swear a 'vow of chastity' to focus their filmmaking on basic principles, moving as far away as possible from conventional Hollywood movies dependent on post-production, CGI (Computer Graphic Images) and complex editing.

Although this seems simple, it is a creative challenge to ensure that the quality of your basic camera work, lighting, mise-en-scène and composition is strong enough to carry your text. *The Blair Witch Project* (1999) was heavily influenced by Dogma principles and is a very successful example, although this success has not been repeated.

Genre texts

There are many genres that provide accessible opportunities for the construction of a short film extract. You might, for example, consider an extract from a new British gangster movie or a new Western. There are many examples of each genre which you can study to identify genre conventions, audience expectations and typical visual and aural codes. You can use these to construct a conventional genre text or a 'modern twist' on a genre for a more contemporary audience. If you choose to produce a text that mocks or tests genre conventions in any way, try to avoid a **parody** of a genre. It is difficult to parody a whole genre successfully and the attempts are not always funny. While there are notable successful parodies, such as *Naked Gun* (1988) or *Blazing Saddles* (1974), there are many more that were unsuccessful.

A conventional Western extract could involve a gunfight at high noon in a deserted Western town. After the hero has dispatched the villains, he would ride off into the sunset across a vast desert plain. A more modern twist on this might involve female gunfighters in a different environment. You can also 'translate' a genre for a different effect – *Star Wars* could be viewed as being a Western but set in outer space.

There are other cinematic traditions that you may wish to focus on. For example, Bollywood films are heavily stylised with much use of song and dance – usually to overlaid audio tracks, fantastical settings, extensive uses of gesture, visual set pieces and symbolism to communicate meaning to an audience and extensive use of production effects including dissolves, **wipes** and picture in picture. These are less common in Hollywood productions but may appeal to you. As with all genres, you should not embark on a production until you have completed some research, but Bollywood extracts can be produced fairly simply. The extravagance and complexity of a Bollywood text is often offered by the lavish and brightly coloured costumes against the fantastical settings. This creates an artificial and symbolic visual environment, but with simplistic characterisation, quickly establishing stereotypes and the expectations to tell a story.

You may wish to produce a more avant-garde text, ranging from a simple piece in the style of early French New Wave, through German experimental theatre to contemporary post-modern films. It is difficult to give general suggestions on how to approach such a project since, by definition, most avant-garde filmmaking rejects conventions and categorisation. If you wish to create an avant-garde piece, you should ensure that you are familiar with the philosophy and practice of your chosen film style. Do not forget that this project must be a mass media text, produced for a specific target audience within a specified institutional context, not an 'art' film which is produced without awareness of audience or cinematic context. It is easy to become self-indulgent, as mentioned before, and this detracts from the nature of mass media text and can be penalised – despite all of your hard work.

DISCUSSION

- The final section of the Dogma 95 'Vow of Chastity' states:

'*Furthermore I swear as a director to refrain from personal taste! I am no longer an artist. I swear to refrain from creating a "work", as I regard the instant as more important than the whole. My supreme goal is to force the truth out of my characters and settings. I swear to do so by all the means available and at the cost of any good taste and any aesthetic considerations.*
Thus I make my VOW OF CHASTITY.'

Consider two films of your choice in light of this statement.
- Most Bollywood films rely on very simple plots. Does this matter? Discuss with reference to at least three recent releases
- Read the article on spaghetti westerns at: http://www.imagesjournal.com/issue06/infocus/spaghetti.htm To what extent do you agree with this overview?
- Compare and contrast an early Western, such as *The Searchers* (1956) with a more modern Western like *Dances with Wolves* (1990). In what ways has the genre evolved? Is the genre dying out?
- What are the key conventions used in Bollywood movies?
- Study three films starring a Bollywood hero such as Gowinda Ahuja. Would a Hollywood hero be presented in the same way?
- Bollywood action movie heroes are based on Hollywood action heroes. Do you agree?
- To what extent does *The Blair Witch Project* conform to the Dogma 95 'Vow of Chastity'? Is the success of the film due to these elements?
- Watch at least two films by non-Hollywood directors such as Tzvetan Tarkovsky or Haile Gerima. What conclusions can you draw about the directors of these two films?
- What makes a Hollywood blockbuster? Use at least four examples
- Baz Luhrmann stated that *Moulin Rouge* (2001) is 'all about a boy who loves a girl'. Others have called it 'carnival of the grotesque', a term used by Rabelais to describe the 'popular culture' of medieval Europe in contrast to the 'high art' valued by the church
- Which do you think it is and why?

Audience research

Once you have planned the context for your extract in this way, you should think carefully about the target audience for your film.

- What is the target audience?
- Is this target audience typical for the genre?
- What expectations will the audience have?
- What representations will be operating in your extract?
- Is your film narrative or genre-led?

Once you have completed this research, you should be able to plan your film more effectively by using the appropriate and successful elements that you have identified above.

Storyboarding

It is vital to storyboard your extract before you begin. If you do not have access to storyboard templates, look back at the film section in *AS Media Studies for OCR* again to see an example of a possible storyboard layout.

Despite the temptation to plunge straight in and start filming, successful and thoughtful, complex texts (as well as more straightforward texts) are invariably carefully constructed on paper before filming begins. Unless the entire production crew is in tune with the director's vision of how to construct the film and locate the appropriate cast, locations and set, the film may be unsuccessful. There are many stories of directors, for instance Ridley Scott, who choose to create their entire film in great detail before they begin filming. They sometimes painstakingly complete every frame in detail and full colour to ensure the vision is clear. Even when less detailed, the direct correlation between storyboard and final result is usually clear for a successful film. Few directors can afford to disregard the storyboard and work with completely ad-libbed camera work when shooting. Filmmaking costs money and wasting money on unplanned shots is likely to be unpopular.

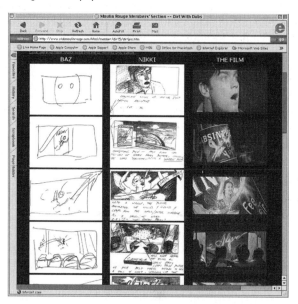

This example from Moulin Rouge *(2001) shows clearly the original sketches by Baz Luhrmann, the detailed storyboard created by the graphic artist and the actual construction of each of these frames, in the film. See figure 4.*

Cinematography and editing

When you are planning your film extract and drawing up the storyboard, many of your creative decisions will stem from your decisions about genre and narrative. If you are working in a realist tradition, you will want to use realist framing, lighting and composition. Your edited piece will be narrative-driven but may use narrative devices such as ellipsis. You would be unlikely to add effects during editing, unless they were simple effects like **fade** to black to suggest a passage of time. However, you would need to think carefully about the shots and edited sequence – could a passage of time be better and more aptly conveyed by the use of a text overlay at the beginning of the new section, to sustain the realist feel?

If you are working with a different genre, your composition and edited sequence will be different and this should be identified during the planning stage. If you are filming an extract from a Bollywood movie, for example, you need to use appropriate composition and mise-en-scène for a musical duet and to use appropriate effects (such as **dissolves**) during editing to maintain the atmosphere. The framing and composition of shots is often more formal and the angle wider than with Hollywood films and close ups are more posed. It is these elements, combined with the more obvious elements, such as the elaborate costumes, that define Bollywood films and highlight the different genres. There are several genres to be seen within a 'Bollywood' movie (see page 181 in Issues and Debates).

If you move further away from the realist tradition, you gain both freedom and responsibility. The more avant-garde or post-modern a text is, the more use there will be of unconventional camera angles, unusual composition and (often) effects-laden editing. Texts which are deliberately post-modern in intent, for example, *Moulin Rouge*, use whirling camera angles, loud noise and fish-eye **lenses** to distort faces so that they seem closer and more aggressive. The frequent use of dissolves highlights the nightmare atmosphere and the fascination that Christian has with the *Moulin Rouge* and this, coupled with the fast-paced movement between different images of the club, establishes the effect it has upon him. Contrast the more fixed shots and close ups in muted light used for Satine and the audience are well aware of the effect she has upon him. This is further exemplified by the contrasting sound when she is on screen – a deliberate parody suggesting that 'the rest of the room just disappears when she's around'. Of course there is more to the text than this and Luhrmann uses cartoon elements in the narrative to sustain this sense of the absurd. Rabelaisian grotesque is employed to prevent audiences from identifying with the characters and being sucked into the narrative instead of viewing the spectacle. Indeed Luhrmann is almost Brechtian in his determination to force the audience to observe and analyse the film, rather than engage with it and he achieves this through the **cinematography** and editing.

You do not have to work in any of these ways. These are examples of how decisions about genre and style will affect your extract from the storyboard and planning time onwards. You can choose to work in any way you wish – provided you know why you are working that way and you know to what extent each **frame** in your storyboard, each transition, each layer on the soundtrack, each title graphic and all your elements are related to this basic decision. The plot of your extract is of secondary importance. After all, you are only offering a brief taste of a far bigger narrative. The presentation of your extract will show more about your understanding of your own working practice and the creation of a credible text than the plot.

PART TWO
Television Production

Television broadcasting is continuing to develop and remains, arguably, the most dominant form of global mass media. Current studies suggest that the average adult in Britain watches 3.25 hours of television every day (source: *The Guardian*, 20 November 2001). Given that most of this viewing takes place after 7p.m., it is clear that watching television is the principal leisure activity for many people. The proportion of active compared to passive viewing is debatable yet *The Royle Family* would seem to be a credible exaggeration of many households at this time. There are important debates about the future of television and these include:

- The impact of **digital** broadcasting and the extending range of channels available
- The balance of **Public Service Broadcasting** (PSB) and commercial television

Production facilities

It is also important to remember that you should not attempt a production in this medium unless you are competent with your available equipment.

Research activities

You will probably have studied television in some form at AS Level and may be studying television in some way for the other A2 units. There is so much information available about television and so many programmes to view, that you cannot expect to cover everything. You will need to decide very quickly what genre you will be working within for your television production and structure your research in relation to that genre.

Case Study

Title sequence for a new gameshow

ACTIVITIES

- Which gameshows are currently being shown on national, local and cable or satellite channels? Identify the institution for each of these gameshows
- Which shows are commercial programmes and which are produced by the BBC?
- Can you identify any institutions producing more than one gameshow? What differences and similarities can you see between them?
- Research the demographics of the audience for one gameshow on a commercial channel and one gameshow on the BBC. What conclusions can you draw about these two audiences?
- What 'genres' of gameshows are currently being shown? What conclusions can you draw about popular genres of gameshows at present?

DISCUSSION

When researching TV production, it can help to undertake some more theoretical research in advance, to prepare for the Critical Evaluation for your artefact.

- Why are gameshows so popular?
- What are the key signifiers of a conventional gameshow and a 'reality gameshow'? Which is more successful and why?
- What influence does the choice of presenter have on the style and format of a gameshow?
- Compare and contrast the gameshows *The $64K Dollar Question* and *Who Wants to be a Millionaire*. What differences and similarities can you see in these programmes?
- Comment upon *Survivor* and *The Mole* in light of the comments from Bernard Crick in the Guardian from August 2000 (see boxed text overleaf)
- What makes *The Weakest Link* successful?
- Is the increasing number of gameshows on television evidence of 'dumbing down'? You may want to refer to *The Truman Show* (1998) in responding to this question.

Bernard Crick

One surfed so easily from those mob scenes in Portsmouth to those outside the Big Brother studio when blowsy Caroline was voted out and Machiavellian Nick met his nemesis. The one mob was, of course, ugly and full of hate, the other was facetiously high-spirited when it screamed: "We hate Nick." But both were mobs. Hannah Arendt, in her Origins of Totalitarianism, distinguished between "the people" and "the mob". The people seek for "true representation" politically whereas the mob "hates society from which it has been excluded" – interestingly she called it "a residue of all classes" (which well fits arrested football hooligans). The mob, she argued, is highly individualistic, all for "number one" as it were, unless a great leader emerges to legitimise its sense of being outside society, to turn spasmodic hatreds into tendency. Our two mobs are excluded from society in different ways: the mob on the Paulsgrove estate was, by many measures of social deprivation, objectively excluded; whereas the mob on the factoid studio set is subjectively excluded; it cheerfully excludes itself from conventional ideas of seriousness and social responsibility. Let us call the two the hate-full mob and the empty mob.

So Channel 4 has, indeed, created or cribbed a brilliant show for the empty mob, a cunning synthesis of game show and debased, dumbed-down documentary which even impels some serious attention. First, it creates the illusion of naturalism. Nearly all tele-dramas, not just the soaps, are for us watching others like ourselves doing recognisable things – there is very little imagination, fantasy or magic realism – even if the frequency of murder, rape, other violent crime and even sex on first sight and adultery, are statistically unusual. They close down rather than broaden imaginative horizons.

Most of us, not all, know that it is all "made-up". I remember having to tell, when asked, a former partner's foster-child that the cowboys and Indians on the box were not really getting killed. This is the twilight zone of the factoids that can fool or confuse even adults. We are too often in a shadow-world between journalism and entertainment. Channel 4 makes fatuous claims that Big Brother seriously reports on how people react under pressure. Considering how heavily cut the film has to be, and how aware the happy family is that they are on camera, this is nonsense on stilts.

Also Big Brother gives the viewers sentencing power: the illusion of popular power, happily in this case illusion. "Crucify him, crucify him!" Not just the tabloids feed this mentality, but increasingly BBC presenters will ask a relative of a victim what the punishment should be, or draw from an allegedly "ordinary person" a snap, prejudiced and often ignorant opinion. Well, if they are not representative, at least they are an "authentic" voice – that magic word that links populism high and low.

Then Big Brother attracted a huge mob to come and watch the expulsions from the anti-Paradise of those voted out. Davina, the presenter, dashes through them, like a frenzied post-modernist Anglo-Saxon messenger in Alice, inciting and feeding their lines, but all scripted, of course, unlike the mob leaders in Portsmouth. She is the apt embodiment of clamorous triviality or the purity of purposelessness. And they can go home and look for themselves on video. True reality!

Lastly, Big Brother turns Orwell's potent metaphor upside down. His Airstrip One was totalitarian. There the "telescreen" was emphatically not for entertainment. But the programme Big Brother pretends to be the voice of the people, or "the empty mob". "Well, we are a democracy, aren't we? Why can't the people have what they want?" Even if this entails what Tocqueville long ago called the "the tyranny of the majority"? No need for knowledge, good education, reasoned judgments, recourse to authorities and experience. All that is what populists call elitism. Beatrice Webb once remarked: "Democracy is not the multiplication of ignorant opinions." Dreadful woman! But pause a moment. Surely the will of the majority must interact with reasoning, liberty and human rights? Consider capital punishment. Perhaps the case for populism would be stronger if those in TV and the tabloids who hide behind "public opinion" while seeking to stir it, made serious attempts to ascertain what it actually is, not just viewing figures and readers' letters. Social survey organisations rarely turn down good business.

Orwell's picture of Big Brother's strategy, however, brings us close to the world of sitcoms, game shows and the prize inanities of the Big Brother show. The party made no attempt to activate the proles in support of the regime. They are simply depoliticised by cultural debasement, dumbed down, kept from even thinking of demanding fair shares. The party looks after the proles by producing for them rubbishy newspapers, containing almost nothing except sport, crime and astrology; sensational five-cent novelettes; films oozing with sex; and sentimental songs which are composed entirely by mechanical means on a special kind of kaleidoscope known as a versificator. There was even a whole sub-section "Pornosoc" engaged in producing the lowest kinds of pornography.

That was not Stalin and Hitler's regimes; it was and is savage, Swiftian satire of the British popular press. A wicked exaggeration, of course; at the time only one paper fully fitted the bill – by happy coincidence the News of the World. Back then, even they got the naughty bits in only by long verbatim reports of court proceedings, in case they appeared grossly sensational, even faced prosecution. What demands they then had to make on the literacy of their readers.

Orwell was deadly serious in arguing that capitalism, faced with a largely literate and free electorate, could only by means of cultural debasement maintain a class system so grossly unequal and inequitable. He knew nothing of Habermas and Frankfurterschule neo-Marxism. Old George worked it out for himself. Seemed obvious; 14-pint common sense.

Rebekah Wade in her seclusion may think she understands the common people or she may just be selling her master's newspapers on the street. But she certainly stirred a mob reaction on an issue that needs sensitive and informed leadership – incitements to thought not precipitate action. The broadsheets, except the Times, did begin to remind us that there were only five children murdered by strangers last year, compared with hundreds of deaths on the roads and that 98% of recorded child abuse is within families; and that while tabloid reports of cases of murder, welfare scroungers, incompetent doctors and so on are usually well-researched and true (for fear of libel), they are usually numerically insignificant. Panics make news, statistics are boring and demanding. When my doctor told me six years ago that I had prostatic cancer, he said: "Do you understand the concept of probability?" I said yes. "Thank heavens," he replied. We sadly agreed that many now believe that they can live in a risk-free world; and that if somebody can't be found to blame, then the law is at fault.

Who knows how Ms Wade's readers would react if presented with less simplistic reactions? Which of us last week did not feel an often unexpected respect for the reactions of police, probation and social services, and dismay at the political leaders who talked far more strongly of the need for new laws (so far unreasoned except that some people seem to demand it) than in rebuke of vigilantes. Stanley Baldwin once rebuked Lord Beaverbrook for exercising "power without responsibility; the prerogative of the harlot throughout the ages". Who says that now to Murdoch? But Baldwin lived in "elitist" not "populist" days. It takes political courage to appeal to the best instincts of people, not the worst.

Orwell understood the difference between "what the public is interested in" and "the public interest". That is why he wrote that book whose warning has been treated with cynical contempt and is itself treated as "prolefeed".

- Bernard Crick is author of *George Orwell: a Life, In Defence of Politics* and recently *Essays on Citizenship*.

The Guardian,
Saturday 19 August, 2000
© Bernard Crick

Constructing the title sequence

Planning

You should start by identifying the institutional context and target audience for as many contemporary gameshows as you can. If you have access to facilities to view or research gameshows from other countries, the comparisons will be useful. Identify a particular style of gameshow you wish to concentrate upon and record the title sequence for at least four programmes of this type.

For each programme, answer the following questions:

● How long does the title sequence last?

- What proportion of graphics, text and live images is used?
- Do they use still images or moving images?
- How does the soundtrack reflect and identify the programme?
- What 'clues' in the title sequence attract and identify the target audience?
- How does the title sequence indicate the style of the programme?

Once you have analysed a range of existing title sequences, you will have a more focused concept of what will be required for the title sequence of your gameshow. It is probable that you will decide to produce a title sequence primarily dependent on still images and/or video clips from the 'programme'. This makes it less likely that you will need to use sophisticated post-production software to create an animated title sequence or to provide sophisticated text effects.

The show

Clearly, you cannot begin to plan the title sequence unless you have a very clear concept for the gameshow itself. You should decide on at least the following factors before beginning to plan the title sequence:

- What is the name of the show?
- What is its target audience?
- What is your institutional context?
- What type of gameshow is it?
- What is the ideology of the show?
- What sort of contestants will you be seeking?
- What image do you wish to present in the title sequence?
- What is the presenter like (a detailed image profile will be helpful here – not only in itself but to help you plan how the presenter may be reflected in the title sequence)?
- What is your **scheduling** context?

Recommended content for Production Log

- Research notes about comparable gameshows, indicating your research and decisions about your title sequence
- A complete and detailed storyboard for the sequence
- A shooting script and possibly call sheets, **prop** sheets, continuity sheets and other paperwork
- Annotated drafts for CGI elements to be included in your sequence
- Samples of possible fonts – again annotated
- Production Log and individual accountability information
- Personal schedules and project timeline

It is the producer's responsibility to ensure that all of the necessary equipment is ready and that material is edited on time. This does not mean that the producer does all these jobs, but that they supervise them.

Titles

When constructing titles for inclusion in a moving image title sequence you can construct them in a variety of ways:

- Using a built in titler in a non-linear editing suite
- Using dedicated post-production software within an editing suite or to transfer to an editing suite
- Creating titles in a graphics package to import into the edited sequence
- Using a titler attached to a linear editing system
- Using an 'on board' titler on a video camera
- Setting up title screens and filming these with a video camera

Each of these approaches will produce different results. Filming a constructed title screen may seem simple but can be used to great effect. For example, as the title graphics for a maths-based programme for children by using coloured pegs on a peg board to spell out the required words. A very 'low tech' approach but very effective in that context. You are unlikely to have access to high end post-production software in your editing suite (or the time to learn the software packages) so you should aim to keep your titles and any required animation simple. If you choose to make your titles in a different application (such as Adobe Photoshop™), you should ensure that you create pictures at the right size and with a transparent background. A resolution of 72 dots per inch (dpi) is fine for screen-based work.

You must ensure you create a transparent background for your title so that the action behind the title can be seen. If you do not use a transparent background, when you overlay the title graphic it will hide everything layered below it. The transparency information is contained in the 'alpha' channel associated with a graphic that has a transparent background in this way. Import the graphic into the video editing programme, ensuring it is placed in a channel or layer where transparency can be discarded. Use the 'white alpha' transparency key in the software (or the equivalent key) and the background will be hidden, and the images hidden below the title screen will reappear.

1. When you create a title screen in a software package, you may need to remember that computers work on square pixels whereas televisions display 'non-square pixels'. To ensure that your text is not distorted when seen on the television screen, you may need to make the titles or images using the appropriate PAL (Phase Alternation by Line) referenced size – 768 × 576 pixels and then change the image size to 720 × 576 when it is finished. If you were simply to compose at or crop to the final size, the image would still appear distorted when you imported it into your editing programme.
2. Remember that the image will appear distorted when you see it in a graphics editor. However it will not look distorted when viewed on the video.
3. You may not need to do this with some newer software packages as they will automatically compensate.

Still images
Many contemporary title sequences use still images from the programme with overlaid graphics or titles as part of the title sequence. You may choose to set these up as still photographs or you may choose to mock up a sequence from the gameshow and take a series of 'action' stills from this filming.

If your gameshow is a 'reality' show, it may be appropriate to use still images as part of the title sequence to introduce the audience to the key individuals in the gameshow and to designate and identify the target audience.

Case Study

Extract or package for a children's news programme

This option requires competence with producing a news programme extract. It involves the very particular demands of working with an explicit, and challenging, choice of target audience. No media text can be created in isolation without direct address to the target audience but in some cases, such as here, the relationship between form and content must be more carefully analysed and constructed to ensure that the text is accessible and appeals to the target audience.

Planning

You should think carefully about the structure and placement of your text before you begin. You may decide to create a news package, for example a 'local news' section for a national news programme. Or you may simply choose to provide an extract from a longer news programme, perhaps with an introduction from a presenter and two items from the programme. Remember that you do not need to produce the whole programme. Five minutes is the maximum length allowed.

In terms of institutional context, you will need to identify a station and thus an identity at the very beginning. You might choose to present a local package as part of *Newsround* or a *Newsround* special report on the environment. If you choose to present an extract as part of a Saturday morning programme on ITV or on a new local cable channel, the institutional context, and thus your text, will be very different.

Questions to ask before you begin

- Are you producing an extract or a package?
- Which station will your programme be shown on?
- What is your target audience?
- What devices will you employ to ensure you directly target this audience?
- What stories will you want to include?
- If you are constructing a presenter for your programme, what image will they present? In what ways will this reflect the character of your chosen channel and identify your programme?
- If you are using reporters, how will they visually and aurally reflect the channel and programme identity?
- What stories will be appropriate for your given context?
- What mise-en-scène will you use? How will this create your context?
- Will your presentation be formal (presenter in a studio with a blue projection screen behind, for example) or more informal and chatty?
- How many items will be in your extract/package?
- Will you be using devices such as musical links between items or overlays to communicate with the viewers? Will you need supporting graphics (for instance, when presenting an item about volcanoes exploding you may feel a graphic to demonstrate the process would be valuable) or interviews with particular people?

You may wish to create the title sequence for the programme as well, since that would be a different project. However, you may want to use a presenter to open the programme, in which case you need to plan and construct an effective 'lead in' to the programme.

As with print production, it is strongly recommended that your reporters source, research and construct their own stories, rather than depend on 'found material'. It is surprisingly difficult to 'own' found material sufficiently securely to be able to effectively manipulate it into a new format. A news item that is regurgitated from another channel and simply **re-badged** for a different context is likely to be fairly awkward in approach, insubstantial and is rarely successful. If the item is heavily dependent on a previous report with the use of found graphics and so forth, it is unlikely that you would be able to display sufficient skills with media construction to merit a high mark at A2.

Although the stimulus for a story may come from a 'found' source, your reporters should ensure that they conduct their own primary research and locate their own interviewees and images. This level of engagement will enable them to produce a far more structured item, showing clear regard for institutional context, news values and choice of material.

DISCUSSION

- Why are there so few children's news programmes?

- Would you say that Galtung and Ruge's 'news values' are applied in the same way for children's news programmes as for adult programmes?

- Identify and justify a list of news values to be applied when compiling a children's news programme

- In *On Television* (New Press, 1998), Bourdieu asserts that, 'With permanent access to public visibility, broad circulation, and mass diffusion these journalists can impose on the whole of society their vision of the world, their conception of problems, their point of view.' Do you agree?

- Does television news sensationalise events?

- Why is television news important?

- The BBC was first created to fulfil the **Reithian** vision of broadcasting to 'entertain and educate' and PSB broadcasting has continued this vision. Do the contemporary news programmes on the BBC perpetuate this vision or is the news becoming entertainment-led?

- Should children's news and current affairs programmes be presented by children or by adults?

News values, the institution and the role of the journalist

News values are the ideological backbone of the journalist and news editor. The most familiar identification of these 'news values' was from Johan Galtung and Marie Holmboe Ruge. Although their research was conducted in 1965, virtually any media analyst's discussion of news values will always refer to their list, despite the fact that it was initially intended to cover only international events. The values they identified are:

- **Frequency:** The time-span of an event and the extent to which it 'fits' the frequency of the schedule. On this basis, motorway pile-ups, murder and plane crashes will qualify as they are all of short duration and therefore nearly always fit into the schedule.
- **Threshold:** How big is an event? Is it big enough to make it into

the news? A fire in the city may be reported on the local news but is unlikely to be reported on the national news unless it becomes more of an event.

- **Unambiguity:** The mass media generally want closure. With an event such as a murder, its meaning is immediately grasped, so it is likely to make it into the news. A more complicated story may not be used as it cannot be addressed sufficiently quickly.
- **Meaningfulness:** Stories tend to be judged in terms of how they relate to the viewers. The closer to home the events, the more likely they are to be reported. A train crash in Outer Mongolia which kills 300 people is likely to be of less interest to the viewers than a car accident on the M25 which caused a 10 mile tailback.
- **Consonance:** The audience – and the journalists – have expectations about how a story should unfold. To make the news immediately accessible, journalists tend to present stories very simply and rarely offer more than one perspective on events.
- **Unexpectedness:** Some events are more predictable than others – parliamentary campaigns may not be reported in any detail because they are not 'exciting.' A walkabout by a parliamentary candidate becomes a lot more exciting if they are attacked by a group of protesters who cover the candidate in baked beans, for example.
- **Continuity:** Audiences quickly come to expect continuation of running stories.
- **Composition:** There is usually a balance of stories in a bulletin.
- **Reference to élite nations:** Cultural proximity is an important factor for journalists – the less cultural proximity for the audience with the events, the less importance will be attached to them.
- **Reference to élite persons:** Some people are more newsworthy than others.
- **Personalisation:** The more human interest in a story, the more likely it is to be heard.
- **Negativity:** News tends to be negative.

Role of a journalist

There are also differences between the neutral and participant role of journalists. **Neutral** is associated with the idea of press as channel of information, **participant** is where the journalist behaves as a representative of the public. Most see themselves as neutral but many political journalists deliberately have an **adversarial** role. Weaver and Wilhoit (1986) further qualified this:

interpreter – analyses events and raises questions
disseminator – the journalist as servant, providing information to the public
adversary – the journalist as challenger, forcing individuals and institutions to answer to the public

DISCUSSION

Watch *Newsround* for a week and consider the following questions:

- How long is each bulletin? When is it shown? Why is it scheduled here?

- How many stories are there each day? From the observation of a week, what conclusions can you draw about the balance of stories to be used each day? How far does this match with adult programmes – or the application of 'news values' in adult programmes?

- In what ways do the presenters of the programme define the identity of the programme (consider clothes, interaction, studio background, register and image as a starting point)

- Compare and contrast the presentation of two stories on *Newsround*, *BBC 10 O'Clock News* and *Channel 4 News*. What similarities and differences in presentation can you observe? What does this reveal about the role and function of *Newsround*?

- What is the target audience for *Newsround*?

Visit http://www.cjetech.co.uk/watched_it/jcnr.html for a detailed history of *Newsround* and consider the changes that have been made to the programme recently. How has the format and style of the programme changed from the early days?

What do we mean by 'children's broadcasting'? Select three 'children's broadcasting 'programmes to research. For each one answer the following questions:

- What is the institutional context (i.e. which channel and at what time)?

- What persona is constructed for the presenter(s) of these programmes? How does this affect the style of the programme?

- How are camera angles and framing used to establish that these programmes are for children?

- What register is used in the programmes?

- What is the format of the programmes? What similarities and differences can you observe?

- Are the programmes successful? Can you account for this?

Case Study

Audience research

Once you have analysed a range of children's programmes in this way, you should think carefully about the target audience for each programme.

- What is the target audience for each programme?
- Is the target audience similar for all of these programmes?
- Is the audience the same for the channel itself?
- Can you account for these similarities and differences?
- How do the programmes 'brand' their identity for their audience?
- Do these programmes have an audience or a community?

Once you have completed this research, you should be able to plan your programme more effectively, using the appropriate and successful elements that you have identified above.

Case Study

Children's Express

Children's Express can be found at http://www.childrens-express.org/html/khome.htm. It is a news portal for children where the reporting is done by children. It is a useful site to visit to find out what stories are being reported, where they are being reported and how they are being reported. There is a range of material on the site and plenty of links to ongoing projects.

There are main bureaus in London, Newcastle and Belfast, with part-time bureaus in Birmingham, Blackburn with Darwen, Plymouth and Sheffield.

Look at http://www.childrens-express.org/dynamic/public/hot.htm to see what stories are 'hot' at Children's Express now. This will give you a good starting point for possible stories in your bulletin.

- Why do you think each of these stories was considered important?
- Follow some of the links to see what stories were created. In what ways are they targeted at children and children's audiences?
- What other children's news organisations can you discover? One other organisation is www.ypress.org, which is a children's news network based in Indianapolis, USA
- What is the target audience for this organisation? Will this be the same audience for your bulletin?
- How many of these stories do you think will be relevant in a month's time?

Administration

Once you have the concept of your programme you need to think about the logistics, such as distributing responsibility for each of the bulletin items or casting presenters. You should plan each story carefully with a lead reporter and a director for each bulletin, so that one person can be responsible for content and one for form with each story. You will need plenty of planning meetings to ensure that there is consistency of form and style across each of your stories. All of your material must conform to the 'house style' that you designate and must reflect an appropriate institution.

If you are working in a group, it is fairly easy to allocate a range of responsibilities to each of the group members and to change roles between stories. This allows for greater diversity of experience and research and, if properly managed, should strengthen Critical Evaluation opportunities.

Editing

Unless you are severely limited by the quality of your editing equipment, you should try to complete each story separately and only combine the sections during editing. It is easier to control shot choice, rhythm, length and focus across all of your stories in this way. Complete the filming of each section (which should be substantially longer than the final time available) and structure the rough cut before editing begins. Look for consistency and finalise the house style for reports, graphics and so forth before you begin editing. You should ensure appropriate time for each story, consistency of overlays and graphics, natural links (if appropriate) and similarity of shot across stories if possible to sustain your bulletin. Assess the relevance to the target audience and the institutional factors during editing.

Framing

When you are filming interviewees, it is usually most effective to allow them to face a reporter standing next to the camera, allowing them to look to the side of the camera.

It is intimidating for an interviewee to be expected to stare straight into a camera, and full frontal shots of most people are unflattering. By allowing people to look to the side, their faces gain perspective and depth and they feel more secure looking at the interviewer during their responses. If you are using a formal studio, remember that the presenters are usually positioned slightly to the side of the frame as well, to ensure eye-line matches on the pivot points. In a formal studio situation, there may well be a blue-screen behind the presenter where the videos can be shown (you can show an opening graphic for a story as a still image in the blue-screen space). Use the **chromakey** option or other transparency filter in your editing programme, to make the graphic appear on the page. Then use a zoom transition to move to a full screen version of the story. (NB: How do they link in this way on *Newsround*?)

If you are using a less formal studio set, it may be easier to lead into the various stories. However, you should make sure that there is still plenty of space in the frame for the presenter to look into as they look off screen to lead off the story. You should also try to use audio 'lead ins' to make the bulletin more cohesive. An audio lead in means that the audio track for the new clip starts slightly before the previous visual image has finished so that it is already playing when the relevant clip starts to appear.

PART THREE
Print Production

Despite the digital revolution, print artefacts are still a fundamental mass media form. Newspapers are currently reviewing their on-line provision, after discovering that even the most techno-literate of their audience have yet to make a full transition to on-screen editions of the daily papers. Readers still prefer to retain the traditional print product and use the on-screen versions as searchable archives, responding most favourably to a 'daily digest approach'. At the time of writing, the introduction of e-books has not remotely affected the global sales of books. Book production figures are in fact increasing. Readers do not seem ready to give up the physical sensations of holding and opening a book or the tactile appeal of a glossy magazine or the expectations raised by the visual construct which is a **broadsheet** front page. *The Financial Times* would not be differentiated and elevated in the same way by an on-line version using black text on a pink background, yet the newspaper is instantly recognised and situates its entire ideology in its format.

The range of possible options for print production work is as varied as the print media themselves, including newspapers, magazines, adverts, pamphlets, leaflets, comics and posters.

Each medium within the production context involves different production skills and different research expectations and so it is logical to consider two case studies individually as examples rather than apply generic principles across such widely divergent media forms.

Production facilities

It would be unwise to embark on print production work unless you feel that you have access to appropriate technologies.

It is assumed at A2 Level that you will have access to computers which have desktop publishing (DTP) and image editing software available on them, just as at AS Level. Again, the industry standards in terms of software are usually Quark Xpress™ for DTP work and Photoshop for image editing but there are many cheaper (and less complex) alternatives available, such as Green Street Publisher™ and Paint Shop Pro™. Without access to such software you will be unable to draft and compose your print artefacts with enough flexibility. DTP software allows a greater degree of adaptability by treating form and content as different units, allowing you to isolate either for redrafting without affecting the other.

The artefacts should be shown in their real size (although billboards might reasonably be scaled down to A3!) and they should be carefully presented and labelled. Laminating the work is often a good way of preventing wear and tear. Hand-drawn artefacts are unlikely to be successful at this level (unless they are necessarily 'hand-drawn', for example, comics), even if well presented. The visual construct of a hand-drawn artefact is very distinctive and would detract from the artefact unless the effect is deliberate. It is also unlikely that work dependent on 'found' images would be successful, unless the images are sufficiently manipulated.

It is useful, but not essential, to have access to an A3 full-colour printer. This allows better printing options and credible presentation of film posters or broadsheet newspapers. At this level broadsheet newspapers are not expected to be presented on a single sheet of A4 because proportions of the font sizes, balance and image sizes would be totally inappropriate. If large format printing facilities are not available, the use of multiple sheets of paper and sticky tape can provide an adequate alternative.

Case Study

Children's comic

There is a wide range of opportunities within the comic genre for print production, ranging from **manga** animations, through comic and graphic novels to underground comics and political/satirical comics. You need to define a specific form and content within the genre and your research and production will be necessarily controlled by this choice. Critical research for a manga graphic novel or a contemporary satirical cartoon on the web would (and should) be very different.

For this sample project we shall look at creating a new children's comic with a primary target audience of children (predominantly boys) between the ages of 8–11. In this scenario you should probably anticipate producing a conventional comic, but constructing a new superhero to demonstrate an understanding of the requirements of constructing such a figure in relation to audience and institutional context. There is always a danger when planning an artefact that a rejection of conventional form and function leads to a rejection of the fundamental fusion between text, institution and audience which is the hallmark of the credible product. A product should not become introspective and self-indulgent or lose awareness of audience and institution in relation to text. It is important to ground the Critical Evaluation in media theory and in a detailed deconstruction of text, audience and institution in order to provide evidence that justifies the artefact as a media text.

Research activities
The obvious starting point for creating a new children's magazine is to research currently available comics and review these against historical trends.

DISCUSSION

- Trace the history of Spiderman or Superman in comics and cartoons from their beginnings to current incarnations

- Discuss the key **signifiers** of manga comics

- Write a detailed deconstruction of the front page of three different comics published in the last month

- Discuss the key features of the American and British comic markets. How do they differ?

- Consider whether style or layout is more important when constructing a comic

- How do your chosen contemporary comics target their audience?

- What has been the impact of *Pokemon* on the contemporary comic market?

- Which is your favourite comic character and why?

Detailed analysis

Select fairly recent editions of three different comics. Try to choose examples from different cultural or ideological backgrounds, for example a manga comic, Marvel comic and another comic. Use the following questions to structure your analysis.

- How are the stories sequenced? Are the boxes numbered or are there narrative links? Which is more successful?
- How realist are the visual codes?
- How many colours are used in the comics that you are researching?
- What is the proportion of text to graphics on the pages?
- What **representations** are operating in the texts?
- What ideologies are operating in these texts?
- Identify the institutional codes operating in your texts – you may need to look at different examples from each of the relevant institutions to draw clear conclusions

DISCUSSION

When researching print production, it can help to undertake some more theoretical research in advance, to prepare for the Critical Evaluation for your artefact.

- Why do comics appeal to an adult audience?

- It has been said that the appeal of comics lies simply in the escapism offered in their pages. Is this the case or is the appeal wider than this?

- How does *Viz* identify and target its audience?

- Theorists have argued that comics directly reflect and subvert the cultural landscape. Do you agree?

- What are the key differences and similarities in structure, institution and audience for comics, comix and graphic novels?

- What is a comic?

Constructing the comic

Planning

In the light of your interests and research you will need to start by deciding what type of comic you are going to produce, the audience and the institutional context. As you will have discovered from your research, the form and content of a comic depends totally on this context.

- What is the Unique Selling Point (**USP**) of your comic?
- What is your target audience? What 'hooks' are used by comparable comics to attract this audience?
- Is there a key 'hero' to your comic? Is it a conventional comic (e.g. science fiction, detective or jungle based)?
- What style of drawings (shape, colour, structure etc.) and layout is appropriate for your comic?
- How does the front cover of your comic define the comic?

There are many different forms of comics today, ranging from the well-known comics like *The Beano* through *Pokemon* comics, Japanese manga, European texts such as *Asterix*, to graphic novels and the 'laddish' humour exemplified by titles such as *Viz*.

Like most forms of magazine, the genre of 'comic' contains an extensive range of texts, yet each text targets a particular audience and operates in a particular environment. Your artefact must identify its audience and exploit it in this way. Even within popular culture, comics are sometimes perceived as having lower status than other media forms. Nevertheless, successful comics are not only incredibly sophisticated and multi-layered artistically, but usually commercially profitable and used as media texts.

Once you have completed this research, you should be able to plan your programme more effectively, using the appropriate and successful elements that you have identified above.

Recommended content for Production Log

- You should have a fully annotated flat-plan for your comic. In addition you should include draft drawings, colour match charts, designs, source material and so forth to show how the comic design was created
- It is helpful to provide annotated research material (e.g. pages of comics which you have deconstructed as appendices to the Critical Evaluation)
- Your Log should include a production schedule and clear information about group roles and responsibilities if you are working in a group
- You will also need evidence about how you identified the target audience and how this influenced the production process
- Show that you have thought about an appropriate institution for the text and have considered how this impacts both on production practice and on the final product

Production

Quantity

An appropriate project length for A2 work is usually about six fully realised pages. This is unlikely to comprise an entire edition of a comic so you should decide which pages you will present and include a detailed flat-plan and mock up for the entire edition in your appendix to show how the complete edition would work. You cannot take random pages in isolation so completing a full flat-plan allows you to demonstrate that you understand the layout of the whole edition. The balance of stories and adverts or inclusion of 'in-depth' articles, interviews or items such as competitions show that you have a good grasp of the genre and its requirements.

You would usually be expected to produce the front page for your comic, possibly the contents page and perhaps two double-page spread stories or one story spread over three pages and a second story over just one page, depending on your chosen style and genre.

Masthead

Your **masthead** is one of the most important elements of the front cover of your comic. It must define the style of the comic and be easily identifiable on the shelf to appeal to both regular readers and newsagent browsers. The masthead becomes a signifier for the comic so it is important to get it right.

Colour, font, size, position, name and background should all be considered carefully in relation to both your target audience and the institutional requirements and expectations. Again, you should be prepared to defend your decisions in your Critical Evaluation and to include examples of rejected drafts in an appendix.

Look at these examples of possible mastheads for a new comic. Which is the most suitable example and why? The name 'Boy's Own' has been used in each example to enable you to focus directly on design issues although a large proportion of your own discussions will involve finding a more credible name for your comic.

Although none of these is a sufficiently dynamic title for publication, they are here to help you focus on the choice of font, layout and possible background appropriate for your masthead. You should also think carefully about the institutional codes which need to be included as part of your masthead and research the styles and formats used by your chosen publishing house.

Now compare these two front covers for *The Beano*. The first edition was published in 1938 and the 60th birthday issue published in 1998. What significant features of the masthead can you identify? How has the masthead changed over 60 years? In what ways is it still identifiably the same?

Key character

Many of the early comics were built around a superhero or heroic figure (it varied among the three principal genres) and this figure was the main USP of the comic. Like the mastheads, the portrayal of these **characters** has changed over time to match the changing target audience and cultural expectations. Consider these three images of Superman on the front cover of his magazine and look at the changing visual signs. If you wish to see further examples of *Superman* covers, go to www.supermanhomepage.com, and choose 'Images'.

An edition of Superman *magazine from 1939.*   *An edition of* Superman *magazine from 1972.*

An edition of Superman *magazine from 2001.*

Superman, Action Comics, and The Adventures of Superman are trademarks of DC Comics.
© DC Comics. All Rights Reserved. Used with Permission.

Analysis

● What elements are repeated throughout all three *Superman* covers?
● What colours are used for Superman? Does this change? Why is this?
● What type of image is used for Superman? Why is this?
● How does DC Comics 'brand' the covers?
● What context is set up for each cover? What does this suggest about the inside of each edition?
● Which elements on each front cover indicate the comic format?
● How does the use of colour and style change over time? Does this reflect the changing cultural context?

Layout of stories

When you analyse the inside of various comics you will see that there are different layouts for different institutions. Just as with other magazines, you will readily be able to identify a house layout for Marvel or DC Comics, for example. You will also see that the layout varies depending on the genre of the magazine and the target audience. Few of the niche market comics use a simplistic or conventional layout. The straightforward layout of a page of a Disney magazine, where a very simple structure and use of an organised pattern of say six images with substantial captions underneath makes the story very easy to follow compared with the cluttered and complex layout of a manga magazine.

Think carefully about how to structure your stories and the layout of the pages to appeal to your target audience, to reflect the style of your magazine and to demonstrate an understanding of the institutional codes employed in the texts.

To help you, complete an analysis of the layout of a story from perhaps three different publications, to identify the key signifiers.

● How does each layout reflect the target audience?
● What clues are used to indicate the pattern of the story?
● Is the story told with narrative description, speech bubbles or a combination of these methods? Can you account for this? Are any other narrative devices operating?
● What are the institutional codes operating across layouts for different magazines from particular publishing houses? How are these adapted for different audiences?
● How does each layout reflect the cultural and social conditions in which it is operating and in which it is published?

Technical issues

Most comics start as hand-drawn artefacts (or rather computer-drawn equivalents). It is therefore entirely appropriate for you to hand draw or computer draw each page of your comic. You may choose to write the supporting text by hand (narrative and speech bubbles) or you may choose to use your DTP software to add these elements. Remember that hand-colouring each image can take a long time and that if you choose to handwrite your text, it must be consistent, legible, using an appropriate font. You may prefer to add the text using your DTP software to create a more professional effect. This gives you more control over the text boxes, style, colour and shadows as well as ensuring consistency and legibility across all of your pages. If you are hand drawing the images, you should draw each image separately and scan them into the computer to put into a number of picture boxes in your DTP programme. Mapping out the layout of each page and drawing on the whole sequence of images at once would make it too difficult to manipulate size, balance, position and so forth for each of the images. It would be very time-consuming to have to completely redraw the page because one element was in the wrong place. If each element is separated in a DTP programme, it is easier to manipulate the ordering of the boxes on the page and control which is most visible.

Whether you choose to create the whole comic on a computer or draw the images and then input them into the computer, you should ensure that the final version is printed out properly and that the pages are either made up into a booklet or clearly labelled with their numbers as well as your name.

Case Study

New tabloid newspaper

You should aim to produce about six pages from a new **tabloid** newspaper, in line with the expectations for other print-based projects. Remember that you will be expected to present your tabloid in a professional way and at an appropriate size.

Beware of designing your tabloid at A4 size and 'blowing up' to A3 size. If your fonts are appropriate on your A4 version or you have carefully managed the quantity of white space visible on your page, remember that the fonts will be too large and the white spaces seem empty when this is blown up to A3 size.

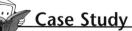

Case Study

A C T I V I T I E S

- Research the current tabloids available in your area – national and local. Identify the institution, target audience, approach and circulation figures for each one
- What are the key signifiers of the local tabloids in your area?
- Write a detailed deconstruction of the front page of three different tabloids. Try to compare one national and two local tabloids if you can and look for editions which focus on the same stories
- Complete an analysis of the audience for each of these publications and explain how they are directly targeted by the publication
- What are the key features of the local and national tabloids? How do they differ?
- What is the balance of visual against text in your chosen texts? Does this vary for different sections of the newspapers?
- How is colour used (or not used) in these titles? Why is this?
- Which do you feel is most successful and why?

Detailed analysis

Select fairly recent editions of three different tabloids (ideally from the same day or at least the same week). Try to choose examples from different cultural or ideological backgrounds, for example a right-wing national tabloid, a daily local news-orientated title and a niche title such as a specialist publication.

Use the following questions to structure your analysis:

- How many similarities are there in the choice of stories?
- Are the registers of each text different? Can you account for these differences?
- How important are photographs to the text?
- What is the proportion of text to graphics on the pages?
- What representations are operating in the texts?
- What ideologies are operating in these texts – how are these ideologies exposed?
- What is the target audience for each text? How are they directly targeted by the publication?
- What are the institutional codes operating in your texts? (You may need to look at different examples from each of the relevant institutions to draw clear conclusions)
- Why have you chosen to research these three texts in detail?

DISCUSSION

When researching print production, it can help to undertake some more theoretical research in advance, to prepare for the Critical Evaluation for your artefact.

- What is a tabloid newspaper?

- What differences in role and function are there for **gatekeepers** on local and national papers?

- Do newspapers report the news or an interpretation of the news?

- Should journalists operate as interpreters of news, disseminators of news or **hegemonic** adversaries? Can they operate a **plurality** of these roles?

- Are the tabloids ever too hungry for 'human interest'? Are we, as readers?

- Why are dramatic and disastrous occurrences such a powerful draw, and why do we not see more good news in the media?

Project
Once you have completed the above tasks, you are ready to begin to plan your newspaper extract.

You should start with detailed research to discover an appropriate market for your new tabloid and define your target audience carefully.

You may prefer to construct a local paper. Since it is expected that you will source and research all of your stories directly, a local focus will simplify the logistics of production. Remember to allow a substantial amount of time for **newsgathering** and research for your newspaper, as well as for the basic construction.

Planning and assembling material
Identify likely local stories, think of an appropriate angle and prepare material, for example, photographs and background research.

If you are working in a group, it may be useful at this stage to delegate responsibility for different stories to different members of the group. One group member could act as 'editor' to oversee the process and take primary charge of the final production. This allows a fair degree of autonomy for group members and ensures direct involvement in the newsgathering, photography, research, organisation and writing and editing of articles.

Source material

You should endeavour to source all of your stories directly. Although your interest in a story may be triggered from another news source, you should follow normal journalistic practice and create your story from scratch. There are some very good reasons for doing this.

The most important reason is that you cannot 'own' the material sufficiently and construct and edit it appropriately for your particular publication if you are dependent on the words, images and research from a different journalist or publication. Having defined the niche and target audience for your tabloid, you are expected to construct a newspaper that relates to this position. There is also great danger if you try to manipulate material intended for different publications because it can become distorted or unfocused. It is far better to use this kind of material as a stimulus and to undertake your own research and take your own photographs to construct the exact image you wish to present in your publication, and to write your own copy which directly relates to your audience.

Photographs

Original images are required. The process of constructing and editing your photographs reveals much about the decision-making involved in constructing your text and it allows far more sophisticated targeting of graphics to audience. If you have simply copied images from a different publication they are unlikely to 'fit' well (physically or as representations) and may constrain the production process unnecessarily as you attempt to fit them in.

Interviews

Most public figures are happy to cooperate with media students if approached in the right way. You should make a polite request, for example, a letter to a local politician asking for an interview in relation to one of the stories you are researching. You should ensure you appear professional 'on the day' (for instance, your tape recorder has fully-charged batteries, the photographer has got a flash gun, the list of questions is already prepared and you are punctual). It is far easier to add credibility to your stories if you have quotes or interviews from relevant people.

Register

Newspapers have a particular register that their journalists employ. For example the style of The Sun is very different to that of The Times. It is important that you think carefully about the register you use for your newspaper and how this will be reflected in the language of each story. Your register should reflect the institution and audience that you have defined for your newspaper.

Ideology

You should also take care to define the ideology of your newspaper before you start. All of your news is likely to be interpreted in the light of this ideology. The most obvious aspect of this is often the political leaning of a newspaper. A 'pro-Labour' newspaper is likely to report Tony Blair's latest Cabinet reshuffle very differently to a 'Tory' paper. A local paper would probably put a very different slant on the building of a new nuclear waste reprocessing plant in its area than a national paper which is produced far away. Your ideology should also be appropriate for your designated institutional context and target audience.

Advertising

You may wish to construct some suitable advertisements for inclusion in your paper. This gives you more opportunity to ensure that appropriate products and adverts are placed but is perhaps less vital than originality with other elements of your paper. It may be appropriate to 'borrow' relevant advertising from other newspapers (which will also cut down on production time). The adverts are not usually controlled by the news or editing teams in a real publication, although the advertising and editorial departments of the newspaper coordinate layout and proportion of advertisements to editorial copy.

If you choose to borrow existing adverts in this way, you should scan them into a computer and insert them as elements into your page layout, just as with stories and images. In this way you are able to manipulate, crop and move the adverts as appropriate for your page design, giving you more control.

Page content

It is likely that you will produce the front page for your newspaper and a range of inside pages. These may be news-based or 'in-depth' interviews or articles (e.g. a newspaper targeting local clubbers may have a double-page spread story about gang warfare outside local clubs at closing time or an interview with a bouncer at a local club). Try to avoid 'filler' pages such as the horoscope pages or letters page if you can – these are difficult to achieve effectively and provide little opportunity to demonstrate your understanding of the processes of newspaper production. Tempting as it may be to construct the range of letters for inclusion in your paper, it is likely to be more entertaining for you than for your proposed audience.

Flat-plan

One important aspect of your research will be to analyse the layout of comparable publications and use this analysis to inform your flat-plan for your newspaper:

- What proportion of text to graphic might be appropriate on the front page?
- What type of story and image is appropriate for the front page?
- Are you going to use colour in your newspaper? If so, where and why?
- What fonts and point size are appropriate for the front page?
- How will you construct the masthead for your newspaper?
- What institutional codes will you use on your pages?
- What fonts and point size are used inside your paper?
- How are the columns, titles, images, pull quotes, captions and so on, organised on the page in your newspaper? Can you justify these decisions in light of your institutional context and target audience?
- How do your images reflect the ideology of the stories they are supporting?
- What use will you make of additional material like advertising?

ACTIVITIES

Compare and contrast these newspaper front pages to see how certain conventions are employed globally.

- How readily can you identify the target audience for each newspaper?
- How is the combination of text and images used to create meaning?
- How effectively do these front pages communicate?

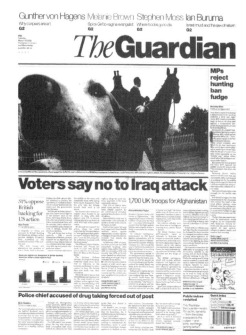

Gunther von Hagens   Melanie Brown   Stephen Moss   Ian Buruma
Why corpses are art   Spice Girl to vagina evangelist   Where books go to die   Israel must end the law of return
G2   G2   G2   G2

TheGuardian

MPs reject hunting ban fudge

Voters say no to Iraq attack

51% oppose British backing for US action

1,700 UK troops for Afghanistan

Police chief accused of drug taking forced out of post

THE Mirror
NEWSPAPER OF THE YEAR   32p

M's OSCAR FASHION SECRETS SEE PULLOUT

Four months ago, Tony Blair said the war in Afghanistan was as good as over.. now 1,700 British troops are being sent in and we're told to expect casualties

WHAT THE HELL IS GOING ON?

FULL STORY AND ANALYSIS: PAGES 4 AND 5

THE Sun

GARETH 4AM FRENZY Page 9

HOT NEW fashion section

WAR ON TERROR

IN WE GO

Royal Marines to wipe out al-Qa'ida

KAT FIGHT

Exclusive: EastEnders girls in scrap at telly awards bash
SEE PAGE 5

What's important? The Times, with more Sport, Business and News every day

'A sad, sad day for the sport I love'
The end of the Umpire?

The lie that changed the war

Why the Pope and I believe trade unions are right - Cherie Booth QC

THE TIMES
40p

Thatcher insists Britain must never join the 'doomed' euro

Marines to hunt Mullah Omar

● Americans call up 1,700 British troops

Hunting lobby's hopes of reprieve dashed

Teabags and sympathy at the passing of another great British institution

Breast screening saves thousands

PART FOUR

Radio Production

Radio production is changing in many ways as many stations are becoming more audience aware and audiences are expanding as digital radio increases listening areas. The range of stations and content is growing all the time. A recent estimate on http://www.anetstation.com/ (a non-commercial music radio station which broadcasts from the Antarctic) is that there are currently over 50,000 web-only radio stations.

Audience and institution

You may have studied digital radio and changing technologies as part of your AS study on New Technologies and so you may have experienced some of this variety already. This gives you a strong background for the Critical Evaluation for a radio project. If you are creating a radio text using some of these digital stations as your context, we would recommend that you choose a station where the relationship between institution, text, audience and society allows you to demonstrate your synoptic understanding of the context and practice of production. In the same way, a campus or school radio station would not fulfil the criteria, since, by definition, the audience is far too limited.

Production facilities

It is also important to remember that you should not attempt a production in this medium unless you are competent with the equipment. While it is relatively easy to produce a simple radio production using a single-track recording system, it would be difficult to create a production to a higher standard without access to some form of multi-tracking or mixing facility. This may be software or hardware based but production values for A2 work should demonstrate this level of competence.

Research activities

Radio is almost overlooked as a media form, with many students and centres concentrating on TV, film and print forms. Yet radio is the earliest of the broadcast forms of mass media, preceding television by many years. In this country, radio broadcasting began with the BBC but has now broadened into a range of national and local BBC stations and a range of national and local commercial stations as well as to global stations and web-only stations.

ACTIVITIES

- Which radio stations are available on FM, MW and LW in your region?
- Identify the institution for each of these stations
- Which are commercial stations and which are run by the BBC?
- Are there any pirate stations or other stations that do not fit either of these profiles? What is the remit of these stations? Are they successful?
- Identify at least five features of each of the major stations that make it easy for a listener to tune in without knowing the frequency. How important are these features for the stations?
- Identify five major differences between the BBC stations and national commercial stations
- Identify at least five similarities and differences between the national and local commercial stations
- Are there any stations that are **badged** for your region? If so, try to listen to equivalent broadcasts from a different region and compare how they are mediated for the different audiences. For example, the GWR group re-badges stations for different regions, using the same format and style but different presenters with an emphasis on local competitions
- Research the demographics of the audience for a national and local BBC Radio station and for a national and local commercial station. What conclusions can you draw about these four audiences?
- The **demographic** of a radio audience changes at different times of the day – in what ways do the morning/daytime/teatime and evening audiences change for your chosen stations? Can you account for these changes?

At some time in the day most of us will turn on a radio. But do we really listen to the radio, or is it just on in the background?

Write a short account of the role of radio in your own life, reflecting on the following issues:

- How often do you listen to the radio and where do you listen?
- When you do listen do you usually switch on to listen to a specific programme or do you simply use radio as background noise – and what programmes (if any) do you concentrate on?
- Why do you choose these programmes?

- Why do these programmes make you want to concentrate?
- What audience **hooks** do they use?
- How far do you fit the audience demographic for these programmes?

DISCUSSION

When researching radio production, it can help to undertake some more theoretical research in advance, to prepare for the Critical Evaluation for your artefact.

- Is advertising the best way to fund commercial radio?

- Based on your earlier research, what conclusions can you draw about the audiences for local and national and for PSB and commercial radio? What are the significances of these differences?

- It has been said that the presenters of a radio programme are the personification of the station and its listeners. Discuss this point of view with reference to the presenters of at least three programmes of your choice.

- It can be argued that the trend from broadcasting to **narrowcasting** has transformed radio speech into an agent and reflection of anti-standard social and intellectual currents. Do you agree?

- Many 'shock jocks' assert that they are the 'voice of truth' in radio, operating against the hegemonic function of talk-based radio. Is this the case or are they merely sensationalist?

- Why does pirate radio continue?

- It is listeners who decide the content of the airwaves, by listening to certain stations and not to others. Do you agree or are there other factors that control the output of the radio stations?

Constructing the programme

The construction process will vary, depending on the software and hardware you have available for the programme. This will be determined by your centre and by your previous experience. Allow enough time for testing and re-recording your programme. It is easy to assume that a programme will be successful when the recording quality is actually too low.

When creating your programme, it is strongly recommended that you have access to either a multi-track recording system with effects units or that you access sound recording software and hardware that allows you to record each track and edit or add effects before mixing for airplay.

You should use as many microphones as you have speakers and ideally these should all be good quality uni-directional microphones to avoid picking up background sound. A uni-directional mike only records in one direction – it only picks up the sound aimed directly at it. An 'omni-directional' mike picks up sound from all around. This is good for background or blanket sound but not so good for a single sound source such as a voice. The microphones on a video camera are usually omni-directional which is why the sound recorded by these mikes during filming is unclear and unbalanced; the microphone cannot sort out the sounds to hear only the important sounds. You may need access to one omni-directional mike to record sound effects or 'studio noise' during the show.

It is very difficult to get good quality radio work at this level if you are working by crash editing onto a single-track recording device like a cassette player or CD player where multi-track is not possible. It is possible to use two cassette players and a basic mixing facility but the reproduction of sound is likely to be weaker even with first generation 'multi-tracking' in this way. However, as mentioned below, you may be able to record a radio play using a single recording source, although you are strongly advised to test your recording beforehand. You may discover that recording from a single microphone detracts from your production because the sound quality is so poor that it cannot be easily evaluated. It is plausible to record a live performance of a radio play using live or canned sound effects, providing you have access to a multi-tracking recording system. You can use more than one microphone and take a direct feed into the mixing desk if you are using canned sound effects.

Whatever method you use you will still need a substantial amount of rehearsal time to make sure that you know what you are doing and to synchronise all the various activities.

Recommended content for Production Log

- A script outline and studio time-plan. In addition you should ensure you have got a detailed production schedule. Remember to allow time for elements that need preparation. It is no good turning up in the sound studio to record the final version of the programme only to realise that the jingles have not yet been recorded and edited for inclusion!

- It is a good idea to construct a script so that you know what information will be available on each section. You may prefer to use memo cards to prevent your presenters and callers from sounding as if they are simply reading aloud. This is especially worthwhile if you are doing a phone-in to help achieve a sense of spontaneity. It is also good to put timings on the script so you know how quickly or slowly you are going. Clearly, if you are producing a radio play, you need a full script with sound effects, additionals and timings annotated clearly so that it can be adhered to during production
- Make sure there is a large clock which can be seen by all the members of the group so you can be aware of timing
- If you are using pre-recorded sound effects, make sure you have clearance to use them – just as you do with music tracks
- A Production Log is necessary to keep track of the creation of elements such as station idents and to keep research information that may be useful to the project. A Production Log also allows you to keep detailed records of objectives for meetings and rehearsals and problems to be sorted out. It also allows you to allocate responsibilities and schedules clearly

It is the producer's responsibility to ensure that all the necessary equipment is ready and that material is edited on time. This does not mean that the producer does all these jobs, just that they supervise them.

Practical exercise 1

Radio drama

When creating video productions, you will frequently run into logistical problems. Even apparently simple shots, such as an actor being chased along a road, can be hampered by bad weather or too much traffic. If your production requires more visual support, for example, if you were trying to film a spaceship landing in the middle of the local shopping centre, you would rapidly enter the realms of special effects and laborious production. However, on radio, these problems are easily overcome. Just listen to the Radio 4 afternoon play or any episode of *The Archers* to hear how effective sound effects can be in creating a sense of time and place. It is easy to tell when scenes in *The Archers* are set in a pub or in a field by the different background sound effects that are used. It is far easier to establish a change of location than when working with visual material.

This is a short script for two people. You should record this script three times, each in a different location. You will need to think about the sound effects and possibly the music that will create the right atmosphere for each of the locations. You will also have to consider how the lines will be spoken.

THE SCENE

Opening music and/or sound effects
Enter J

J: *Are you there? I can't see a thing at the moment.*
                          (Shouting) Are you there?

Enter P

P: *I'm right next to you. Keep your hair on!*

J: *OK. Let's get this thing open and see what's inside.*

P: *There isn't much time left. You know what might*
                          happen. So, you go down that end, and when I say
                          'now', lift.

J: *Right. On the count of three; one, two, three . . .*

P: *Now!*

TOGETHER: *What is that?*

This is a very short scene but you can make it as long as you wish with sound effects and additional music.

Location

So, where will this be? You must choose three from the following list:

- A graveyard at midnight
- A main road during the morning. Two workers looking at a manhole cover
- Two archaeologists in an ancient Egyptian tomb
- Two space explorers on Mars
- Two people mending a lavatory cistern at home
- Two surgeons in an operating theatre

There are obviously a number of decisions to be made with each of the locations. You will need to think about:

- What is being opened
- What music to use to set the mood at the beginning
- What other background noises or music to use in order to keep the mood going
- What opening or use of presenter's voice you will use at the beginning and end to open and close your piece

When you have finished this production, test market it on an appropriate audience.

- Can they identify the locations and atmosphere you created?
- Which elements of the recording did they consider most effective? Why?

Practical exercise 2

Jingles

There are now many more radio stations and so it is important for each to make sure that its audience can identify the station as quickly as possible. One way we identify stations is by the regular 'jingles' which tell us that we are listening to 'Wonderful Radio Whatever'. The jingle must reflect not only the station but also the particular programme or item about to come on the air. A jingle for the 'News' would be very different to a jingle for a 'Top Twenty' music programme. You should try to listen to as many stations as possible, listen to their jingles and try to work out the images projected for both the stations and the programmes.

Now compose jingles for the following programmes on the following types of station. You have been given a brief profile of the station and the type of audience it hopes to attract.

Radio Oldie

This station plays nothing but records from the 1960s, 1970s and 1980s. It has a profile audience of 30 year olds plus, although it is discovering that more and more teenagers are tuning in. You must compose jingles for the following:

- A station jingle for Radio Oldie
- A jingle for the news
- A jingle for the '20 Year Top Twenty'. This is a daily programme

immediately following the breakfast programme, which plays the top 20 from this day 20 years ago

Radio Nose Stud

This dance station broadcasts to the local area. It is heavily alternative in approach, with an audience profile comprising young people, age 16–21 who like the club focus and local dance scene information available on the station. Compose jingles for the following:

- A station jingle
- A jingle for the local traffic bulletin
- A jingle for the local club update programme

Classics Radio

A classical music station, aimed at a sophisticated A/B audience with an age profile between 25–50. A national station it plays classical music with the occasional programme which reviews new releases and gives background information on different composers. Compose jingles for the following:

- A station jingle
- 'Composer of the Week' – a look at the music of one individual composer
- A programme that reviews new CDs

Case Study

Alternative phone-in programme for a station

If you choose to create a phone-in programme for a station, you should aim to produce a maximum of 5 minutes worth of material. You do not have to produce the whole programme so you may choose to do the beginning, middle or end. In 5 minutes you cannot hope to produce a whole programme. You may wish to include some of the following:

- The opening link and opening sequence
- The opening monologue
- Jingles
- A travel bulletin
- A news bulletin
- Several 'callers'
- The closing sequence and lead out

Most phone-in programmes are live, so you should probably aim to record the programme whole while it is 'on air' to get this sense. However, remember that the opening and closing sequences, jingles and possibly the opening monologue are often recorded for live radio work. Ensure these are pre-recorded and lined up ready to play with no delays or confusion during the recording of the programme. Although the programmes are 'live' it is customary with all live broadcasting of this kind to allow a delay time between recording and transmission. In the case of radio phone-in programmes this is usually about 7 seconds which allows enough time for a presenter to fill quickly if a caller has to be terminated abruptly, or if they use inappropriate language which must be screened out before transmission. On some phone-in programmes the member of the production crew with their finger on the 'bleeper' is kept very busy!

However, there is no reason why you cannot pre-record the entire programme and then edit it as required, if that is more convenient. The only approach that is unlikely to work is pre-recorded 'callers' where your presenter(s) try to time their comments for the gaps in the call – this quickly becomes out of synch and detracts from your work.

You should also experiment with the sound quality available for your programme. Ideally, you should run the microphone for callers through an effects unit, either while recording or during editing to create the ambiance of a telephone call. Failing this, you should experiment with other methods. If you have a good quality microphone available and a multi-track recording system, it may even be possible to record a genuine telephone call by holding the microphone close to the phone! However, using this method may result in problems with feedback.

When you are constructing the programme, the content will be far easier to author if you spend some time at the beginning of the project constructing the format. For example, you should define:

- What station the programme is for and the time of day of transmission
- Target audience profile
- What 'hooks' are given in the programme for the audience
- The name of the programme and the presenter
- The presenter's persona and attitudes (for each presenter if there is more than one)
- The factual content of the programme (i.e. what the programme is about)
- The attitudes and opinions of the presenter(s) and how these will be revealed
- Catch-phrases and slogans which may be used in the programme
- The outcome (which may not be a conclusion) to the discussion

Concluding the programme
Remember that it is not necessary to end your programme with a fight or a shouting match. While many alternative phone-ins are presented by shock jocks who gain notoriety before respect, your programme may be less convincing if it descends into anarchy at the end. Skilled presenters keep the programme just within the boundaries of civilised behaviour while not missing any opportunities to provoke their callers. This is what most listeners regard as the entertainment value of these programmes. If the programmes always degenerated into anarchy, that would become boring, as it does not make good radio.

Callers
In addition to deciding on what each caller is going to say, it helps to create a persona for each caller. As with visual work, your radio work will not be marked down on the quality of the acting. However, the more convincing the construction of each caller's thoughts, opinions and motivations for calling the programme, the easier it is to present them with conviction.

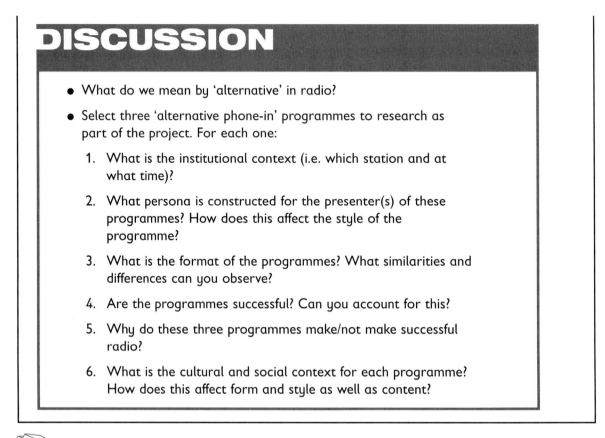

DISCUSSION

- What do we mean by 'alternative' in radio?

- Select three 'alternative phone-in' programmes to research as part of the project. For each one:

  1. What is the institutional context (i.e. which station and at what time)?

  2. What persona is constructed for the presenter(s) of these programmes? How does this affect the style of the programme?

  3. What is the format of the programmes? What similarities and differences can you observe?

  4. Are the programmes successful? Can you account for this?

  5. Why do these three programmes make/not make successful radio?

  6. What is the cultural and social context for each programme? How does this affect form and style as well as content?

Case Study

Audience research

Once you have analysed a range of phone-in programmes in this way, you should think carefully about the target audience for each programme.

- What is the target audience for each programme?
- Is the target audience similar for all of these programmes?
- Is this the same audience as the audience for the station itself?
- Can you account for these similarities and differences?
- How do the programmes 'brand' their identity for their audience?
- Do these programmes have an audience or a community?

Once you have completed this research, you should be able to plan your programme more effectively, using the appropriate and successful elements that you have identified above.

Create a radio play

You should aim to produce an extract from a radio play that is no longer than 5 minutes. You do not necessarily need access to multi-tracking recording equipment or sophisticated sound software to record a radio play. You could record the play live with the use of live sound effects. However, the station idents around the play can be pre-recorded to limit the amount of live recording to be done at one time and to make the project easier to handle.

Project

You may choose to create an original play or adapt a scene or chapter from a book for radio. You should not try and produce a play that has already been written for radio as this will not allow you sufficient freedom to create something which will show your understanding of text, audience and institution. If you start with a previously written text, the production context and audience are already defined (your only audience-related question becomes 'does this play suit this station's target profile?', which is a much more limited question). To ensure an artefact appropriate for A2 production work, you should be able to demonstrate how you have constructed the product within your chosen institutional context.

You should probably consider a clearly defined audience – you need to choose your institution and define your target audience carefully before you can plan your extract. The institution and audience for *The Archers*, for example, is now so much a part of the public expectation of the programme that the episodes are almost defined before they are even written. A Christmas story written for children and presented on local radio, based on the displays in the local department store would be very different to a family-based serial presented by Kazakhstan National Radio intended as a unifying drama for expatriate Kazakhs across the globe. When *The Archers* started, one of the key motivators for the programme was to provide a focal point and education base for farmers scattered across Britain who were feeling isolated in rural communities.

Possible suggestions
- An extract for a new episode of *The Archers*
- An extract from a radio adaptation of one of the later Harry Potter books
- An extract from a spoof comedy series for radio such as *Big Brother is listening*

Once you have decided on your extract and deconstructed the institution and target audience you will be able to script the extract.

Your extract may be from the beginning, end or middle of the episode or play but you should think about the following elements:

- Are you creating an extract from a one-off play or an episode of a serial?
- How does your choice of institution affect the register of the actors?
- What atmosphere will the sound effects need to establish?
- What is the target audience and why will this programme appeal to them?

Once you have the concept of your programme you will need to think about the logistics. These include the arrangements for the actors, rehearsing the sound effects or splicing them all onto one tape or CD for easy access during recording, and constructing the context.

If your extract is from the beginning of the play or episode, you may want to use a station jingle to lead in to the play. This will help to set the audience expectations for the play. You may want to use a narrator or presenter to introduce the play, although make sure that your introduction is not too long and does not detract from the play itself – about 20 seconds is probably about right.

Equally, if your extract is the finale, you will need to establish the climax, close the play and lead out to the next programme. This can be challenging to construct but does allow plenty of opportunity for complex and dramatic sound effects – depending on what happens at the end of the play or episode of course!

5 PART FIVE
ICT/New Media Production

There are a variety of options available within this area. You might choose to create a website for a new band, a new computer game, a Dorling Kindersley presentation on CD-ROM about film noir or a short animation for the web.

It is important to remember that you should not attempt a production in this medium unless you are competent with the chosen software. While it is relatively easy to transfer skills between different video editing programmes, for example, it can be far harder to transfer skills between multimedia software – not least because the programmes are intended to achieve very different outcomes.

You should present your project on CD-ROM or on floppy disk and make sure that the disk you use has been scanned for viruses before you give it to your teacher or lecturer to be marked and before it is sent off for moderation. It is NOT acceptable to offer a web address for a site and ask for 'live' marking, because it is impossible for the marker to determine when you have edited the site. Your work may be sent for moderation and viewed three months after you created it. To be sure that you have not amended or improved your site between submission and viewing, the moderator must view a fixed version of the project. You should also provide a hard copy of each page. A video 'walk-through' can be a very successful method of presenting a website.

Case Study

Website for a new band

If you choose to create a website for a new band, you should aim to produce a homepage and at least six other pages for your site. You may wish to include 'stills' of the band performing, gig memorabilia, information pages, tour schedules, biographies and maybe samples of the music or clips from videos made by the band.

Some of this is complex to put on a website and you should be confident that you have the necessary skills, expertise and backup to create, for example, a streaming video or to ensure that your images are 'web ready'.

If possible it would be better to find a local band to work with. This has advantages in many ways:

● You are likely to know at least one of the band members which makes access easier

- You will know the music fairly well which will enable you to construct a site that reflects the band and their music
- You will probably have access to stills and possibly video footage that you can use
- You should be able to get facts for biography pages, information pages, gig guides and so forth fairly easily

The disadvantages in working with a real band are that they may expect to make some contribution and structure the design in some way. There may be a difference between the site that you wish to author for your A2 work and the site that they want to see go 'live'. Compromising and negotiating a solution is very much a part of the design process (hence it is assessed as part of your project planning).

If you choose to work with a real band, make sure that you set up a series of meetings at the beginning of the production process. Initially you should simply talk to the band about their music, philosophy, image and future plans. Then you should talk in detail about how they see a website benefiting them and what material they would like to see included. You should always have an agenda for these meetings and make sure that you stick to it and that one member of your production team keeps notes. You may even decide to video these interviews (and get some useful footage to feature on the website). It is important to appear credible and professional during the production process and so you need to be organised and disciplined in this way.

If you decide to work with a mythical band, you free yourselves from the constraints of diplomacy and negotiation with clients, but you do not get the access to visual or aural material which would benefit your site. In this instance you are strongly recommended to take the time to construct some stills of the band, for example, 'in performance' or 'rehearsal', so that you are not forced to rely on found material that may detract substantially from your site. It is unlikely that you will be able to create live action video material in the time given, but you may be able to use a 'talking head' video, an audio file for a biography page or a sample track from the 'new album' to add interest and depth to your pages.

If you are constructing a mythical band, the website will be easier to author if you spend some time at the beginning of the project constructing the group. For example, you should decide:

- What type of music they will play
- How many band members there will be
- What the band members look like (physically, but also the image they present)
- What previous material they have produced (titles and genres may suffice for most)
- Future gig guides, reviews of CDs, gig reviews, biographies, press releases and other supporting material
- Constructed stills of the band – these could be individual shots or group shots, or a mixture of the two!
- The name of the band

While you do not want to use up too much of the planning time, if you do not construct the group effectively at this stage it will be difficult to define an identity for the website because there will be no group identity to reflect.

Planning your site
Having made the decision to either work with a local band or create a mythical band you should begin to plan the site itself.

A C T I V I T I E S

Look at the examples of websites for different bands and artists here. For each site a web address has been given so you can look at the site properly but there are also images of pages for each site. How far does each site brand the band or artist? Are there strong similarities between the sites and the CDs they are promoting? Each site involves interactive elements that cannot be shown in a book. When you are analysing the sites, think carefully about how integral these elements are to the style of the sites and also how integral they are to the information provided and marketing purpose of the sites.

www.madonnamusic.com

The entry page for the current Madonna site. How effectively is it branded? Is it welcoming to a fan? Is it accessible to a casual viewer? See figure 5.

www.travisonline.com

The homepage for Travis. A very different style of site in line with the different style of music. There is interactivity on most pages, even if this is just scrolling text. In what ways do the images reflect the differences between Travis and Madonna? See figure 7.

www.westlife.com

The homepage for Westlife. The target audience for Westlife is different. How is this reflected in the design of this page? Is this page appealing to casual viewers as well as fans? See figure 9.

Another page from the current Madonna site. See figure 6.

A typical page from inside the Travis site. Notice how the design elements are consistent across all the pages. There are sections for lyrics/chords, discography, chatrooms, e-lists, merchandise, competitions and more. This is a very comprehensive site. See figure 8.

Is this simplistic design more accessible for the target audience? See figure 10.

www.eminem.com

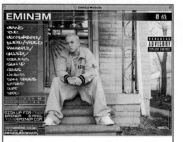

The homepage for the official Eminem site. In what ways does the site reflect the (deliberately) controversial style of the rapper? How does this site attract its target audience? See figure 11.

ACTIVITIES

Identify at least five sites for bands within a particular style of music that already exist on the web. Try to choose a style of music relevant to the band you intend to promote and choose a variety of **mainstream** or well-recognised artists and more independent or less well-known bands.

For each site, audit the content information available:
- How many pages?
- How many sections?
- What are the key section headings?
- How much emphasis is placed on hearing the music?
- How much emphasis is placed on stills?
- How much emphasis is placed on video material?
- Do they provide background, such as biographies?
- Are there opportunities to be interactive, e.g. by e-mailing the band/joining a web community to talk with other fans or by buying merchandise/CDs etc?
- How effective are these opportunities? How well designed are they?
- What is the basic design of each site?
- How does this relate to the ethos of the band?
- Why have they designed the site this way?
- How successful do you feel this design is?
- What fonts and colours are used? Are these successful?
- Do you feel the sites reflect the band appropriately?
- What differences can you observe between sites for more mainstream bands and more indie bands?
- Do you feel this site is an appropriate marketing tool for the band?

Audience research

Once you have analysed a range of similar sites in this way, you should think carefully about the target audience for each site.

- What is the target audience for each site?
- Is the target audience similar for all of these sites?
- Is this the same audience as the audience for the band?
- If there are differences (for example the target audience for the website may be a subset of the main audience), how do these manifest themselves?
- How do the sites 'brand' this style of music for their audience?
- What elements on the sites identify the style of music to the audience?

Once you have identified and differentiated the target audiences in this way, you should select three sites that you feel are successful and test them on members of the target audience.

What responses do you get?

- Do they feel part of the target audience?
- Do the sites appeal to them?
- Which one is the most/least successful for them? Why?
- Do they respond to the music, the band or the site? Does this matter?

Once you have completed this research, you should be able to plan your site more effectively, using the appropriate and successful elements that you have identified above.

DISCUSSION

- Would you say that a successful band website should be primarily a marketing and promotional tool or a representation of the band?

- By what criteria can we define a successful band website?

- De Certeau in *The Practice of Everyday Life* (University of California Press, 1992) argues that everyday life is creative primarily because we construct our own version of reality across a range of media and mediums. To what extent would you say that the use of new technologies, such as band websites, constructs our responses to the music we are interested in?

- Do you feel that the global nature of music websites affects the image and style of bands? Is it different for global stars?

Project

Producing a site map

When planning the site, the place to start is with a site map. Depending on the style of music you are working with and the proposed target audience, you may choose to structure the site differently.

A **linear** structure may be appropriate for a simple site – perhaps a band with a young target audience or a new band with limited pages.

A **hierarchical** structure may be more appropriate for a conventional band or a heavily information-based site, acting primarily as a band resource.

A **mesh** structure would suit many bands and styles of music – it allows for freedom of navigation, which may be more appropriate for indie bands or rappers, for example. It also allows more navigation choices which may suit a site with a large amount of information or one which is offering an e-commerce option (buying merchandising) as part of the site. (NB: You are NOT expected to produce the e-commerce pages for your band.)

Task

Consider these examples of how each type of site might be laid out. The mythical band here is called 'Itzcool'. What does each design layout suggest about the target audience?

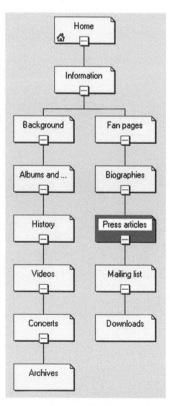

Linear structure for Itzcool site.

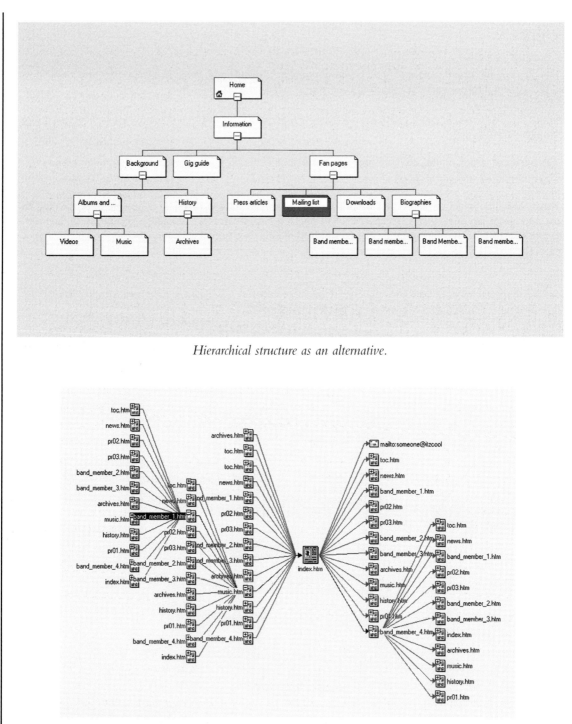

Hierarchical structure as an alternative.

Mesh structure for site – all pages are linked to all of the other pages – perhaps by using a navigation bar as a fixed element.

Site design

Having planned the basic structure of the site, you need to design the site appearance. How are you going to use visual codes to reflect and present the band? As starting points, you should think about the choices of background, which fonts to use, type and placement of graphics (including the possible use of a background image), use of design elements such as frames, focus points on the page, possible placement of adverts and balance of information/space. From there you need to work on creating an on-line identity for the band. Effective band sites reflect the (current) image of the band and highly successful sites identify the band or music for the viewer before they even know who the site belongs to. Visit http://www.michaeljackson.com and load the front page into your browser (if you have the Flash™ plug-in.).

> Flash™ is a multimedia plug-in for Internet Explorer™ or Netscape™, which allows you to see web animations. If you have a fairly recent browser (Internet Explorer 5™ or above, for example) you will already have Flash™ on your computer. If you are using an older browser or an older computer, you may need to download Flash™ from http://www.macromedia.com. It is a free plug-in which is very useful for sophisticated websites.

From the animation that plays as the site is loading, the style of Jackson's music and the expectations about his image and performance are defined. Try experimenting with dynamic sites such as this — how quickly can you identify the sites without knowing who the site belongs to?

ACTIVITIES

Look at each of the possible site designs for Itzcool. What is the impact of each design? What expectations does each design create about the band and their music? Each of these is produced as a different 'theme' in Microsoft Front Page. These themes are an easy way to brand a site and can be tweaked to suit your band. However, you should be aware that many people are familiar with these themes and so they may not seem as unique and dynamic as you would wish. It is also important to remember that using these Front Page themes can make it difficult to upload your site onto a 'live' server once it is complete.

> Sites made with Microsoft Front Page will usually only display correctly on servers that use the 'Front Page Extensions' provided by Microsoft. If you want to look at the site you have designed on the web, you should check with the ISP you intend to use to host the site about whether they have these extensions. Remember of course that you only have to produce a CD-ROM version of your site for the A2 practical unit.

For each of these designs, make notes about the following things:
- The colours used and their impact
- The fonts used and their impact
- The effect of the colour scheme and style on the image constructed
- Your personal response to this design scheme
- Your opinion about whether elements of this scheme would be suitable for your artefact
- Is a different image created by each different scheme for Itzcool?
- There are no graphics on these design samples. Why is this? What would be a suitable band image for each of these designs? How would that affect our assumptions about the music?

Six possible site designs for Itzool. **See figures 12–17.**

Developing the pages

If you are working in a group, you may decide to make each person responsible for a group of pages, or perhaps one group member could take charge of creating a series of images of the band and preparing them for web use. One member of your group should also undertake the responsibility of project management and make sure that all the required elements are prepared and assembled on time. It is sensible to have a range of paper-based planning materials. Not only will these help you to prepare the site, they will provide the necessary evidence for your written work to illustrate how you planned and prepared the site.

Recommended content for Production Log

- A storyboard or site map. This may include a site map along the lines of the examples shown above or you may map out your site differently. Once you have designed the basic site map, it is a good idea to construct the storyboard so that you know what information will be available on each page. You can use a simple arrow with a page number above the arrow to indicate which pages link to which. You may prefer to do a separate site map and storyboard or you may prefer to combine the two in one planning document
- Draft layouts for at least three pages from the site so that you can analyse the design process and explain how you reached a design consensus
- Original copies of stills used on the pages, annotated to show how and why you selected and manipulated images
- An asset sheet for each page so that you know what elements need to be inserted into each page and who is responsible for them. An asset sheet can be laid out in various ways but one example is given here

Constructing the site

You should construct each page of your site in line with your production schedule and allow enough time to create each of the required elements well in advance of their insertion into the relevant page. It is usually a good idea to assign a group member to be responsible for each type of asset here. In this way, one group member is responsible for taking and editing the pictures of the band, another group member prepares music tracks for inclusion in the site and a third group member writes all of the biography sections.

The construction process will vary, depending on the software you have chosen to use. This will depend on what is available at your centre and your previous experience. Remember to allow enough time for testing your site. It is

Example of an asset sheet listing all of the files required for each page when constructing a website.

easy to assume that a site will be successful when there are technical problems with the site. You will provide a hard copy of the site and therefore you will not need to complete extensive testing to see if the site will download quickly, but you should try to test your completed site in a different browser before submission. If you are working on a PC, the browser which you are using and familiar with is likely to be Internet Explorer™. However, Macs use different browsers and there are different browsers available for PCs as well. You are strongly recommended to test your site in Netscape Navigator™ as well as in Internet Explorer™. If your site displays correctly in both these browsers, it is reasonable to assume it will display correctly in all browsers.

It is strongly recommended that you create your site with a web-editing package. Many word processing packages (e.g. Word) or DTP packages (e.g. Microsoft Publisher) have a 'save as web page' option which can make site production seem quite straightforward. Sadly, the output from these packages does not always work and in extreme cases may be impossible to save properly and copy to CD for assessment.

Lastly, do not forget that you need to put a copy of any file that you insert into your pages on the CD along with the pages themselves. The professional way to ensure that all the images, video, music tracks and so on are safely copied for assessment and moderation is to copy them all onto the CD which you will be submitting *before* you start designing the site. You can then tell the web-editing programme to look at the copy of each file that is already on the CD, as required.

Case Study

Create a website for a new film

You should aim to produce the homepage and at least eight other pages for this site, perhaps with accompanying media files. For example, you might want to include stills from the film, downloadable files, poster images and maybe even trailers or 'interviews' with people involved in the film. If you integrate many of these elements, you may need to reassign your project to 'cross media' but this should not be a problem. However, you cannot work in the same medium as you chose at AS Level. Also remember that you should produce an official site, not a fan site, in order to adequately research and evidence the institutional determinants on production.

For the purposes of this project example, we will focus on the website itself and not on these associated media. Nonetheless, there will be some suggestions about more complex technologies involved, like streaming media.

This Case Study should be read in conjunction with the previous 'Website for a new band' Case Study. Most of the information about research, planning, construction and evaluation is similar, if not the same, for both examples and therefore has not been duplicated in this second Case Study.

Research task
Identify a range of contemporary film releases that have associated websites. Identify at least three different production studios (ideally three mainstream and one independent). What similarities and differences can you see between the sites?

Now find sites for at least two other films produced by the same studios (or equivalent independent production companies). What common elements can you identify between the sites? Can you identify a corporate identity for the studios? To what extent are the sites formulaic?

Now complete the same exercises for at least three different genre of film. Analyse the elements of these sites to identify common elements – is the layout or the style of the sites similar for example? Do sites within a genre tend to rely on similar selling points such as freebies and downloads, for example? What methods do they use to 'hook' the audience? How do they communicate about the film? How do they establish a sense of 'community'? You may find the sites make use of bulletin boards or chat relays. How popular are these? Do they affect the success of the film in anyway? Why are they used?

- Which comes first – the trailer or the website?

- How much money do studios invest in websites for new releases? What evidence is there that this results in increased revenues? If websites are seen as 'loss leaders' are they important? Why?

- Some sites are more substantial than others. Is there any evidence that these sites have a different purpose? What examples of substantial or insubstantial sites can you find? Do they affect your responses to their films at all?

- What trends can you identify in film websites? Can you account for these trends?

- Do you prefer to visit official film sites or fan sites? Why is this?

- David Gauntlett, in his book *Web.Studies* (Arnold, 2000) dismisses film sites as largely irrelevant to cinema and to film marketing. Do you agree with him? Why do you think the studios consider it important to create sites for new releases?

- Ben Bachmair, writing in *Intertextuality and the Media*, Meinhof U and Smith J [Eds] (Manchester University Press, 2000) comments upon a new formula for audience segmentation constructed by a German television station in 1994, which identifies 'media surfers' as an audience group who engage with a wide variety of media texts and mediums in a critical but non-judgemental way. Is this the most likely target audience for these sites or would you define the audience in a different way?

Project

Once you have completed the above tasks, you are ready to begin to plan your site. You should start by thinking about the film that you wish to promote.

What genre is the film?

Just as there are generic elements and conventions for a film poster, you will see the same conventions reflected in a website for a film. Indeed it would be unlikely that a studio would not ensure consistency across a campaign and establish a 'look' for the site which does not identify the film and establish familiarity.

Who is it produced by?

Just as there are key genre elements, there are institutionally driven elements in the promotional campaign for any film. For example, the campaign designed for a Film Four Production will use the recognisable institutional signifiers for Film Four. It would be unlikely that a website dedicated to a new Film Four release would not also make use of the elements of colour, layout, fonts and logos. If you are creating a website for a new film, it is made within an institutional context and the institutional codes and conventions should be defined and expected at the beginning of the project.

What is the target audience for the film?
There are two important elements when identifying the audience. You need to identify the audience of the film and then the sub-audience for whom the website is likely to be an attractive marketing tool. It may be that the site can also extend the initial audience – perhaps by promoting the film or creating a cult identity or a community or fan group for the film. For instance, the target audience sub-section who access the site may be keen to find out about the film prior to release or to gain access to images to use as wallpaper or screen savers, to reflect their enthusiasm for the film. A successful site will create a strong identity for the film and this can become a very successful marketing ploy. A good example is the now infamous *The Blair Witch Project* site which became a cult site. Elements of a site which entice surfers to revisit the site or engage them for some time – perhaps by offering games based around the film – can act to both heighten interest in the film among the target sub-set, but also to extend this across a wider community (by word of mouth – mail usually) and establish a sense of 'belonging' and involvement which may cause more people to feel familiar with the film and to choose to go and see it.

Choosing the film
Once the broader context for the site has been established, you should spend some time thinking about the particular film. Unless you have thought about the film in detail, you are unlikely to be able to isolate it and establish a strong site branding.

You may wish to create your own film and write a short treatment, define stars and select a studio and so forth, as you would do when creating film posters and video covers. Alternatively, you can choose to create a site to re-launch an older film for a new audience (perhaps even a digitally remastered version of an old black and white film!). You need to have the basic packages constructed before you can begin to plan the site, as with the previous case study. Much of web design work consists of creating a basic design and using it as a casing for other media elements, for example, stills of the cast, extracts from the storyboard, trailers and copies of posters.

Constructing the site
Once you have defined the film and thought about the target audience, institution and genre of the film as suggested above, you can begin to plan the site, knowing what you are seeking to achieve and why. You should look through the previous Case Study suggestions to give you some ideas about how to structure your site and about the possible planning documentation you can use.

Remember to allow enough time to complete the site and test it before submission – especially if you are constructing posters or even trailers which will be available on the site. If you do decide to create these artefacts rather than just using mock-ups to indicate how and why they would function, you should be prepared for the substantial amount of additional work that could be entailed.

PART SIX

Cross Media Production

There are many contemporary media texts that operate across or require skills from more than one medium. There are other texts that require skills and knowledge across several media for construction. Therefore, the 'cross media' option at A2 is intended to allow these more specialist and highly skilled texts to be offered. As suggested below, it is unlikely that you would want to embark upon one of these options without previous knowledge and experience, since they are more demanding because of this very 'cross media' nature. Of the two options suggested here, pop video is likely to be a popular choice for many students, but animation is offered as an alternative so that you can choose to work in this medium if you wish. You should remember that it is extremely time-consuming and requires painstaking attention to detail in order to be successful. If you already have experience and interest in animation, you would be in a position to offer an animated text at A2 Level.

Case Study

Music video

Possible examples:
- A video for a new release composed and performed within school or college
- An animated video for an older track, re-badging for a new audience
- A video for a re-release of a track not previously released as a video

If you are going to make a music video, you need to start by deciding what sort of music video you wish to make and decide on your purpose.

While it is not essential to compose and perform an original track for this project, it is often highly successful. It is far easier to integrate sound and vision when the composer, performers and video director can integrate as a team. In the event that an original piece is presented in this way, the music is not assessed, but the freedom of control allowed is usually very beneficial. In many centres, there has been an opportunity for work across departments, with music technology students composing and performing the track and the media students constructing the video.

It is generally accepted that pop music began in 1950s' America, with the birth of rock 'n' roll. In the last 50 years pop music has developed into a global economy, going far beyond the expectations of those early performers and audiences. The extensive range of musical types and styles in the contemporary scene presumes a sophisticated and experienced audience that is readily able to identify and analyse music. However, music video is a far more recent phenomenon. The fusion of image and sound in a video adds a further layer of complexity and creativity to a band's output. Early music videos were little more than edited 'live' recordings, which progressed from live cuts to multiple performances spliced together or a combination of live and rehearsal shots. Later videos added a narrative sequence as well as the performance, usually closely related to the lyrics. From this came the complex narratives and abstract interpretations that defined music video as a genre in its own right, leading to the multi-layered representations that comprise contemporary music video. Each new popular music style and genre is a development of the early rebellion that was 'rock n roll' and it is perhaps for this reason that the music video has developed into such a complex and varied media text. The forms and conventions of moving image text are challenged and manipulated endlessly in music video and it has clearly transmogrified into a complex form in its own right. The combination of live performance, narrative, computer graphics and animation within a single video is both the epitomy of a post-modern text and a rejection of the realist conventions.

Indeed, the videos may be more appropriately defined as 'spectacle' than as narrative. This presumes the different modes of address and representations that operate within a music video. The videos operate both as fantasies constructed around the music embodied within the text and also as definition and limitation for the music presented. The visual construct both extends and defines the reception of the musical track that is presented as spectacle in this way.

Video style now tends to be related to the genre of the music embodied in the video. A hip-hop video is likely to be different in form and conventions to a rock video, a punk video or lyrical ballad. We readily identify different visual codes with different musical genres. The target audience for any video identifies with the video very quickly because of this use of visual conventions. The vast sums of money spent on videos by artists such as Bjork or Madonna and the publicity campaigns around the release of the latest Michael Jackson video suggest the importance of the video in the lexicon of the artist's work. Indeed it has been suggested that the visual has been more influential for some artists such as Madonna (who reinvents her image with each new video) than the music they promote.

Research tasks

- Trace the career of a particular star/band through their videos (e.g. Michael Jackson, Madonna, *Blur*). In what ways does their image change through the videos? Why is this? Which comes first, the video or the image change?
- Select four music videos for different musical styles which you think are especially influential. Provide a detailed reading of each video, justifying your choices. Identify the specific target audiences for each of these texts. In what ways do the music videos target their audiences?
- What is the ideology of these texts? How is this revealed within the texts?
- Use the internet to research examples of music videos from other cultures. What differences and similarities can you see between these and those you have already studied?

DISCUSSION

- With the increase in digital channels and more demand globally for video material for these channels, will music videos become such significant promotional tools that there will no longer be a CD release for many tracks?

- Has the rise of the music video changed the bands and artists who produce the music in any way?

- Do you feel that manufactured bands that only produce videos and cannot perform live deserve equal credit with more traditional recording artists?

Deconstruction

When deconstructing the videos, or your own video after production, you may find the following list of prompts helpful:

- What representations are set up by the visual image?
- What media forms are used within the video?
- Does the video depend on the music for its context or does it define the context for the music? Why is this?
- What themes are set up within the video?
- In what ways are colour/style/fashion and make up used to define this image or contextualise it?
- What are the social, economic and cultural contexts being employed in this video?
- What narrative is being constructed for the audience? In what ways is it constructed?
- What image is constructed for the band/artist?
- Are there other texts referenced within the video? What is the effect of this referencing? To what extent does it presume a knowledgeable audience?

DISCUSSION

When researching a music video production, it can help to undertake some more theoretical research in advance, to prepare for the Critical Evaluation for your artefact.

- 'Rock videos take many forms, including narrative and spectacle and their meaning varies depending upon the context in which they are viewed, and the context or positioning of the viewers or fans'.

  'Music video: questions of performance, pleasure and address', Sally Stockbridge, *Continuum*, The Australian Journal of Media & Culture, Vol. 1, No. 2, 1987.

  Do you agree?

- 'Video music clips and their associated accessories such as fashion and style are not simply standardised new commodities reinforcing dominant discourses nor are they completely subversive or the products of a rebellious, non-conformist or avant-garde impulse. Rather, they allow for a range of interpretations and uses because of their lack of uniformity and because of the various and different contexts in which they appear.'

  'Music video: questions of performance, pleasure and address', Sally Stockbridge, *Continuum*, The Australian Journal of Media & Culture, Vol. 1, No. 2, 1987.

  Analyse this statement in the light of three different music videos

- The pop music video has both reflected and influenced popular culture, fashion, advertising, cinema and television. Discuss with reference to three music videos from different decades

- Trace a history of music video using six examples, to chart the development of the genre. Why have you chosen these examples?

- Would you say that music videos are the salvation or the destruction of pop music?

Sample project
A video for a re-release of a track not previously released as a video.

Planning
When planning your video production, probably the most important decision to make is on the quantity of live performance to include. This is crucial to the structure of your video but may be determined by the technology available at your centre.

When shooting the live action strands to the narrative, you should apply the theory and knowledge of video production that you learnt earlier in the course. This basic knowledge will not be repeated here.

Your planning should include:
- A complete copy of the lyrics of the track and detailed timings
- Identified target audience (with research notes and evidence)
- Narrative breakdown for the composition of the video
- Themes which need to be incorporated into the video
- Storyboard for the video
- Detailed breakdown of the visual codes to be constructed
- Props list and shooting schedule
- Equipment list

Live performance and sound recording
Most contemporary videos utilise a multi-layered narrative, combining live performance and other elements to construct a narrative. However, although there may be four or five different strands to the narrative constructed, the soundtrack is usually singular and consistent. In many cases, the narrative comprises a live performance supplemented by other narratives. The soundtrack will usually be taken from the live performance with other narrative strands used as cutaways. This creates a complex and sophisticated structure for the video. Clearly, if constructing a video for a re-release of a video track, you would not want to use pre-recorded commercial material (even if it were available) as extensive use of found material is always discouraged. Therefore, to lay down this kind of visual structure for your video and soundtrack you would require access to a group who could perform the track (copyright permitting) and the equipment to film the performance from at least three angles, while taking a live feed from the sound desk into one of the cameras to use as the basis for the video.

Once you have decided how you are going to produce the soundtrack to be laid down, there may be no need to record audio for the filming which you undertake, which obviates the need for microphones and sound equipment.

Music sources
- If the band is performing acoustically, you may not have access to a sound deck to mix the sounds together for a feed into one of the cameras

- Few centres have microphones that are sophisticated enough to record live music sufficiently well to use as a soundtrack. Poor quality sound recorded in this way may detract from your video. It is important to note at this point that your work is never penalised for the quality of the technology available to you – only if you make inappropriate use of that technology. If, for example, you were able to make a live sound recording that was adequate for examination purposes, although not produced to commercial standards, it may be acceptable
- A more successful solution is usually to use a pre-recorded version of the track and to film the group performing to the track. However, you should try and ensure a live feed from the recording equipment to one of the cameras again, to ensure that the sound and visuals are in synch
- If you do not have access to such equipment you should think carefully about the quantity of 'live' performance material that you wish to include in your video. If you are going to use live performance without recording sound and vision simultaneously, you should ensure that the same recording of the track is played during filming (you can ignore the audio when filming in this case) and then use the SAME track for the soundtrack on the video. In this way the audio timings should be identical and it should be easier for your group to mime in synch

Choice of music and performers

As suggested above, the ideal arrangement for your video is to work with an entirely original track from an original source such as a local band or the music technology students at your centre. Remember that just as with actors, the video performance of your musicians and the musical performance are not assessed as part of your project. However, clearly the fusion of sound and vision is so important that a lacklustre performance is unlikely to help your project. If your musicians are not performers, you may wish to consider actors, but remember that this complicates the logistics of your project planning.

Pre-released material

If you have decided to go with a pre-recorded track, you should think carefully about the choice of track. You need to first decide upon genre, style and target audience and then find a suitable track, simply to narrow down the choices. You may prefer to work with a track that inspires you but you must think about a wider target audience than just you and think carefully about whether the track is a good choice for visual representation. Some heavily sampled dance tracks would present immense problems for a video and may require full animation if a video is to be constructed at all, simply because of the way the images need to link with the sound. Equally, you should try to choose a fairly unknown track – it might be very difficult to create a new video for Michael Jackson's 'Thriller' or *Pink Floyd's* 'Another Brick in the Wall'. If you choose a track that is too well known (especially if the video is also very well known) you may find that your target audience responds less positively to your video because it is 'different'.

Mise-en-scène

If you are using a set for one element of your narrative, you should try to film all of those clips at the same time so that the set can be dismantled as soon as that shoot is complete. This eliminates most continuity problems with the set – and probably with costume for that strand as well. You may not have the facilities available to shoot a performance against a blue-screen (for example, to supplant the screen with images from a desert island) or indeed shoot on location in Barbados to begin with, so you need to choose a mise-en-scène that you can credibly create and work with. The videos produced by artists such as *Travis* may provide some examples and inspiration for possible formats.

Live action filming

If you are filming a live performance, you should try to use three cameras and shoot from different angles. If you try to film the performance three times from different angles you may run into substantial continuity problems when editing.

As far as possible, it is probably best to try and shoot each strand of the narrative as a batch, possibly even in one go. If you are constructing a conventional narrative as one of the strands of the video, you may find it helpful to treat this as a mini-production and plan it separately to the live performance filming. You may even be able to distribute responsibilities amongst your group for the different sections to ensure that everyone is fully integrated.

Clearly this does not apply to any computer graphics material or animated material that you are integrating.

Miming

If your video is going to include footage of the band miming to the music, you need to establish the context of this fairly quickly. Is this to be obvious miming (such as the band performing in a strange location with bizarre representations of instruments) or is it going to be presented as live action? If you are filming the former, you should work from the same copy of the track that you will be using for the soundtrack, but you do not need to record any audio while you are filming. The advantage of this approach is that it allows for more mistakes and slips if the audience is not anticipating perfection.

If you are filming 'live action' mime, you should try to feed the track into the camera as above so that your action is tied as closely as possible to the music. If your camera does not have the connections to take a feed it will be difficult when you edit because you will have to try and manually line up the visuals with the music for each clip. It is unlikely that playing a CD player next to the camera mike while miming a performance would provide an audio track of high enough quality for you to edit accurately and produce a product you can be proud of. Although the technology should not restrict your work, if you are limited in this way, you would be advised to construct a narrative which does not require these live elements and to reflect briefly in the evaluation on the ways in which the limited technology impinged on your decision-making process.

Visual image constructed for the band

Depending on the narrative layers that you have planned, you may choose to construct similar images for the band members in each of the strands or you may choose different images. Michael Jackson often combines these approaches, using a fusion of live action and narrative-based strands (sometimes presented with words almost as a film alongside the song) and combines the images in different ways. He frequently maintains his own costume throughout a range of fantasy scenes and live action for example. Madonna works primarily with a narrative construct and the visual images are subservient to this construct, again more like a film than a music video at times. Lenny Kravitz uses more variety and different strands, each with a very different visual construct. Whichever approach you choose to take, you should remember to justify the decision-making and result in the Critical Evaluation.

Editing

This is likely to be the most complex and challenging aspect of the production. If you have prepared your storyboard well and shot the required material with a range of shots and pacing as required, the assembly should not be too painful. You may find with a complex narrative that it would be a good idea to shoot a couple of different versions of many shots to allow for 'matching up' with the soundtrack. It is usually not a good idea to change the speed of a clip to make it fit a particular space – unless this is done specifically for a purpose and the change is explicit. Usually you will need to cut clips carefully to fit the soundtrack. You have more licence with a music video than with conventional narrative material so you can repeat clips or use longer transitions than normal.

Some editing packages allow you to see the audio waveform while you are editing and enable you to match sound and vision more carefully. In Adobe Premiere™, to do this you click on the triangle to the side of the name of the audio track to reveal the waveform. Remember that you can layer up the soundtracks (as Michael Jackson does) as well as layering the video (such as when adding titles).

Titles

These can also be created elsewhere or within your video-editing programme. They can be integrated into your project and layered up as conventional titles at the beginning of the video or may be more restrained as simple overlays at the beginning of the video. You may prefer to place the titles before the video itself, either against a black background or against one or more stills so that the titles do not interfere with the video. If your video text is complex, you may prefer the latter approach so that your audience can concentrate on the narrative strands presented to them.

Computer graphics

Many contemporary music videos make use of computer graphics to create a narrative strand or within the narrative of a video. These can be effective and are easily integrated into the project. They can be made in 3D software applications such as Lightwave™ or 3D Studio Max™, which can be very expensive. A more budget solution is software like Poser™ (which creates figures and creatures that can be animated fairly simply). Computer graphics can also be made as cartoon sequences, either as animations (which would probably result in a project too complex and time-consuming for the requirements of A2) or as narratives in 2D software such as Flash™ or Hash Animator™.

Shapes, text and colours and so forth can be easily animated to provide abstract strands in a music video. This is sometimes used for the big screen videos shown on video walls at outside events. The shapes and colours are animated to the music to create an abstract narrative in its own right. This can be effective but usually requires skills beyond those you are expected to develop at A2 for competent results. However, the integration of some animation in this form, for example, animated shapes or images of the band members using software such as Adobe After Effects™, can be readily integrated and highly successful. Simple text and graphics effects of this kind can also be established in most video-editing software (e.g. Premiere™) where a combination of movement, distortion and fading text and shapes in and out can create a surprisingly effective animation for your video without being too time-consuming. Remember that your final A2 project is not the time to be experimenting with new software because of the standard of proficiency expected at this level. If you are not already competent with your chosen equipment and technology it is probably best to rethink your idea into a format where you can be more competent.

Case Study

Animation

There are many different forms of animation that you might choose to work with for your practical project. Generally, however, these fall into distinct categories:

- Claymation (such as *Wallace and Gromit*, *Morph* or *The Plonsters*)
- 3D animation (*Cyberworld*)
- Manga cartoons (*Armageddon*, *Ninja Scroll*, *Angel Copy*, *Bubble Gum Crash*)
- Children's animated cartoons (Disney/Pixar animations, *Pokemon*, *Scooby Doo*, *Tom and Jerry*)

If you are going to make an animated film, you need to start by deciding what sort of animation you wish to make and decide on your purpose. For example:

- An animated trailer for a new animation release
- An animated Public Information Film
- A short children's animation film

Sample project

An opening sequence for a new animated children's programme.

ACTIVITIES

- What is the difference between an animation and a cartoon?
- Watch at least four television animations and deconstruct them in detail. What differences and similarities can you find between the animations?
- Identify the specific target audiences for each of these texts. In what ways do the animations target their audiences?
- What is the ideology of these texts? How is this revealed within the texts?
- Use the internet to research examples of children's animations from other cultures. What differences and similarities can you see between these and those you have already studied?
- From your study of these animations, would you say that visuals or sound are more significant when constructing an animation? Why is this?
- Watch the opening sequence for at least four different children's programmes aimed at your target audience. What key features can you identify? How do they differ from adult programmes?

DISCUSSION

When researching an animation production, it can help to undertake more theoretical research in advance, to prepare for the Critical Evaluation for your artefact.

- Adorno suggested that media institutions churn out a mass of unsophisticated, sentimental products which have replaced the more 'difficult' and critical art forms which might lead people to actually *question* social life. Do you think this is true for animation or are there exceptions? Are there different forces at work in animations which allow a different approach?

- Early folk humour, which was often based on mockery and grotesque exaggeration was generally considered a lower cultural form than high art. Do you think this is also true for animation as a contemporary cultural form?

- Mikhail Bakhtin in *Rabelais and his World* (1965) published by Indiana University Press wrote about the role and function of carnival in medieval Europe. He suggested that the carnival was a necessary escape for medieval people, offering a non-authoritarian, non-ecclesiastical and apolitical environment – is this a tradition reflected in the form and function of contemporary animation?

Planning

Having researched similar products and constructed a theoretical scaffold for your product you can now begin to plan properly.

Animation is very time-consuming. Animation is usually shot at 24 frames per second and each of those 24 shots is constructed and shot individually. So a 1-minute film comprises 24×60 shots, i.e. 1440 different shots! Animators generally try to shoot 'in twos'; that is to film just 12 frames for each second of video, which cuts the work in half. If you were creating a very fast action piece you might find that this would be too slow, but for most animation work this is more than adequate. Almost all of *Wallace and Gromit* was filmed in 'twos'.

If you are animating the opening sequence of a new television programme you will probably find it helpful to start with a *treatment* for the programme.

Your planning should include:

- An outline of the entire series/serial
- Identified target audience (with research notes and evidence)
- Treatment for the first episode
- Hooks/themes which need to be incorporated into the opening sequence
- Storyboard for the opening sequence (which will probably last no more than 1 minute)
- Props list and design schedule
- Equipment list

You may want to use a shooting script, as you would for live action work to ensure, for example, that you shoot all of the shots against a particular background at the same time. However, most animators find that the dope sheets can be used as a shooting script as well.

Production
Things to think about

Using a blue-screen

It is often effective to shoot a claymation scene against a 'blue-screen' or a single colour background, which can then be 'keyed out' in your video editing software and a more appropriate background added. This technique takes practice but does allow for more choices. If you have to design and build a fully realised set for your claymation action, this can be very time consuming. It can be very simple to draw or design a background and simply superimpose your figures over this background. For example, the children's programme *Blues Clues* makes extensive use of blue-screen techniques to combine the live presenter with the cartoon graphics to create the interaction. The presenter is filmed against a blue-screen and this film is layered above the background information using a post-production editing package with the background keyed out, to create the final action. This effect can be achieved with most video editing software using an 'effects' option and choosing either the 'chroma key' option or image control effect and then selecting a colour to be transparent. The most important factor for success here is to ensure that the background is as solid and flat a colour as possible. The more variations in colour in the background (even those caused by the effect of light and shadow on the screen) the more difficult it will be to accurately key it out, without unwanted distortions. A suitable blue card is available from most theatrical and film suppliers and can be brought in sheets suitable for small scale animation work but also in rolls suitable for full size studio backgrounds.

This technique has been used to great effect in many other films and television programmes. Another very famous example which merges live action and cartoon graphics is *Who Framed Roger Rabbit?*, where Bob Hoskins interacts with the very glamorous cartoon figure of Jessica Rabbit throughout the film.

Audio

If you are using characters in your animation, you should try to avoid using dialogue. To create effective lip-synch is very difficult and can involve 30 or more different mouths for a character to create the sound shapes. It is better to add a simple audio track to your animation — perhaps a piece of original music you have created on a keyboard. It is often easier to create a piece of music which matches your action than try to edit your animation to match the music. Unlike most live filming, you are unlikely to have extensive choices as to which shots you use in your final animation. Although for a conventional film you probably shoot at least three times as much material as you think you might need, to do that for an animation would triple your workload!

Sets

If you are using a set behind your characters, you should aim to keep it fairly small (a set built on a table top is useful as it is easy to film from different directions) and make sure you stick everything down very firmly. Putting something back even slightly misplaced because it was knocked over can look very clumsy on film. If you are constructing a room, leave at least one wall missing and try to ensure that one of the other walls can be removed if necessary, to allow for different camera angles.

Camera

Your camera *must* be on a tripod and you need to think about the camera angles very carefully. If you shoot a scene over several days, make sure that you mark the position of the tripod, just in case. If it is moved even a fraction, this can affect the final result quite dramatically. You can use a video camera set to single-frame recording (if your camera can do this), manually controlled or controlled by the editing software. If you do not have access to

The set for Morph. *Notice the storyboard attached out of line of the camera! Taken from* Cracking Animation: the Aardman book of 3D Animation.

this kind of video camera, you can use a digital stills camera instead and then upload your images to the computer more frequently.

Lighting
You cannot create an effective claymation without lighting your set properly. You need several lights to ensure you only get the shadows you want. Desk lamps are usually fine – try experimenting with different wattage bulbs, different colour bulbs, filters over the lamps and different positions to create the effects you want. Do not forget, however, that if you are using clay models they will melt if they get too hot!

Models
You can create a relatively sophisticated animation with models that do not move, for example, Lego characters or small dolls/animals. Alternatively, you can build your models using plasticine or modelling clay. Make sure that you use a modelling material that does not dry out too quickly and try not to handle your models too much once you have made them. It is usually better to have five heads showing different expressions to swap between frames, than to try and mould your figures between frames. Make sure your hands are clean and dry when working with the modelling material (you can even wear gloves to be sure) and use some talcum powder if the modelling material becomes too oily. You can build small models successfully without a frame, but larger models benefit from a frame. You can buy specialist 'armatures' or frames or simply make a basic shape from chicken wire to build around. Glass eyes and bits of bead are useful to give substance to your figures.

Lego kits
There are kits available now which allow you to make a simple animation using proprietary software and models such as the Lego Studio kits. These can be just as effective for creating a set, lighting it and creating models as more traditional methods. You might choose to use proprietary kits like this to build your animation, yet use more sophisticated cameras and editing to create a very strong animation.

Editing
When you import your frames into your video-editing programme to create your animation, it is important to check the default values for still images imported into a project. This varies depending on the software programme, but most of the programmes assume that if a still image is imported into the project, it should be visible on the screen for at least 1 second. This would make for a very slow animation and needs to be changed before the frames are imported. In Adobe Premiere™, the standard default is for still images to span 150 frames when they are imported (1 second at 15fps). This must be changed before the frames are imported so that they import correctly. This can be done by going to Edit>Preferences>General and Still Image and changing the default duration from 150 frames to 2 frames if you are working 'in twos'. Although you can change the duration of each frame manually on the timeline, this might take quite a while if you have imported 500 images.

Stop-motion capture

Another way to import your footage into Adobe Premiere™ is to use the Stop-Motion Capture facility within Premiere, if you have a compatible video recorder. This will allow you to operate your video camera through Premiere, shooting single frames and importing them directly into your project. This can be a very quick way of working as you do not need to spend time uploading your images from your camera to the computer and then importing them into Premiere. It also makes it quicker to see if a shot is wrong and to correct it.

Backgrounds

If you have not created a fully-realised set for your animation or if you have only created the foreground set, you will need to design a background for your animation. This could be hand drawn, scanned in and then put into the animation as a layer behind the action (make sure you import it and put it into a lower level layer on the timeline or it will appear in front of the action). Or it could be created in Photoshop™ or with a drawing programme. Some animators make an animated background using software such as Macromedia Flash™ and import that behind the models to create a multi-layered piece.

Titles

These can be created elsewhere or within your video-editing programme. They can be integrated into your project and provide an easy way of extending your project by some seconds without needing to shoot so many model frames. If you are fortunate enough to have access to more sophisticated software such as Adobe After Effects™ you can create some good special effects to support your animation. However you make the titles, they are a vital element of an opening sequence and should be created with as much care as your claymation.

Section 2
Critical Research Study

Introduction

The Critical Research Study is an exciting area of the course because it allows you to independently research and analyse an area of the media that you find particularly interesting. You should view your study as an opportunity to use the research skills and critical abilities you have gained so far within your Media Studies A Level course in order to produce a comprehensive and challenging piece of work. This section aims to define what is expected from you within a Critical Research Study and to give you guidance on how to research and present your chosen area in the most effective way possible.

To help you produce a detailed, wide referencing, organised and challenging study, the following areas will be covered:

- A description of the exam
- A description of the eight areas of investigation that have been specified by OCR
- An explanation of the areas of investigation that need to be discussed within your study
- Detailed guidance notes on how to approach the unit
- Guidance on research methodology
- Case study examples from the eight areas of investigation
- Examiner hints

The Exam is 2 hours long and breaks the unit down into two areas. You will have to answer two questions on your chosen topic. The first area is *research* and you will be asked to give an account of the research you have undertaken, commenting on a range of **primary** and **secondary research**. The following areas should be addressed, although the degree of detail for each section may vary according to the specific area of study:

- Institution
- Academic criticism
- Popular criticism
- Audience reception (including yourself as an audience member)

The second part of the exam asks you to *Analyse and Present* your research. You will need to comment on:

- The findings of your research
- The creation and development of your thesis, referring to research and textual evidence, where appropriate
- Your conclusions

The eight set topics

Below is a list of the eight topics of study, as specified in the OCR syllabus. Further on in this section we will look closely at each of these topics in turn and consider a selection of more specific study areas.

1. Women and Film
2. Popular Music and Youth Culture
3. Politics and the Media
4. Children and Television
5. Audience Research
6. Sport and the Media
7. Community Radio
8. Concept to Product

Areas of investigation

As with any independent academic study, your research needs to be active and rigorous. Your set topic will be chosen from the eight offered within the OCR syllabus, but the specific area of study will be chosen by you. The Critical Research unit asks you to create an investigative area and you must choose something which you feel you have the enthusiasm to research and analyse in detail.

Once you have chosen your topic and specific area of investigation, you need to make sure that your research includes audience, institutional and critical perspectives. Remember, however, that one of the most important aspects of the study is that you should try to formulate your own critical thoughts. Your research findings should be used to lead you towards independent analysis. Your own thoughts and not those of established critics should be the focus of conclusions about your chosen area.

When looking at the issue of audience within your study, try to consider not only the profile of the audience you have defined, but also how they reacted to the media texts they were offered. You could bring in theories of audience consumption here, but use them sparingly. Make sure that if you discuss theories, such as **suturing** or 'mediation', that you make your comments directly relevant to the topic, research area and media texts you have chosen. Your own audience surveys could be as relevant to this unit as established theories and can be an invaluable element of research. You should also recognise that you are an audience member yourself and that your own reception style and readings are important points of reference.

Institution is the second area which needs to be covered and should be considered in terms of the people who have a role in the production process of media texts, the companies and organisations they represent and the processes of production, distribution and marketing in which both are involved. The institutional research which you carry out will provide information on attitudes towards your chosen topic area and the ideological and historical contexts in which texts were produced.

As we have already identified, perhaps the most important critical perspective that you will discuss in your study is your own. This should be informed by other critical thoughts and frameworks and you should make sure that you include analysis of both academic and popular criticism. You will need to research existing academic critical work, but you should also look out for discussions within the press, TV programmes and sites on the internet that may have a more popularist attitude to your chosen area.

Guidance notes on approaching the unit

As you can see from the outline of the exam, the Critical Research Study needs to be detailed and organised in a way which allows you to easily access relevant information. The main body of this section will offer you case studies that discuss not only the possible content of your chosen area, but give you areas to consider and a way of working which will cover the requirements of the exam. These areas are outlined for you below and should form guidance for your investigative work.

Generating the research title

Once you have chosen your topic, you should then brainstorm areas that may be of interest to research. Make sure that you choose an area you will be able to fully explore, one in which you will be interested and one around which you can build an interesting thesis. It might be useful to create a more specific research area under one of the following general headings:

- Issues of representation
- The relationship between product and audience
- The individual producer's relationship with the industry in which they are working
- Historical changes within the chosen area
- The role of the medium in which an individual producer is working
- Conflicts or controversial issues within the topic area

Finding references and materials

There are three main sources that you can access when searching for references and materials: the internet, print publications and visual materials. The internet can be used to find reviews, critical writing, popular criticism, surveys and institutional information. Make a note of the websites that you use and the authors behind the materials so that you can give correct references in the exam. Print publications may be books of media criticism, media-related magazines, biographies of particular individuals, newspapers or guides relating to specific texts. You may need to photocopy the particular materials you wish to use, and you must note the author's name, the publication's title and the date of publication. Visual materials do not have to include texts only related to individual or institutional producers, they could include TV programmes that discuss an issue concerning your chosen area. DVDs of films frequently have very useful documentary material as 'extras'.

Keeping organised notes and using reference materials effectively

You will need to organise your notes and materials in such a way that allows information to be easily accessible to you. You should use sectioned folders to store your findings but you also need to break these down into particular areas. Below are some headings that might help you to organise your Critical Research Study.

- Original research – once you have chosen a topic, you should look at all of the sources you have located and create your own means of finding appropriate information. You could create questionnaires for target audiences and consumers, try to contact people within the industry, post questions on websites for people to comment on or answer and note your own responses to texts which are associated with your chosen topic area

- Secondary textual analysis – notes on academic and popular criticism that have been written on texts related to your chosen area
- Biographical information – information concerning particular individuals who are significant within your chosen area
- Contextual information – information on the social, political and ideological context relevant to your area. You may have looked at, for example, the impact of political shifts on your chosen topic area, the role and perception of producers or texts in a particular period, or controversial issues which may be relevant to institutions or textual production
- Institutional detail – your notes will include details of the companies and organisations that are significant within your research area. You may have information concerning their attitudes to and intentions behind the media texts produced, their role within new developments (either technical or ideological) or their attitudes to certain groups of people who work within them
- Audience related research – you should have information concerning the audience for the texts related to your particular area in terms of their profile, expectations, modes of consumption and contexts. This section should include any academic research that you think is relevant concerning audience reception, as well as details of audience research that you have carried out

Finding and applying critical frameworks

Remember that this unit has been designed to enable you to use the materials you have created during your research in order to develop an independent critical response. Whichever idea and framework you use from established critical work should be incorporated into your own arguments. However, established theorists can be challenged and your study should include discussion of the relevance and the pros and cons of using certain critical frameworks. The Case Study sections of this chapter will give you more specific ideas concerning critics and critiques that may be appropriate to the Set Topics.

Creating your own critical response

Your own ideas and responses should always be systematically argued and fully substantiated, using examples from your primary research. Your ideas may challenge much of the existing criticism you have read and this can provide a thought-provoking study if your argument is supported by specific examples. Remember to refer directly to your area of research when you are creating your own response and not to formulate ideas that are not relevant to your title.

Presenting your findings

You will be allowed to take four A4 sides of notes into the examination and some of these should be selected so that you will be able to show evidence of the following:

- Your reasons for identifying your topic of study
- That the topic has been thoroughly and appropriately researched
- That you have made relevant use of existing criticism
- That you have considered the profile, expectations and text reception of your identified audience
- That you have understood the nature and impact of institutional questions
- That you have considered historical and social context as factors which influence your topic area

Research methodology

The exam asks you to comment on the investigative findings and process of your research. You should make sure, therefore, that you adopt a systematic approach to this study in order to gain the most effective results and be able to discuss your methodology clearly in the exam.

Your research will be mainly **qualitative**, in that it will consist of active investigation, analysis and evaluation of texts and institutions. Below is a possible model of the different stages that may occur during your project and this should be used in conjunction with the guidance notes on approaching the project to ensure that both content and process are thorough.

Research methodology model

You could use this section as a tick list of areas to cover while you are involved in your research.

Define your sub-topic clearly

You need to do this both for yourself and for the examiner when you come to do the exam. What kinds of areas will need to be discussed within your sub-topic? What kinds of information do you predict that you might find? You could create a spider diagram for yourself outlining the ideas you think will be pertinent to your study (obviously the contents of this diagram will be added to or amended by the end of your study, but the comparison and contrast in itself will provide you with possible developments within your investigation).

Identify the breadth of the topic

Even sub-topics have huge investigative potential and you need to create some limits for yourself in order that the project is manageable. It is much better to research a specific area thoroughly than to offer a vague, overly broad and therefore insubstantial account in the exam. In your planning, you need to describe the limits of your project. They may change slightly as the research progresses, but in your final account make sure that your project and findings address one specific aspect of the sub-topic thoroughly.

Be realistic with the secondary information you collect

When you are browsing the internet, searching through libraries or reading through back issues of magazines, always keep your specified topic area in mind. It is very tempting to download everything you find connected with the general topic or try and read through every piece of critical work that refers to it. However, you have given yourself limits for your research area and you should stick to these. You may have chosen to research 'Children and Television', but only a small percentage of the information concerned with this massive topic area may be relevant to you. You may have been more specific and have begun to research issues of the effects of violent TV images on children, but even within this narrower sub-topic there is still an overwhelming amount of information. However, if you have already decided to limit yourself to violent images in certain types of programmes and have defined the exact age group of children you are going to be studying, then the information available to you will be that much smaller and your study will have more investigative weight.

Evaluation of information

As we have already discussed, it is essential within this study that you develop an informed, personal response to the sub-topic you have chosen. Part of the process of doing this is to evaluate the information you have collected. Try to comment on the advantages and disadvantages of certain pieces of information for your study. If you have found some connected data or critical responses, try to evaluate their usefulness. They may be biased in some way, out of date or reflect differing views on your topic. Evaluation is an extremely useful critical procedure, because it allows you to prove to an examiner that you have not merely absorbed and regurgitated secondary critical thinking.

The process of evaluation must also extend to the whole project when you are near completion. Read back through your notes and comment on what you find. Do you think you have created a comprehensive project? Are there any questions that you feel have been left unanswered? What kind of conclusions have you come to through your study and do these challenge or confirm established critical positions?

Providing accurate references and organising your project

For any piece of information or secondary source you gather, make sure that you have logged the source, the author and date of publication. If you note down a quotation for your project, also give its originator and source.

When you come to write your project, it needs to be developmental and systematic. Make sure that you refer back to the section on 'Keeping organised notes' in order to do this.

Case studies

These parts of the section aim to offer examples of how to generate areas of investigation around the eight set topics, to explore methodologies of research and present research findings. The examples given do not indicate an exhaustive list and you should use the sections to guide you in the creation of your own research topic and set of comprehensive notes.

PART ONE
Women and Film

The topic Women and Film allows for many areas of study connected to the varying roles that women can occupy within the film industry. You may decide to look at issues connected with just one filmmaker or to consider a group of female filmmakers and the issues raised by their work or their position in the industry. There are many areas of study on which you could focus within the general heading of Women and Film. Below is a selection of possibilities.

Gender issues within the film industry

You could take an historical perspective and trace the position of and attitude to women in the film industry. What developments can you see? What difficulties and restrictions have meant that women still occupy a minority percentage, especially within the realm of directing?

Issues of gender representation in films

This section considers the interior world of films, rather than being a direct analysis of female personnel and so you could study texts by both male and female directors. You could analyse a group of similar texts (the group could be constituted by nationality, genre or historical period) and research the different representations of women offered. You could look at the developments and shifts within the representations of certain female character types or investigate what expectations audiences have concerning the women they see on the screen.

Jodie Foster,
figure 18.

A still from Little Man Tate, *see figure 19.*

Feminist or other critical perspectives

An analysis under this heading might consider the approaches and theories of different feminist critics or look at how feminist criticism approaches certain groups of films. You could take a more contextually-driven approach and discuss the dynamic between feminist criticism and films produced within a particular decade.

Audience reception of films by female filmmakers

The first stage of a study under this heading would be to choose a group of female filmmakers. You do not have to limit yourself to directors, but could include female producers, actors and editors as well. If the films you have chosen are not explicitly female driven in some way (i.e. they do not have central female characters, discuss a female agenda or are from a female film director), then your analysis will be more difficult because audience reception will not be of the film as a piece of female filmmaking. It would be more straightforward to choose films that the audience recognise as being 'female' in some way. Once you have your film group choice, try to gather a range of critical responses, from academic to popular. You then need to pose yourself a question that can be answered from the criticism you find.

- Are films targeted at female audiences?
- Are these films from a particular genre?
- Are they successful?
- Are there expectations involved in the audience's viewing of a film by a female filmmaker?

Female filmmakers within Hollywood or the independent system

Within this area, you could study the different ways in which female filmmakers are treated within Hollywood and the independent system (remember to avoid any literal preconceptions about one system being the polar opposite of the other). How have female filmmakers risen within both systems? Is there any crossover between the two? Remember that you do not have to limit yourself to American or British female filmmakers.

Whichever sub-topic you decide upon, it is important to remember that

The director,
Gurinder Chadha.
See figure 20.

A still from Bhaji
on the Beach
*(1993). See
figure 21.*

the research project needs to include at least the majority of the areas outlined in the Guidance Notes section. You should not limit yourself to providing points of textual analysis, but also extend your research to include institutional and contextual information.

Case Study

Sally Potter: films, context and reception

Original research

With an individual filmmaker, it is probably best to begin with research into their filmography. This will give you an immediate sense of the genres of film produced, the period in which the filmmaker was or is working, and their range of talents. Sally Potter, for example, has worked as a director, writer, composer and actress as the list below indicates.

Director	*Thriller* (1979)
	London Story (1980)
	The Gold Diggers (1983)
	Tears, Laughter, Fear and Rage: Tears (1987), TV
	Tears, Laughter, Fear and Rage: Rage (1987), TV
	I am an ox, I am a horse, I am a man, I am a woman (1988)
	Orlando (1992)
	The Tango Lesson (1997)
	The Man Who Cried (2000)
Writer	*Orlando* (1992)
	The Tango Lesson (1997)
	The Man Who Cried (2000)
Composer	*Orlando* (1992)
	The Tango Lesson (1997)
Actress	*The Tango Lesson* (1997)

The director, Sally Potter. *See figure 22.*

A still from Orlando *(1992). See figure 23.*

The rest of your original research should revolve around seeking answers to specific questions relevant to your chosen sub-topic. You could create questionnaires for your fellow students asking them if they know of Potter's work and what they thought of any texts they have seen. You could post questions on film websites, like the http://www.IMDB.com (Internet Movie Database), in order to gauge responses to Sally Potter's work. You should also aim to note your own critical responses to some of the texts relevant to your project. In the case of this particular case study project, an analysis of *Thriller, Orlando* and *The Man Who Cried* would provide notes on the developments and changes in Sally Potter's career.

Secondary textual analysis
It is important in this section of your notes to try and find both academic and popular criticism connected with your chosen area. You may discover differences in the reception of particular texts or in attitudes to particular filmmakers in the criticism you find. This kind of difference could provide a fertile argument within your study. For Sally Potter, the examples of critical response below offer useful comment on texts, context, director's view and audience reception from both an academic and popular perspective.

User Comments:

Melissa
Seattle, Washington

Date: 31 January 1999
Summary: Thoroughly Engaging, Fun, and Visually compelling

Tilda Swinton was born for this role. She is Orlando. But that preoccupation aside, the first striking aspect of this film is the costumes! It opens on a scene with Orlando in Elizabethan finery, and moves through several historical periods, not least of them 18th Century literary England. That's something to see. The film is, as you would expect, very literary. You don't need to have read the book, but a working knowledge of typical euro-centric history and literature is helpful, I guess. Quentin Crisp plays a perfect Queen Elizabeth, the grotesque institution herself, opposite Swinton's birdish Orlando. The photography is clear and even luminous at times, and the story moves along quite well – I consistently wondered what would happen. The exploration of gender, while it was obviously 'the point', was not overdone, in the last analysis. Our freakish Orlando turns out to be quite human, which is a relief. The film is very well done; Swinton is a rare bird, never boring, and not to be missed.

Source: IMDB.com

Walter Donohue

Against crawling realism:
Sally Potter on 'Orlando'

In the 70s and 80s, Sally Potter was a controversial figure in British independent cinema, making films that blended narrative invention with theoretical and formalist concerns. Her 1979 short *Thriller* has long been a staple on film courses for its deconstruction of opera's sexual politics through a re-reading of *La Bohème*. She followed it up with her feature debut *The Gold Diggers* (1983) with Julie Christie, and *The London Story*, a Technicolor spy musical. More recently, Potter has worked in television: making *Women in Soviet Cinema* (1988) and *Tears, Laughter, Fear and Rage* (1986), a four-part series on the politics of emotions.

Potter's feature *Orlando* is produced by her own company Adventure Pictures, which she formed with Christopher Sheppard. A free reading of Virginia Woolf's historical fantasia, *Orlando* represents Potter's first venture into more mainstream narrative, but it also continues some of her past concerns. Her Russian connection carries on in the co-production deal with Lenfilm and the use of a Russian crew that included Elem Klimov's cinematographer Alexei Rodionov. Potter also co-wrote the score with David Motion; her past work as a composer includes the song cycle *Oh Moscow*, and she has also run her own dance ensemble, the Limited Dance Company. All these diverse concerns find their way into *Orlando*, which with its elaborate staging and exuberant cultivation of artifice gives a new twist to the British costume drama.

Walter Donohue was the film's story editor. (*Sight and Sound*) Location: Blackbird Yard, Ravenscroft Road, and like birds alighting on a field Sally Potter and I are sitting here in her workroom in the renovated London shoe factory where one draft after another of the script of her new film *Orlando* was exposed, criticised, knocked into shape. Almost a year since the troop set off for St Petersburg to film the Frost Fair sequences, this interview took place.

Walter Donohue: It's strange to be sitting at this table where so many of our script discussions took place. Can you describe something of the process of adapting Virginia Woolf's novel into your own film?

Sally Potter: It was a process of reading, re-reading and reading again; writing, rewriting and writing again. Cutting characters, stripping things right back to the bone. I did endless skeleton diagrammatic plots, all to find the guiding principle and then reconstruct the story from the inside out. I also went back to research Woolf's sources. And then, finally, I put the book away entirely for at least the last year of writing and treated the script as something in its own right, as if the book had never existed. I felt that by the time we were getting ready to shoot I knew the book well enough, was enough in touch with its spirit, that it would have been a disservice to be slavish to it. What I had to find was a live, cinematic form, which meant being ruthless with the novel. I learnt that you have to be cruel to the novel in order to be kind to the film.

Where did your interest in 'Orlando' begin?

When I first read *Orlando* as a teenager, I remember watching it as a film. And from the first moment I considered doing an adaptation, I thought I could see it, even if parts were out of focus. The book has a live, visual quality to it – which was affirmed in Woolf's diaries, where she said that what she was attempting with *Orlando*, unlike her other books, was an 'exteriorisation of consciousness'. She was finding images for a stream of consciousness, instead of using a literary monologue.

But the single idea that was sustaining enough for me to live with the project for so long was immortality, or the question: what is the present moment? And the second idea was the change of sex, which provides the more obvious narrative structure, and is a rich and lighter way of dealing with the issues between men and

93

women. The more I went into this area, and tried to write a character who was both male and female, the more ludicrous maleness and femaleness became and the more the notion of the essential human being – that of a man and woman both are – predominated. Clearly here was just a character called Orlando: a person, an individual, a being who lived for 400 years, first as a man and then as a woman. At the moment of change, Orlando turns and says to the audience, 'Same person, different sex.' It's as simple as that.

But Orlando – a character who is both a man and a woman – has to be embodied in an actor. And you chose a woman to play this part. How did you deal with the maleness and femaleness of the characterisaton?

We worked primarily from the inside out and talked all the time about Orlando as a person rather than as a man or a woman. Then there was a mass of small decisions which added up to a policy about how to play the part – for instance, we decided on no artificial facial hair for Orlando the man. Whenever I've seen women playing men on screen, it's been a mistake to try to make the woman look too much like a man, because you spend your time as a viewer looking for the glue, the joins between the skin and the moustache. I worked on the assumption that the audience was going to know from the beginning that here was a woman playing a man, and so the thing to do was to acknowledge it and try to create a state of suspended disbelief.

I was attracted to Tilda Swinton for the role on the basis of seeing her in Peter Wollen's film *Friendship's Death*, where she had a cinematic presence that wasn't aligned to what our cinematographer Alexei Rodionov called 'crawling realism', and in the Manfred Karge play *Man to Man*, in which there was an essential subtleness about the way she took on male body language and handled maleness and femaleness. Tilda brought her own research and experience to bear on the part; as her director I worked to help her to achieve a quality of transparency on the screen. The biggest challenge for both of us was to maintain a sense of the development of the character even when we where shooting out of continuity and with the ending still uncertain. The intention was that there would be a seamless quality about the development that would carry that suspended disbelief about maleness, femaleness and immortality.

The idea of suspended disbelief – was direct address to camera one of the devices used to maintain this?

The speeches of Orlando to the audience took many forms during the writing, and during the shooting they were the hardest things to get right. The phrase I used to Tilda was 'golden thread': we were trying to weave a golden thread between Orlando and the audience through the lens of the camera. One of the ways we worked in rehearsal was to have Tilda address those speeches directly to me, to get the feeling of an intimate, absolutely one-to-one connection, and then to transfer that kind of address into the lens. Part of the idea was also that direct address would be an instrument of subversion, so that set against this historical pageant is a complicity with the audience about the kind of journey we're on. If it worked, I hoped it would be funny; it would create a connection that made Orlando's journey also the audience's journey; and most important, it would give the feeling that although Orlando's journey lasted some 400 years and was set in the past, this was essentially a story about the present.

The function of the voiceover at the beginning and end is to dispatch with certain issues as neatly as possible – for instance, the film begins with Orlando's voice saying, 'There can be no doubt about his sex.' I also wanted to state that though Orlando comes from a certain background, which has certain implications, he is separated from this background by a kind of innocence. One is born into a class background, but that can change.

Was there any governing idea behind the transitions from one period to another?

I tried to find a way of making transitions through a characteristic of the period (dress, poetry, music), that could launch us into the next section. And what I found was that you can be much bolder than I ever thought in the way you jump, cinematically, from one period to another. Ironically, the most striking transition is where Orlando enters the maze in the eighteenth century and emerges into the Victorian era, which was the one I hadn't worked out in the script and was still struggling with in the shoot. The decision to effect the transition by having Orlando enter the maze was made simply because there was a maze at the location which I knew I wanted to use; its final form was found in the cutting room.

Perhaps we could discuss one or two of the myriad aspects of the craft of filmmaking – such as framing?

Framing is the magic key, the door through which you're looking. The quest in shooting *Orlando* was not just for a frame or possible place to put the camera, but for the only place. This became my driving visual obsession. To transcend the arbitrariness of where you put the camera became a joint process between Alexei and myself. And one of his great strengths as a cinematographer is that he won't settle for an obvious or easy visual solution. He's trying to peel back the layers and find this transparent place – and this search for the right frame became a parallel process to trying to achieve a transparency of performance.

Technically, we worked with a monitor, and every frame was adjusted – up, down, right, left – until there was a frame which he and I agreed was *the* frame. If we couldn't agree it was an unhappy moment, and a lot of energy was spent on that kind of tussling. Alexei's intention is to be a mediumistic cinematographer; he says that the greatest compliment Klimov paid him after *Come and See* was that Klimov felt as if he had shot the film himself. That's a very ego-free statement for a cinematographer to make, and for me it was an incredible gift, as well as a challenge that was initially almost too great to meet, because it put the gaze back on me: what did I really want? I didn't always know what I wanted; I was groping to start with. But by the end of the shoot I felt that Alexei and I had one eye.

You're credited, with David Motion, with the music for the film. How did that come about?

A lot of people commented that the sound was often mentioned in the script. And I wanted a sound-effect structure and score that would mirror the scale of the film. Our policy during the mix was to make a broad dynamic range and then highlight certain evocative or pointed sounds – such as the peacock's cry when Orlando is walking down the gallery of long white drapes, or the sound of the ice cracking, or of rain taking over the soundtrack.

As far as the music is concerned, I originally wanted to use Arvo Pärt's *Cantus*, which I had been listening to over and over again. I even got permission, but it became clear that to use it would create as many problems as it would solve – it was a piece in its own right that couldn't be cut or repeated. So I started on a journey to find out what it was about that piece of music that was appropriate to the film, and then to look for another way of achieving this. What I discovered was that a lot of the music I had been listening to for pleasure, and as a sort of spiritual reference for the film, was based on an A-minor triad, or the related C-major triad. This seemed too much of a coincidence, so I drew up a chart of the score and we mapped out a structure based on the A-minor triad and related keys. And the more I got to think about the score, the more I was hearing the music in my head. So eventually we decided to go into a studio to record what I was hearing using my own voice. I recorded an 8-track voice piece for each of the major cues and David Motion wrote instrumental parts around them. Some of the voice parts were lost, but others became the background to the cues, or were fitted around sections he had written and arranged. Fred Frith then improvised some guitar lines around the cues. The end song was written slightly differently: I wrote the lyrics and suggested the key; David provided some musical cues on tape; Jimmy Somerville wrote the vocal tune and then David arranged it. It was a score that was made possible through the use of a sampler and the editorial capacity that machine gives you. It was a score that was constructed rather than composed in the usual way.

The novel ends in 1928, but in order to be faithful to the idea of making the film contemporary, it had to finish in 1993. How did you devise the end?

It reached its final form after everything else had been shot. What became clear was that the correct way to approach it was not just to stick an ending on the story, but to think myself into Virginia Woolf's consciousness. What might she have done with the story had she lived until 1993? It was a strange game, a sort of second-guessing that consisted in me re-reading what she had written after *Orlando*; her thoughts on issues post-1928. It seemed clear that I had to refer to the First and Second World Wars and the effect they had on consciousness. And because the book itself is almost a commentary on the history of literature as the vehicle for consciousness, there had to be a cinematic equivalent of what had happened to that kind of consciousness post-war. In other words, the fracturing of that consciousness and the arrival of the electronic age.

What do you want the audience to feel when they've reached the end?

I hope they are thrilled by the rush into the present, by the notion that finally we are here, now. And a feeling of hope and empowerment about being alive and the possibility of change – which comes through the words of the song and the expression on Orlando's face. I want people to feel humanly recognised, that their inner landscape of hope and desire and longing has found some kind of expression on screen. A gut feeling of release and relief and hope.

Melissa's review concentrates on the text. It identifies characterisation and casting as major factors in the generation of textual meaning. She discusses the target audience for the film obliquely, suggesting that a prior knowledge of the historical period and the source literary text would be useful. Donohue's essay puts *Orlando* into a context of Potter's filmography. It gives some institutional detail concerning the fact that it was Adventure Pictures (Sally Potter and Christopher Sheppard's production company) which produced the film and gives a transcript of an interview Donohue conducted with Sally Potter in which she gives her own analysis of the film and discusses production issues.

Biographical information

This section is important when considering influences on filmmakers within your research project. If you have chosen to concentrate on a particular filmmaker, then it is of particular significance when considering both the filmmaker's texts and their responses to the film industry. The biographical detail on Sally Potter (see below) is useful in identifying the significance of dance and performance in her filmmaking. It also highlights an interest in theatre and literary text (*Orlando* is a literary adaptation from Virginia Woolf's novel), and gives details concerning the critical reception of Sally Potter's films (*Orlando* has won more than 25 international awards).

Sally Potter

Sally Potter started making films when she was a teenager and, at about the same time, started learning how to dance. The parallel paths as performer and director continued until The Tango Lesson, when, for the first time, she has performed in one of her own films. Sally trained as a professional dancer and choreographer in the 1970's at the London school of Contemporary Dance, and went on to join Richard Alston's innovative dance company, Strider, before founding her own company, The Limited Dance Company, with Jacky Lansley. During the same period Sally made several short dance films, including Combines (1972), shot in black and white and colour, and projected on three screens at The Place contemporary dance theatre in London.

Sally went on to become an award-winning performance artist and theatre director with a reputation for work that managed to be both challenging and entertaining. For the theatre, Sally created solo shows as well as large-scale theatrical performances (for example, Mounting; Death and the Maiden; and Berlin; all collaborations with Rose English). In addition, she is a lyricist and singer, has performed in various improvised music bands and collaborated with composer Lindsay Cooper on the song cycle Oh Moscow – which she performed throughout Europe and North America. She also co-composed with David Motion the soundtrack to Orlando.

Sally's short film Thriller (1979), a critical re-working of Puccini's opera 'La Bohème', was a cult hit on the international festival circuit and brought her work to a wider audience. This was followed by her first feature film, The Gold Diggers (1983), starring Julie Christie; and then a short film, The London Story (1986); a documentary series for Channel 4, Tears, Laughter, Fears and Rage (1986); and her film on women in Soviet cinema, I am an Ox, I am a Horse, I am a Man, I am a Woman (1988).

The internationally acclaimed Orlando (1992), was Sally's highest profile film to date – starring Tilda Swinton and based on Virgina Woolf's classic novel of an Elizabethan nobleman who lives for four centuries and changes sex half way. In addition to 2 Academy Award nominations, Orlando has won more than 25 international awards, including the 'Felix' awarded by the European Film Academy for the best Young European Film of 1993.

Audiences around the world have delighted in its wry humour and its bold look at gender, sexuality and the English class system.

After completing Orlando, Sally returned to script writing. Of the four new screenplays she has written, The Tango Lesson is the first to go into producton.

Source: Sony website, February 2001.

Contextual information

Context is an important element to discuss within your research project because it will give a background to the particular filmmaker or group of filmmakers you are discussing. Try to investigate how the female filmmakers you are focusing on were received by the industry and the public. Were perceptions of them positive or problematic?

For Sally Potter, for example, the route to industry and audience acceptance was not smooth. Potter's contemporaries, like Derek Jarman and Peter Greenaway, who also created texts with strong ideological agendas, were quicker to find funding for their projects. Potter directed a few documentaries, while Jarman and Greenaway were being given money to create their personal visions. She gained most of her early directorial experience by choreographing and performing avant-garde dance and music projects in Europe. When Potter did gain experience of film directing, she was often criticised for obtrusive feminist discourse and incomprehensible narrative. She frequently used an all-female crew on her films, which many in the industry interpreted as feminist flag-waving. Given the industry view that her films offered ideology over substance and Potter's own uncompromising method of filmmaking, it is remarkable that her vision has remained as true as it has. However, very early on in her career, Potter gained a loyal following of viewers and there were critics who were able to see beyond the labelling of her work as merely flag-waving feminism. With increasing critical acclaim and awards, came an expanding audience and when Orlando arrived in London it grossed more than both Malcolm X (1992) and Scent of a Woman (1992) which were being circulated at the same time.

Institutional detail

Notes under this section should include both institutional detail and any comment on the role played by filmmakers or the texts they produce in technological developments. You may have chosen a female filmmaker who is associated with a particular production company or one who has instituted technological initiatives. For example, Sally Potter, in association with Simon Sheppard, formed her own production company – Adventure Pictures– which produced *Orlando*. This allowed for the original vision of the piece to be retained. *Orlando* was also a significant production in that it was produced in conjunction with the Russian organisation Lenfilm. Potter used a Russian crew, including cinematographer Alexei Rodinov.

Audience related research

This section of the project allows you to research into the audience profile of any texts produced by your female filmmakers. You will need to distinguish between blockbuster and independent audiences and attempt to create a demographic profile of the audience you have identified, describing age, sex, cultural background and expectations.

Sally Potter's audiences are extremely varied. Her films have been accused of having an impenetrability generated by their ideological messages. Sections of her audiences often try to claim films as their own when identifying a narrow range of individual readings. Potter herself is often more pluralist in how she sees her audience. If her film audiences were solely made up of the highly literate or politicised, then her films would not have gained such mass appeal. The Peter Travers interview from *Rolling Stone* magazine (June 1993), includes Potter's own thoughts on the appeal of her films. She discusses the impact and reception of *Orlando*, but also sheds light on the many ways in which her films can be interpreted and the many possible audiences they have.

Extracts from interview with Sally Potter by Peter Travers

PT: How do you lure people to *Orlando* who associate the name with Disney World and Virginia Woolf with an old Elizabeth Taylor movie?

SP: Look, your'e not talking to an academic here. I left school at fifteen. Why should people know who Virginia Woolf is the day they're born? I read *Orlando* as a teenager with a sense of burning excitement because of the images in it and not because of some literary journey. Woolf was breaking all boundaries, turning sexuality on its head.

PT: So you weren't afraid of Virginia Woolf?

SP: I was not afraid, not afraid at all.

PT: How about being afraid of your parents for dropping out of school?

SP: My parents let me alone. They were busy doing their own thing. My father was designer, also a sometime poet. My mother wanted to be a singer, but her career was somewhat on hold while she brought up my younger brother and me.

PT: Did you have trouble supporting yourself?

SP: [snickers] I often laugh because since my early twenties I've lived off my work, which means often living in debt. I've learned to improvise around nothingness. Oh, there's sex, with all it's joys and pains. But what I've been part of all my life is a raggedy community of passionate individuals for whom work is their life.

PT: Would you describe yourself as driven?

SP: I've hesitated for years to use that word because it feeds into the myth of the neurotic artist. But I am driven.

PT: Does this make you a monster on the set?

SP: I'm prepared to be unpopular to serve the film. You don't have to be a monster; you do have to be in charge. There were a few occasions when I did shout, and loud. I don't give up until things are right.

PT: With all that drive, why did it take four years to get *Orlando* financed?

SP: Because I wanted a sense of scale, nothing itsy-bitsy. I wanted to go to Russia and shoot scenes of big, frozen wastes. Eventually a coproduction deal was arranged with Russia, Italy, France, Holland, and England. But for years nobody would touch it. The financiers were deeply afraid of the sexual transformation.

PT: How do you get audiences to accept Tilda Swinton in the role of a man?

SP: By taking them into our confidence in the first minutes of the film when Orlando talks to the camera. That establishes a state of suspended disbelief. Then in comes Quentin Crisp as Queen Elizabeth – so we've got a double gender twist.

PT: How does the film differ from the book?

SP: The language is very modern – none of that "ye olde" stuff. The book stops in 1928, but the film is brought to the present day. Key crisis moments are clearly motivated. When Orlando changes from a man to a woman, there's a reason. The film has the pace and energy of now.

PT: What should people take from the film?

SP: A sense of largeness of their humanity – that their invisible life has been made visible and recognized on the screen. I hope they'll leave the cinema feeling pleasured, moved, and empowered.

PT: Have you been empowered?

SP: Four years ago I was knocking on people's doors. They're now knocking on mine. If *Orlando* can be done without compromise and people are coming to it in droves, that's power. Not just for me but for anyone wanting to follow a dream. Cinema is the big dream, isn't it? It's the consciousness of the population up there on screen, and it's beautiful.

Source: *Rolling Stone*, 24 June 1993.

Finding and applying critical frameworks

It is here that you can explore the wealth of critical response that will have been generated around your filmmaker and their associated texts. It is different from the critical information you gathered for the secondary critical response section, because here you will be evaluating critical frameworks and discussing their relevance to your chosen topic. You might, for example, look at media effects debates or feminist criticism and describe how useful they are in offering fruitful comment. You could select pieces of criticism and discuss them in relation to your own critical response.

With a study of Sally Potter, an analysis of the feminist criticism around her work is perhaps the most obvious place to start. Rather than try to contend with all possible arguments within a feminist critical stance, you should try to identify a particular argument and discuss its relevance. Feminist critics Laura Mulvey and Tania Modleski have contributed much debate to the function of the **gaze** in cinema: who is the object, who might be the 'perpetrator' and what can be found within that dynamic. Within Sally Potter's work 'the gaze' and who controls it is a fascinating area. *Orlando* is a text that debates the nature of gender, the individual and by extension, the position of the genders in relationships. When Orlando becomes a woman, she encounters a repositioning of 'the gaze' and finds herself at first the object of it. At a literary evening she is discussed and derided by Jonathan Swift and Alexander Pope, caught as the object of their critical attentions. However, when she encounters Shelmerdine, it is he who is positioned by both Orlando and Potter's direction as the object of attention. Desire thus rests with the female character and in this way Sally Potter is able to offer the viewer her comments on the 'gaze' debate. The genders and our preconceptions about them are held up as less fixed than traditional film representations would imply. The extract below from the essay 'Turning the gaze around and *Orlando*' by Nuria Enciso, furthers this debate and, for the purposes of this section of our study, gives more evidence of the usefulness of this type of feminist critical framing within debates concerning Potter's work.

Turning the gaze around and *Orlando* by Nuria Enciso

Mulvey's thesis states that visual pleasure in mainstream cinema derives from and reproduces a structure of male looking and female "to-be-looked-at-ness" (whereby the spectator is invited to identify with a male gaze at an objectified female) which replicates the structure of unequal power relations between men and women. This pleasure, he concludes, must be disrupted in order to facilitate a feminist cinema. I think it is important to note that the term 'female gaze' does not necessarily mean a 'feminist gaze'. The question of differences between women are a reminder that when arguing the case for a feminist gaze and an effective feminist intervention in mainstream culture it is prudent to consider just who is looking at whom. At the same time, sex does not guarantee the gaze to be female. Many women, particularly those who gained initial acceptance into mainstream texts did so by presenting the male gaze from a patriarchal perspective. Therefore being a woman producing texts does not guarantee a feminist gaze nor does being a woman ensure a homogeneous female gaze. Black women, older women, younger women, working-class women, and lesbians are just a few of the marginalized groups whose dissenting voices have felt a need to fight for a place within Western feminist discourse. Age, ethnicity, sexuality and class determine the female gaze as much as sex does. Mulvey maintains a heterosexist perspective by assuming a heterosexual male protagonist and a heterosexual male spectator. What happens if the protagonist is a woman? There exists a range of female looks: where does lesbian desire fit in within her theory? It can only be theorised as 'masculined'. In privileging gender as the category which structures perspective, psychoanalytic criticism such as Mulvey's tends to depoliticise other power relations in our society – most notably those of class, ethnicity and generation. A feminist analysis can perhaps afford autonomy in terms of its interest in gender but not, Marshment and Gamman would suggest, if it produces a theory which cannot relate gender inequality to other structures of social inequality. Politics of power underlie feminism – differences between women give the lie to any claim for a single female, or even feminist, subjectivity.

Source: *Orlando* website, 2001.

Creating your own critical response

This section allows you to assimilate your findings and generate your own comments. It should refer directly to the title of your study. The title of this example study was 'Sally Potter: films, context and reception' and the information gathered above enables a variety of questions to be answered. It would be reductive to speak only about the feminist qualities of Potter's films and our findings have evidenced the importance of debates concerning the nature of the individual, time, nation and history, as well as gender in her work. Potter's direction often elaborates on ideological discussion that is overt within dialogue and characterisation. Her camera comments on, as well as reflects, the action that we see. The information on the context of her filmmaking illustrates how important biographical detail, budget restrictions (due to lack of funding) and adverse critical reception (from some quarters of the cinema establishment) are in the look and ideological content of her work. Deductions concerning the reception of Sally Potter and her work offer a picture of increasing critical acceptance, widening audiences and more profitable projects.

PART TWO
Popular Music and Youth Culture

Popular Music and Youth Culture is a broad heading. It allows for many areas of study that discuss the relationship between the two parts of the title. However, it should not become a study in personal music taste but offer analysis of the dynamics that exist between the music industry and the various sub-cultures it caters for. There are many avenues of potential study under this topic heading, but the general areas that you may like to investigate are as follows.

The nature of youth and sub-cultures and their relation to mainstream popular culture

The first stage of any study within this area would be to offer a definition of the term sub-culture. Is the particular sub-culture you have identified resistant to the dominant values of mainstream culture or does it conform to them? A sub-culture, remember, does not have to be a subversive or revolutionary group. You will have to discuss the extent to which the music industry influences particular parts of youth culture. Does popular music influence attitudes, dress and taste or is it the choices made in connection with these things that influence musical taste?

The relationship between the music industry and other industries

For example, fashion, film, television, video, live performance, the internet and newspaper and magazine publishing. The music industry has become increasingly linked to others because of ever-expanding modes of consumption. Whether it is for promotional, entertainment or informative purposes, most music genres will have connected press publications, TV programmes, video sales and internet sites. You need to debate the extent to which the original sub-culture associated with particular music styles is authentically retained when it is translated into other mediums like magazines and TV shows. Does an associated glossy magazine, for example, dilute the original identity of the music and its sub-culture group?

The Face *magazine cover.*

Issues of ideology and the representation of youth culture and young people

If you choose to concentrate on this area for your study, you should investigate how music sub-cultures are represented by various sections of the media. You could, for example, compare magazines targeted at a particular audience with press stories concerning the target audience and their lifestyle. Analyse the way that the dominant morality, voiced by a particular paper, is presented as conflicting with the deviant morality designated as part of the sub-culture. You may also think about investigating niche media publications that construct a particular sub-cultural 'look' and discuss whether this type of publication reflects or exploits its target audience.

Case Study

The Ministry of Sound: music, magazine and website

This case study, under the broader heading of Popular Music and Youth Culture, would fall into the second of the previously-defined headings: the relationship between the music industry and other areas. Here we will look at the relationship between the original music associated with the Ministry of Sound and the 'products' that have been created around it.

Original research
When part of your specified sub-topic is a website, you have an easily accessible means of gathering information available to you. You should begin by defining the sub-genre of music on which you are focusing and for the Ministry of Sound it is predominantly club music. You could include details of some of the artists promoted on either

the website or in the magazine and describe the lifestyle represented by the images and references included in each text. The http.www.ministryofsound.co.uk site has a chat board on which questions to the target consumer can be placed. Questions should take the form of enquiries about how the website and the *Ministry* magazine reflect the lifestyle and interests of the target audience. You could investigate the extent to which the lifestyle offered on the site and in the magazine influence choices made by the consumer.

Secondary textual analysis

For this kind of study, where you are primarily investigating the relationship between a particular music sub-genre and its associated texts, secondary textual analysis could come in a number of forms. You may find information on the companies associated with a music sub-genre and how they grew to afford press publications, websites and so on that publicise the music. You may find analyses of the associated texts themselves and how they represent their target audience. Richard Wray's article below, from *The Guardian*, offers comment on the rise of the Ministry of Sound 'empire'. It identifies the business that has grown up behind the music and in the context of this case study illustrates how the relationship between music and associated text is an extremely lucrative one. When company sales top £100 million and product diversity is growing, is it possible to retain the exclusivity and cultishness of a music sub-genre?

Ministry of suits

3i to take a 20% stake in Palumbo's dance club group

Richard Wray

Venture capital group 3i is expected this week to disclose that it is swapping its suits and ties for tight T-shirts and trainers as it buys a stake in Ministry of Sound, the dance clubs to music magazines group.

3i is understood to be buying a stake of about 20% in the firm which was created by James Palumbo, son of property tycoon Lord Palumbo. The deal could value the group at up to £100m but sources close to Ministry of Sound described speculation of an imminent flotation as "premature".

Many of 3i's recent investments have been in the technology industry. However, the company is increasingly widening its interests to cover consumer brands and funded the management buyout of British Airway's budget airline Go in June.

Mr Palumbo, a former merchant banker, set up Ministry of Sound in 1991 in a rundown warehouse in Elephant & Castle, south London which he bought for £250,000. It quickly gained a name in the underground dance scene and as the popularity of dance music exploded Ministry of Sound became a household name.

Mr Palumbo has attempted to grow Ministry of Sound into a global brand, moving into CDs, clothing, books and even launching a magazine. The company is reported to have sales of more than £100m and its founder's personal wealth was recently valued at £150m.

The group has continued to organise dance events, expanding out from its original warehouse to hold events across Europe. It organised a New Year's Eve bash at the Millennium Dome in Greenwich.

Earlier this year Mr Palumbo teamed up with Pierre-Yves Gerbeau, the Frenchman hired to save the dome, to launch a bid for the arena after plans by the Legacy consortium to turn it into an e-business park collapsed.

Mr Gerbeau's New Dome Partners pulled out of the bidding in March, complaining that the cost of redeveloping the site was too high without public aid.

The consortium wanted some of the proceeds raised from the sale of parts of the Greenwich site to be ploughed back into the re-development scheme. The request was rejected.

Source: *The Guardian*, 6 August 2001.

Biographical information

For this particular case study, the most significant individual within the Ministry of Sound organisation is James Palumbo. The article above outlines how he began the Ministry in 1991 at a warehouse in the Elephant and Castle in London. He then developed the company's interests by diversifying into CDs, books, a magazine and clothing. You could extend this information by finding out details of Palumbo's perception of the music sub-genre with which he is associated and how he describes the typical consumer of dance music and Ministry of Sound products. It would also be useful, here, to look at the **editorials** that appear in the Ministry of Sound magazine and describe how the editor approaches his target reader. Below is an example editorial from the October 2001 edition of *Ministry* magazine.

Editor's letter

Spliff. It's put Cadbury's profit margins through the roof, burnt holes in a million hooded tops, eased untold nasty comedowns and made years of endless *Star Trek* repeats bearable The Student's Favourite over the counter! But exactly how will the big tobacco companies flog it to us? On page 44, we ask three branding experts to give us their take on advertising weed. (Thankfully, there wasn't a fancy-dress chicken in sight, and no one went down the "With this skunk you are spoiling us …" route.)

Portugal, of course, is already ahead of the game in the decriminalisation of class As – they did it in July this year. Cue: tabloid frenzy and much talk about British rave monkeys making a bee-line to go and 'ave it in Albuferia. "Where the bloody hell," demanded disgusted of Tunbridge Wells, "are we going to play our golf" Well, I wouldn't throw those putters away, Marjorie … as you'll see from page 62, it looks like the Algarve has got a way to go before it rivals the White Isle.

Daily Mail readers aren't the only ones moaning about clubbers. On page 72, we meet the night-shift workers that spend their lives dealing with pie-eyed party-goers. Trust us, they know you do look spangled. (I, however, refuse to believe that the staff in my local store thought that we were anything but straight when we bought £237 of, er … fudge vodka after Serious' fifth birthday party at The Cross.)

Elsewhere in the mag, we meet the new stars of laidback house Royksopp, catch up with anthem kings X-Press 2, review the monster festival that was Knebworth and tune into the new wave of stars appearing on Ministry Radio (87.7FM) in October.

Oh, and we also get the bottom line on drug testing at work. I would suggest none of you go and work in the States …

Enjoy!

Ollie

As with many magazines, the comment is delivered through direct address to the reader: 'I would suggest none of you go and work in the States …'. By doing this the Editor positions himself as a kind of seasoned participant of the club scene. At once familiar and slightly distanced by the informed comment, Quain is somebody who is about to take the reader into a world of lifestyle, pastimes and arguments, of which he is a seasoned exponent. The article is informal in its grammar ('pie-eyed party-goers') and makes reference to the drugs debate which assumes a knowledge of 'spliff' smoking ('Spliff. It's put Cadbury's profit margins through the roof'), new music on the club scene ('we meet the new stars of laid-back house') and other Ministry mediums (Ministry Radio). It projects a sense of knowing about the club scene and its lifestyle as well as being part of it. It is always important in this type of publication for the reader to be able to identify with those who have selected materials for them. The editorial comment about the marijuana debate constitutes about 80 per cent of the article space, whereas the music reference is minimal. The comment positions the magazine very clearly against the opinions of those it sees as '*Daily Mail* readers' and 'Disgusted of Tunbridge Wells'. Middle England, conservative values and those who impede a Ministry lifestyle are held up as rather petty and uninformed about the debate. The reader, Ollie Quain implies, is informed and realistic about issues related to him or her. He or she is in agreement with the editorial's position. So, whether the Ministry reader is somebody who is on the club scene or is new to it, they are expected to be in agreement with the arguments of the magazine, as well as being interested in the music and fashion which its advertisements and articles illustrate.

Contextual information

Rather than concentrate on political shifts in this area, it would be more useful to concentrate on the movement of this music genre from underground to mainstream and how this has affected or changed the profile of the music fans. The original context for dance music was small clubs (we have already mentioned the first Elephant and Castle venue for the Ministry of Sound). The associated fashions were on display in clubs, not on the pages of magazines. It was different to other music forms around at the time and was only evident in the charts in a diluted form. The plethora of new consumption modes which have developed recently, like the internet and MP3 files, mean that dance music has many more formats on which to be played. It also means that as well as word of mouth, dance music has many more routes through which to be advertised. Once a sub-genre of music and its fashions hit the high street and become marketable, they become mainstream. What was once a particular look or music style becomes accessible to all. Dance music is no longer the exception to the listening norm, it is one of the standards.

Institutional information and audience related research

Because of the specific nature of the title chosen for this case study, the institution and company information and comment on target consumer has already been given. You would not need to repeat information under this heading.

Finding and applying critical frameworks

There is much critical thought around the area of sub-cultures and youth culture. Rather than trying to use a wider critical framework (like feminist debate) with this topic, you may find that looking at particular texts which investigate the dynamic between music and those who consume it is a more useful way to proceed. For this particular case study, John Fiske's *Reading the Popular* (Routledge, 1989) would be a good text to begin with. In his study, Fiske offers comment on how particular sub-cultures and their associated artists and fashions provide symbolic reference for those who consume them. Dance music would have originally symbolised a state of rebellion and difference, although as we have seen the popularising of any music form often means a dilution of both impact and potential non-conformist status.

Creating your own personal response

As with any of the topic areas we are studying, personal response needs to summarise and concentrate investigative findings. This study on the Ministry of Sound points towards a link between mainstreaming and the dilution of the original impact. As the potential consumer group for dance music has broadened, because of increased consumption contexts and formats, the symbolism of difference has lessened. The branding of the Ministry of Sound and its development into a company that includes magazine publishing, franchised music events, clubs and CDs has translated what was underground into a marketable format. Of course, a lessening of the 'rebellion' symbolism of the original music is not something that would impact or affect those who consume the music in its mainstream form. It does, however, provide evidence for the argument that unless a music sub-genre fails to capture an audience, it will eventually be picked up by the music industry, made digestible for the mainstream and used to generate vast amounts of revenue; thus creating something very different from the original.

PART THREE

Politics and the Media

Initially this topic can seem quite daunting. You might think that you know relatively little about contemporary British politics. However, look carefully at the potential sub-topic areas below and you will probably find areas about which you already know a substantial amount.

Party political broadcasts, campaigns, photo opportunities and lobbying

The General Elections of 1997 and 2001 have been part of your media experience over the last four years. You may not have studied them closely at the time, but you may have seen the party political broadcasts or passed a hoarding of the poster campaigns. As a media student in your second year of study, you are already something of an expert on the effects of visual campaigns on an audience.

You will have studied the ways in which colour, **iconography**, representation, framing, language and cultural signifiers are used to attract an audience and you will be able to discuss the ways in which the audience consumes what they see. Why not transfer this knowledge to the study of a political campaign?

You could look at a poster campaign, political broadcast and series of photo opportunities connected with a particular party during the last election and evaluate both the messages they are trying to deliver and the effectiveness of that delivery. You could compare and contrast two campaigns, broadcasts and photojournalistic treatments, evaluating the relative success of each one. You could compare and contrast a particular party's campaigns over two or three elections, noting the changes in cultural signifiers, target audiences and even media technologies.

You do not necessarily have to base your work on General Elections. You may prefer to concentrate upon local or regional elections. If you choose to base your research project on lobbying, you could examine the media products attached to an interest group and how they have been used to try and influence political action. Greenpeace campaigns on posters and television could provide an interesting debate. What do the campaigns include? How do they attempt to influence public and political opinion? Are they successful?

Government press secretaries, public relations managers, spin doctors and the media

This could be a fascinating area of investigative research because it asks you to consider how the political 'personality' of both party and individual is constructed. An evaluation of the role of press secretaries and public relations managers could consider press releases, for example offering an analysis of the content and the desired effects. You could choose a particular event, such as Peter Mandelson's fall from power, and look at how New Labour dealt with the situation through press releases. The role of spin doctors can be assessed in relation to how particular political events or incidents concerning individual politicians are 're-worked' in order to either confirm positive readings or attempt to avoid negative readings. You could analyse the press reports around a particular politician's actions and try to identify how, through TV interviews and comment from other politicians, the incident was 'spun'. It would be essential for you to assess the effectiveness of the 'spinning'. Did John Prescott ever detach himself from the press reports that labelled him a 'bruiser' for hitting the demonstrator who threw an egg at him?

Media commentators

This is an extremely broad area to contend with and it would be useful at the beginning to identify the particular area of media commentating that you are going to investigate. You may wish to limit yourself to analysing press political commentary, possibly looking at the differences between broadsheet and tabloid coverage of a particular political event. You could investigate the stories themselves or comment on how the editorials of certain papers respond. You may decide to concentrate on photojournalistic commentaries and investigate the differing representations of politicians and political events delivered to the reader through the photographs chosen by different newspapers. You could compare and contrast the various newspaper cartoonists' readings of politicians and events. For all of these areas you will need to employ your knowledge of both intent and consumption. What is the ideological and political stance implied through the cartoons? Are they supposed to

Private Eye *cover.*

confirm the target audience's thoughts or introduce new arguments? What impact do the cartoons have on the political landscape? Are they influential?

Television and radio are the other main mediums for media commentators on politics. Your study may identify the programmes that aim to deliver political discussion and comment and assess them for format, delivery, target viewer and political comment. You would not need to restrict yourself to **terrestrial** channels if studying television and it would be interesting to investigate the different kinds of programmes available within both satellite and digital channels. As for press analysis, you should consider content, format, delivery and target audience and assess the effectiveness of the programme against what it assumes it is delivering. You could even compare and contrast programmes from different mediums, which may bring up issues of audience response to differing consumption formats.

The media commentators you choose do not have to be of the 'traditional' variety and political satire is a particularly fertile area of study. You may like to look at one political event or a political party and investigate how they are satirised. The scope for this sub-topic is huge and the texts available to you are probably ones that you have encountered already. Rory Bremner's brand of satire through impersonation could provide the basis for a research project, as could Chris Morris' shows *The Day Today* or *Brasseye*. *2DTV*, which delivers its brand of the satirical through television cartoon, would also provide rich comment, as would an investigation into the purpose and impact of the satirical magazine *Private Eye*. There is a great tradition of satirists offering a counterpoint to 'straight' political commentary and, as well as focusing on content, format, target audience and impact, you could extend your analysis by noting the ways in which the current crop of satirical texts are treated by those who they satirise. Are they deemed to be useful or obstructive by those who act as satire's 'targets'?

Stills from Brasseye *and* 2DTV.

Impartiality versus editorial or owner's values

A study within this sub-topic would consider the issue of whether or not a media text and its content can be independent of the value system and the beliefs of its owner or editor. Within a study of the press, both the editor and owner would need to be considered in terms of their influence. Where there is a high profile owner, for instance Sky/News International and Rupert Murdoch, first you would have to identify the political stance and value system of the owner and the mission statement of the company and then look at the extent to which this influence permeates programme type, article content and scheduling. Does owner influence affect the type of political coverage offered or the format in which it is delivered? How much influence is the owner legally allowed to have? In the case of less-conspicuous individuals, you could evaluate the role of the editor of a newspaper in shaping comment and bias. Does the comment you read at the beginning of a paper provide an ideological or political model for how the articles are written (and by extension how they are supposed to be consumed)?

The relationship between media owners and government legislation

This area of study asks you to consider the relationship between those who own media companies and the government legislation that is in operation around them. You will need to assess whether you think that legislation is helpful or restrictive to the production of media texts and describe the changes in various pieces of legislation attached to different media areas. Also consider the shifts in type of legislation that occur from one government to the next. It may not be that a new government party wants to legislate differently. The same party might change particular laws either because of a shift in ideological climate or, to give a more cynical reading, because of political expediency. You could look at the laws that inform censorship in the media, for example, those that have informed the shifts in assessment criteria for the **BBFC** (British Board of Film Classification). You could look at the 1990 Broadcasting act and identify not only what it specified and how this was a change from what had gone before, but also the changes in programming it caused and any resistance there was to it.

Public Service Broadcasting and politics

A research project on this area would need to go much further than a basic definition of Public Service Broadcasting. The BBC should not be seen as the sole provider of PSB. The original Reithian view of PSB as completely separated from commercial interests should be thoughtfully examined. Although the BBC, and to a lesser extent ITV, remain constitutionally independent from the state, they have both been subject to regulation and organisation by public bodies. Your study could identify the regulatory bodies that have been connected to the BBC (as an example of PSB) and assess the extent of their influence. You could examine the political programming available within the BBC and discuss how this might be considered public service. You could look at how the idea of Public Service Broadcasting has been influenced by the advent of new technologies, both in terms of production and consumption.

Case Study

Political poster campaigns for the 2001 General Election

Original research

The first stage for this project would be to locate the poster campaigns that you are going to use as your focus. You could search for back issues of newspapers that include examples or look at websites that include them. *The Guardian Unlimited* website allows you to search through its archive and includes many colour examples of poster campaigns used within the last election. You could also look at political party websites in order to find comment on campaigns connected with the election. Of course, perhaps the most important thing you need to do, for original research, is to analyse the posters you have found for iconography, representation of both party politics and politicians, **intertextual** reference (if appropriate) and target consumer. Below are three posters from the main parties involved in the 2001 election and some analytical points about them.

- The poster is constructed as if it is advertising a film. The layout, colouring and imagery point to an action/disaster movie.
- The fact that it is a sequel implies that the Tories have already been given one chance by the voting public and if given another, will fail again.
- The byline 'Coming to a home, hospital, school and business near you' defines the sphere of potential damage as including both commerce, essential services and personal lifestyle.
- Michael Portillo is represented as a falsely optimistic, insincere character whose character name 'Mr Boom' is at odds with his party leader, an unhappy, depressive 'Mr Bust'. An inconsistency in party politics and lack of unity within the party is implied.
- The ratings circle includes 15%, which would be the (frightening) interest rate, if the Tories were elected.
- The target audience are New Labour voters who will have their fears confirmed by the connotations of the poster and new voters who had not fully considered what a return to Tory government might mean. The format and intertextual reference within the poster could indicate a young target audience.

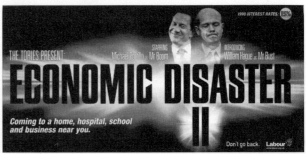

Economic Disaster II: Part of the Labour Campaign.
See figure 24.

- The image is of Tony Blair, pregnant with promises that the Tories state have not been delivered. The representation is of a party leader who breaks his promises and who may smile (as in the poster) when he makes them, but whose words are hollow.
- The sub-heading identifies the areas in which the broken promises have been made: class sizes, numbers of police and taxation. As with the main heading of the poster, these words are in red, building a connection between the red of the Labour Party and the red warning sign.
- The fact that Blair's head has been 'mapped' onto the body of a pregnant woman could also imply that the health service, waiting lists and waiting times are also an area in which Labour have failed to deliver.
- The poster functions as a direct attack on New Labour, and as with the first poster, says nothing about what the party will do and everything about what the opposition did not.
- Its target consumer would be existing Tory voters and those who may have voted for New Labour in the last election, but are now concerned that promises have not become reality.

Pregnant Blair: Tory campaign. See figure 25.

- The focus of the poster is the quotation, which is large, bright white and bold. Charles Kennedy is pictured looking directly at the camera (and by extension the audience). This form of direct address is generally used to imply sincerity and earnestness.
- This is the only poster we have looked at which uses a political leader from the party who originated the poster. The quotation can be assumed to come from Kennedy and is framed as a type of philosophical maxim, i.e. it is something which the Liberal Democrats are implying we should or already do believe. The quotation states that any civilised society privileges the education of the young and the care of the old, any party that does not do this is fundamentally at fault. Both New Labour and Tory policies on education and the old are the implied targets; neither, we are drawn to conclude, have 'measured' up.
- The poster is not one of high production, unlike New Labour's, and neither is it taunting the opposition, as the Tory example does. It is plain, simple, to the point and speaks to its audience of fundamentals rather than surface issues, as do the Liberal Democrats, we are led to believe.
- The target audience for this poster would be established Liberal Democrat voters, as well as those who might respond to a more direct approach.

Charles Kennedy poster. See figure 26.

Secondary textual analysis

With this project, it would be extremely useful to analyse not only what political commentators said about the individual elements of the various poster campaigns, but whether or not the whole campaign was considered effective. Has the huge range of modes of consumption and high production values often seen in campaigns today, made the campaigns seem less authentic and meaningful than in previous years?

Biographical information and institutional detail

For biographical information within this case study, you could identify any individuals who were behind the various poster campaigns. You could look at other publicity campaigns they may have done within the political field and compare them to your study. Institutional detail is covered by this kind of investigation because the companies with which any individual might be associated are of relevance. Does the company or organisation have a pre-existing relationship with a political party?

Contextual information

In order to put your chosen posters into context, it would be useful to compare them with previous poster campaigns. This would allow you to comment on the differences in party and political representations and also the dynamic between the parties. Below are two examples of previous political posters. One is an extremely early example and the other much later, but they both provide a fascinating insight into the social context of their exhibition.

January–February and December 1910: Labour fought two general elections in 1910, winning 40 seats in January and 42 seats in December. They were led by Arthur Henderson for the first campaign and George Barnes for the second. This poster embodies the radical spirit of the Labour party in its infancy — it was only founded 10 years earlier. The demolition of the House of Lords, though never achieved, certainly inspired many of the newly enfranchised working men to vote Labour.

Labour clears the way.

This is an example of a political poster from 1910. There were two General Elections in this year and this poster was used for both. It pictures workers storming the House of Lords in an attempt to break both the class system and its attendant privileges. The Labour Party voter is represented as a working-class man who is prepared to act on his political beliefs. It is not really an incitement to violence, but a statement concerning the fervour with which the infant Labour Party (it had only been around for 10 years at this time) was prepared to act on its beliefs. It is an interesting text in contrast to those recent examples from New Labour, which are often glossy and targeted at a much broader audience. The modern posters are not pictures of radical fervour, but rather attempts at representing New Labour as a viable government option for a cross-section of the electorate; working class or otherwise.

This poster and the others within the campaign became the subject of much debate during the 1997 election. The cloaked and shrouded threat, with evil eyes, presented New Labour as being dangerous, even malevolent. The Tories were hoping to play on a number of voter fears. Firstly, those who had experienced previous Labour Governments were being encouraged to see that time as one of 'dark days'. Secondly, the new voter was presented with an image of an unknown threat. One that may sound plausible, but is in fact at core destructive. The image is created to play on the voter's worst fears, that of the evil lurking behind the curtain. The curtain could also be theatrical and implies that New Labour are offering mere performance, rather than substantial reality. In contrast with the Tory campaign of the 2001 election, this poster is not about policy (previous New Labour policies from their last government would probably not be remembered), but about staying with the known (the Tories) rather than inviting in the dangerous unknown (New Labour).

The long goodbye? March 18 1997: Fear is the key to PM's hopes – Major back on soapbox in early start to marathon election campaign.

'New Labour, New danger'. See figure 27.

Audience related research

You will have made comments concerning the target audience for the different posters you have chosen. To extend your analysis, you could show some of the posters to your peer group or other individuals and obtain their opinions on intention and impact.

Finding and applying critical frameworks

It is not so relevant within this type of study to evaluate the usefulness of a particular critical framework. The articles concerning the posters you have chosen and the feedback you will get from discussion and questionnaires will be of more relevance.

Creating your own critical response

This is where your own analysis of the posters, their context, their audience and impact is of vital importance. You could also ask yourself extension questions. Why is it useful to look at political poster campaigns? How have they changed over the years? What do you think they may look like in the future considering shifts in the expectations of the voting public? What do you think your study has revealed about the place of posters within a political campaign?

4 PART FOUR
Children and Television

This topic is usually extremely popular because it describes an area that we have all experienced at some time in our lives and also because it appears more accessible than, say, 'Politics and the Media'. However, the latter, on closer analysis, includes many sub-topics that are both approachable and potentially fascinating. With Children and Television you need to be careful because unless your sub-topic is clearly defined, the research projects produced can be vague and insubstantial. Having direct personal experience of a topic does not necessarily make it easier or a better subject for close critical scrutiny. Although this may seem to be a warning, you should not be put off studying this area if you have a clearly defined topic that you are prepared to research in depth.

Broadly speaking, this topic asks you to research the relationship between children as subjects of media representation and as consumers of television. There are many potential sub-topics that could provide the focus of study with examples shown below and explanations of the possible content.

Children's television genres

This is an interesting area of study, because it asks you to consider whether children's TV genres are any different from adult ones. You may find that the genre headings are the same but the conventions involved in them are different. You may find yourself 'naming' new genres. Whatever your findings, however, you will need to debate the effect of children's genre categories on the child viewers. If genre works as a mechanism through which media texts become more recognisable to the viewer, is the effect of children's genres and their conventions to offer the same kind of predictability and safety? To what extent do you think that children might 'look' for certain conventions within genres of programmes? This is the kind of question that you may begin to answer through focus group interviews with children.

Television advertising, targeting and using children

This sub-topic actually includes two areas. One is adverts that specifically target children and the other is the kind of advertising that may use children in a representational way. It is probably advisable to choose only one of these areas.

If you are investigating adverts that are targeted at children, there are many possible analytical avenues. You could look at the way in which stylistic features, like the use of colour, iconography and camerawork, are employed to engage and hold the child's attention (and influence the parent). Are common stylistic features evident within adverts for a particular target audience, across a range of products? Are there conventions within advertising for different age groups? You could explore the ways in which children, their families and their interests are represented in a selection of adverts for children's products. How do adverts for children's products use the children within them to sell? Is it the scenarios in which the children are placed, the responses they are shown to have or the actions or responses of an associated adult which advertise? Do not forget that one of the questions you will always find yourself asking within the particular sub-topic is: who are adverts really aimed at, the child or the parents? Any investigation concerning adverts which target children needs to also contend with the context in which the adverts are delivered. Does the scheduling or time of day or channel make any difference? Does the context of film or music associated with particular products affect the way a child would experience the advertisement? Remember that you also need to address and examine the ideological context of your chosen adverts and investigate the content in relation to what is current in social debate. If the children are depicted playing in a certain way, does this fit within a current psychological or sociological model? If the adults in the advert do not constitute a nuclear family unit, does this show a breaking away from 'traditional' representations?

If you decide to study the latter area within our sub-topic, you will also need to consider the ideological context for your chosen set of adverts and explore whether or not you think they confirm or challenge a dominant ideological position. The focus of this type of study will be those adverts that use children in order to sell products to an adult market. The first thing you need to do is collect a range of adverts for different products that use children in this way. Try to ensure that your chosen product range is diverse and you could even collect examples from different decades in order to provide comment on changing representations (and thus changing ideological contexts). When investigating the ways in which children are used in your adverts, there are a number of possible questions you could ask yourself. What connotations surrounding a child/childhood are being 'exploited' in the name of advertising? What are our current thoughts or fears about children that are evoked by the advert? How has the representation of children within campaigns targeting adults changed over the years? What does this indicate to you about the changes that have occurred in our perception of children?

Representations of childhood and gender

Representation is an area of analytical study that we have already touched upon above. A study that appears too driven by either a sociological or a psychological model should be avoided here. You are a Media Studies student and you should bring to this area your knowledge of how to analyse media texts and the representations that are constructed within them. You should begin a project on childhood and gender by describing the limits of your study. The first stage is to collect texts that include representations relevant to your study. You could look at programmes that are aimed at children and also those that are aimed at adults, but that include specific representations of children. You could look at a TV guide in order to find examples, but make sure that the examples you choose include enough variety. For example, you may have identified *Rugrats* as a programme aimed at young children that attempts to represent childhood as a time in which children are able to articulate thoughts about their worlds. This may be in terms that are separate and different from the expectations that adults have concerning children's understanding. You may then look at a programme like *South Park* which is aimed at adults and creates a more cynical and comedic view of children's experiences.

You could then focus on issues of gender and select programmes that comment on apparent divides in the experiences of boys and girls. Through almost caricatured representations, *The Simpsons* depicts Bart and Lisa's separate (but sometimes poignantly similar) experiences of school, their parents and the world around them. With Bart, boyhood is full of scrapes and scams. He challenges authority figures and tests himself against what he considers to be the adult establishment. At other times he can be vulnerable and the mask of bravado slips. Lisa seems initially to act as a counterpoint to her brother's lack of seriousness. She is conscientious and committed to making her world safe by working hard at school and achieving her potential. However, both children sit in front of the violent cartoon *Itchy and Scratchy* and laugh at the horrors being inflicted by one character on the other. What you need to consider at this point is whether or not the depiction of Bart and Lisa's genders is indicative of reality and whether it is a vehicle for some ideological comment on childhood from the makers of the show.

Academic perspectives

The magnitude of critical writing on children and television will initially seem daunting, which is why it is essential that you give your study some parameters. You cannot possibly consider all of the critical perspectives at once, but you could research under specific headings, such as 'Children and TV violence', 'How children watch TV' or 'TV and behaviour modelling'. Do not forget that your task is not merely to relate the perspectives you have found to the examiner, but to evaluate and assess them too. How have academic perspectives changed over time and why this has happened? Which do you think are the most effective and useful theories around your chosen heading?

Television as education

There has always been much debate surrounding the question of television as a potential educational medium. One place to begin this sub-topic is with the current programmes on television which purport to be, and are explicitly, educational. The BBC *Bitesize* series would be a good example to use and you could evaluate both the educational content of the programme and the means by which the content is delivered. You could then extend your thinking into the study of those programmes that have a slightly less obvious 'educational' tag. In this case something like *Blue Peter* might offer an interesting study. In order to extend your study still further, however, you would need to decide what the term educational means outside of explicit examples. If you think that children are educated through role modelling or through scenarios that encourage them to develop critical thinking processes, then the potential example 'net' can be cast further. Can a soap opera encourage children to explore notions of **stereotyping**? Can a literary adaptation encourage understanding of narrative patterns and human relationships? Can watching an extended story help build attention spans?

Research on the effects of television on children

The 'effects debate' around children and television has been ongoing since the first televisions were introduced into the home. A study under this sub-topic would need to consider not only what the various

Blue Peter. *See figure 28.*

The Tweenies. *See figure 29.*

arguments in the debate are, but how established study can be measured alongside the conclusions you draw from your own interviews, questionnaires and research. The effects debate seems to polarise around two schools of thought. One viewpoint holds that children are active participants within the TV viewing process, that they have strategies to deal with problematic information and images they encounter and that the effect on them is not something which encourages copycat behaviour or violent tendencies. The alternative school of thought asks us to consider the child as a passive recipient of the messages and images delivered through the TV screen. The child here becomes desensitised when, for example, shown violent images, and is then capable of copycat behaviour. Within the former argument, the media is not 'at fault' for subsequent behaviour patterns. If a child has a disposition towards problematic behaviour, this may be made worse by certain types of viewing, but television does not 'cause' the child to act in anti-social ways. Within the latter framework, the child who views traumatic subject matter may become more aggressive or anti-social, regardless of whether they are disposed in that way or not. Your study would need to look at the theorists and the specific theories connected with these two schools of thought and evaluate each, using your own findings as a backdrop.

Children as participants in television programmes

There are many TV programmes that use children as participants and not all are aimed at children. You may even argue that there are programmes that use children 'in absentia' as participants, for example, *You've Been Framed*, which has many examples of children doing apparently 'funny' things. You could discuss the function of child participants. If the programme is aimed at the same age group as the participants, it may be a strategy to engage the viewer or reflect his/her own interests. If the programme is aimed at adults, what function do the children on the show have in engaging the audience? To answer this, you would have to identify how the programme was representing the children. Are they shown as cute or quirky or are their skills being presented?

Views of parents, teachers and children on television and childhood, effects debates, violence and theoretical models

This sub-topic begins with your own individual research and asks you to evaluate your findings. This type of project will only work if you begin with some questions that you hope may be answered during your research. Establishing a clear methodology when asking for views from such diverse focus groups will be extremely important and you would need to frame questions which are both appropriate to the target focus group and which allow for the gathering of useful information. It would be impossible for a child, for example, to comment on an effects debate argument and so you would have to ask much simpler questions relating to the child's own experiences and/or create role plays which could be observed. Furthermore, do bear in mind, that showing a child a piece of violent footage and then sitting back and observing their response would be highly unethical!

Case Study

Research into the effects of television on children

Secondary textual research

This would be the starting point for any research project under this heading. As outlined in the previous section, you need to collect and assess information regarding the various researchers who have worked on the two general schools of thought. Some of the project headings that we have used in the previous case studies will be irrelevant here because of the nature of the project. This case study will present some of the ideas that could be used, but it is by no means exhaustive.

For the purposes of this example, we will restrict ourselves to research that has been conducted around the effects of problematic TV images on children. The work of Australian researchers, Hodge and Tripp and the British researchers, David Buckingham and Dr Sonia Livingstone, will provide us with one side of the debate. The studies of American researcher, Huesmann, will be used to exemplify the contrary point of view.

Hodge and Tripp's research took place in Australia in the 1980s. The work was qualitative in its approach and used 600 primary school children as its subjects. Some of the main findings of the project, published in *Children and Television* (Polity Press, 1986), were that:

● Children have the ability to be active decoders of the television they watch
● Media violence is viewed by children as different from real violence
● Children's ability to distinguish between reality and fiction on television is improved through watching TV

David Buckingham has conducted many pieces of research into the effects of television on children. In findings he published in 1996, he highlighted the following points:

● Negative responses to television programmes (crying, worry, fright etc.) are common, but the kinds of programmes that provoke these responses are varied
● Children develop a variety of coping strategies to deal with distress from their viewing
● Children learn to question the reality status of what they are viewing and this provides them with one of the coping strategies referred to above
● There is no evidence to suggest that children are less upset by real life violence as a result of watching fictional violence

Sonia Livingstone is a researcher at the London School of Economics. The article printed opposite describes a study she conducted with a team of researchers into the effects of television viewing on children. It includes not only her findings, but also opinions of others concerning the extent of influence that television viewing has on children. It provides discussion points at the heart of the debate of this particular case study. Articles such as these provide an interesting and relevant reference point within a study and you should try to locate those that would be of relevance to your own work.

The youngsters with no life beyond the bedroom

By RICHARD ALLEYENE

In their free time, they rarely venture beyond the bedroom door. And there they stay, keeping themselves entertained for up to seven lonely hours a day.

The first survey of its kind for 40 years concluded that more and more youngsters are retreating from the real world into a 'bedroom culture'. Their parents, concerned about their safety on the streets, are apparently happy to let them do so.

Two-thirds of children now have TV sets in their bedrooms and some spend up to seven hours a day watching programmes, according to the survey of six to 17-year-olds.

One third of those admitted they regularly watched programmes after the 9pm watershed.

The research, by academics at the London School of Economics, showed for the first time that more households in Britain contain televisions than books.

The study – called Young People, New Media and sponsored by various media bodies – alarmed other academics and family groups.

Lord Alton, professor of citizenship at Liverpool John Moores University, said: 'We should be asking the question, "Is it advisable for young children to spend so much time by themselves?" It is obviously going to be at the expense of outdoor exercise and social interaction.

'Letting a child watch television on their own in their bedroom is like leaving them alone with a stranger. TV and other media are useful aids but they should not be allowed to dominate their lives.

'It creates a world of virtual reality and children find it very hard to work out what is real and what is unreal.

'Advertisers spend £5billion on television and they would not be doing that if they felt it did not have an effect.'

Valerie Riches of the pressure group Family and Youth Concern, said: 'I find these findings very, very worrying. Many studies have shown that it does have an effect, especially the violence. Children spending so much time in front of the television cannot be good for their development.'

Dr Sonia Livingstone, the study's project leader, said: 'The survey was carried out to provide information for debate. It was not supposed to draw conclusions.

'Our research does not support moral panics about children addicted to computer games or mindless entertainment on television. Compared with 30 years ago, children do spend more time in front of the TV or the computer but we have to decide whether that is a good thing or not.' The survey concludes that watching television is the most popular leisure activity, with children viewing an average two and a half hours of programmes a day.

One per cent watch up to seven hours a day. A quarter of those with computer games play them daily.

The report blames these high figures on insufficient outdoor activities available to young people and parental fears that allowing their children outside to play is dangerous. 'Possibly by way of compensation, increasing numbers of young children are provided with a rich media environment at home,' the study says.

The survey further reinforced trends showing the declining popularity of books. It said: 'Overall the image of books is poor. They are widely seen as boring, old-fashioned, frustrating and requiring altogether too much effort.'

Young People, New Media was funded by the Advertising Assocation, BBC, BT, the Broadcasting Standards Commission, ITV, and others. More than 1,300 children filled in questionnaires and 32 families gave in-depth interviews.

Source: *The Daily Mail*, 19 March 1999.

Huesmann, the US researcher, conducted his research from a behavioural/experimental psychology perspective. He often worked with 'test' cases and interviews. A condensed version of his findings is represented below:

- That the audience for a text is the passive 'victim' of the media
- That children do not have the skills to discriminate between real and fictional violence
- That the effect of exposure to television violence is desensitisation and thus a greater propensity to copycat or present violent and anti-social behaviour patterns

The above represents a 'potted' version of a selection of relevant theories and theorists. Your own study would need to go into much more detail.

Original research

Once you have outlined the researchers' findings concerning this sub-topic, you need to create the means by which you can conduct original research. As previously discussed in this topic section, the kinds of questions you create for any focus group of children you wish to use in your study need to be appropriate. You need to make sure that your questions are comprehensible, concise and relevant to the child's experience. If you interview parents, again be careful with the questions you create. Try to avoid questions which are too 'open', for example, 'What do you think about the effects of television violence on children?' Opt for those questions which allow the parent to make observations and deductions based on actual events and examples.

Creating your own critical response

Having investigated established researchers' views and conducted your own research, you will then need to draw conclusions. Do your findings position your thinking with the researchers you have mentioned or do they point to new or different conclusions? How effective do you think the research conducted by both yourself and the established figures was? Do you think there are any gaps in the information you have gained? Are there new factors that you have identified in the debate concerning the effects on children, which have not been highlighted before?

Audience research

This area asks you to investigate the ways in which research into the audience is carried out by media industries and/or academic researchers and how it is used, either by media institutions or in debates about the media. You would be identifying research methods and analysing their strengths and limitations. The sub-topics below are possible examples of how to make this kind of Critical Research Project more focused.

Qualitative and quantitative methods

The very first thing you need to do if you choose to look at qualitative or **quantitative** methods is to find a clear definition of the terms. Put simply, qualitative research is conducted by using focus groups, interviews and questionnaires, which are analysed for opinion and experience, rather than for data. Conclusions evaluate responses and opinions, rather than statistical information. Quantitative methods are very different and can range from units put in the home that record data, to questionnaires that provide a statistical outcome. Conclusions here are based on data outcome. (See also references to BARB and RAJAR on page 126).

Both of these research methods are used by media industries to evaluate the impact and popularity of media texts and the range and profile of consumption. You would need to evaluate the effectiveness of these methods. This could be done both by focusing on a particular media industry and investigating how it uses qualitative and quantitative findings, and conducting your own qualitative and quantitative studies in order to assess the kinds of information gained and the usefulness of it.

The purpose of industry and academic research

At the beginning of this type of project, you need to identify some examples of industry and academic research and then discuss its purpose. You may restrict yourself to a particular media industry, for example, television, radio or the press and then identify both the research that particular industry does and the academic work that is associated with it. You will need to discriminate between qualitative and quantitative research findings and consider how each is used. Ask yourself some questions. Is the purpose of research to analyse the impact of media texts or to inform the creation of them? Does industry and academic research work in a regulatory way, checking and assessing the kinds of texts produced or can it be used to justify decisions made? Is the purpose of research to provide information for the general public or solely for the industry?

Moral panics

A **moral panic** ensues after a number of different stages:

- Something or someone is defined as a threat to values or interests
- The threat is depicted in an easily recognisable form by the media
- There is a rapid build up of public concern
- There is a response from authorities or opinion makers
- The panic recedes or results in social change

Both words within the phrase 'moral panic' are highly emotive. For the threat to be moral, it is seen as a threat to the 'fabric' of society itself; something that is capable of destroying the social order. A panic is an extreme event, so a moral panic is a dramatic response by society to a threat that it perceives as potentially destructive. In order to create an effective project on moral panics, you would need to evaluate not only the stages of the process itself and what the social function of a moral panic is, but also to identify and discuss examples of moral panics. Ask yourself evaluative questions. How useful are moral panics in dealing with social concerns? Do social panics demonise the media and absolve others from social responsibility? Are the social and legal changes that result from moral panics effective and do they have appropriate 'targets'?

Effects research

Within the topic of Children and Television, we considered the part of the effects debate that is concerned with children's responses. Within the topic of Audience research, the potential areas of investigation are far greater. Because of this, you will need to restrict your 'investigative field' and pinpoint a particular aspect of effects research. You may decide that you wish to focus on audience responses to media violence, or on effects research into how audiences consume different types of media texts or on studies of how the effects of media texts may change from childhood to adulthood. Once you have chosen your topic and collected relevant information, you will need to discuss the effectiveness of that research. From a media student's point of view, do you think the information you gathered expands your knowledge of the ways in which media texts (and maybe industries) affect their audiences? Do you think that the type of effects research available and the types of conclusions drawn tell you anything about the perception of the media at a given point in time? Have effects debates concerning your chosen area changed over the years? If so, why have they?

Case Study

Qualitative and quantitative methods

Original or secondary research
This will investigate the organisations that conduct research concerning the media and the methods they use. Help with defining what constitutes qualitative and quantitative methodology is available in the previous section and you should make it clear to the examiner that you understand the differences between the two methods. Try to make sure that you achieve a balance of qualitative and quantitative examples.

Finding quantitative styles of research surrounding the media is relatively straightforward. There are extensive websites available for the main organisations that conduct industry research and, as well as useful data, these include comment on how the data is used and the rationale behind the methodology. **BARB** (Broadcasters' Audience Research Board), for example, conducts quantitative research on television and is used by TV companies and stations to monitor viewing figures and assess the popularity of programmes. **RAJAR** (Radio Joint Audience Research) is a company which collects data on radio and it also has an extremely comprehensive website. The **NRS** (National Readership Survey) is a non-profit making, but commercial, organisation that estimates the number and profile of people who read UK newspapers and consumer magazines.

In terms of qualitative research, finding information will require a little more initiative on your part. You could look at how TV companies try to ascertain the potential of a TV programme. Find some examples of pilot shows and contact the companies who made them about whether or not they used focus groups to gain target viewer feedback. You could also question companies and production staff about how they might use focus groups in order to create a TV programme, an advert or a magazine for a particular target audience.

Alongside information on industry audience analysts, you should create your own findings through qualitative and quantitative methods. Why not set up a target consumer focus group for a potential media text that you have created or ask them for feedback on a text they already consume? You could write a questionnaire that would create data about the reception of or audience profile for texts produced by a particular industry.

Creating you own critical response
This project mainly focuses on your evaluation of existing examples of qualitative and quantitative data and your assessment of these two research methodologies. From your research you will need to ask and answer a variety of questions. Here are some examples of questions you may pose yourself:

- Why do media industries use both qualitative and quantitative studies?
- What different types of information are gained from these two methods?
- Are they used to improve and evaluate media products?
- If the answer to this question is 'yes', then how do they do this?
- Are there any problems you have found with either qualitative or quantitative methods?
- Are there any types of information that they do not offer?

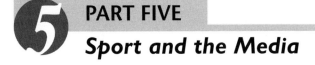

PART FIVE

Sport and the Media

You will need to confine yourself to the British media if you choose this topic, but you could look at international sporting agencies. The general purpose of your project is to investigate the relationships between sport agencies and the media. Below are some of the sub-topic areas that could be investigated.

The attraction and retention of audiences via sport in order to promote other products

The popularity of sporting events to many groups within a television audience, means that these are often used by television companies to entice new viewers or retain audiences. Digital television operators and companies such as Sky, promote the sports content of their programming vigorously. Exclusive coverage of events or new ways of watching events, for example, through interactive technologies, often encourage viewers to pay for access to certain channels or to move away from standard, terrestrial reception modes. The possibility of watching exclusive coverage of a boxing match or being able to decide which **camera angle** you desire at any given point in a football match is often a heavy incentive to buy a particular package of services or access to a particular channel.

If you choose to study this particular sub-topic, you need to investigate which channels offer such exclusive viewing and how this acts as an incentive, and also the profile of consumer who deem it attractive. Is the profile of audience member attracted or retained the same? Does the issue of monopoly arise within this kind of channel marketing? Are some sports given more coverage than others by particular channels in order to retain or attract viewers?

The representation of ideology such as global unity, nation and gender

Do not be put off by the term ideology. As a second year student of Media Studies you will have encountered it many times before. In the context of this sub-topic, an investigation into ideology requires you to analyse what messages are being delivered to you through sporting events and types of coverage. For example are we being encouraged to view the world as a unified place through the presentation of Olympic games coverage? If the answer to this question is 'yes', then how are we being encouraged to do this? Is it through equal coverage of different nations' sporting achievements, through an equality of encouragement from commentators or by the very fact that we are introduced to athletes from different nations who we have not seen before? If the answer to this type of question is 'no', then are we being encouraged to be nationalistic through the process of competition? Are the events selected for coverage chosen because of their involvement of a British athlete? Are these kinds of global events a unifying mechanism through which nations pride themselves in their national difference?

Minority interest sports

You do not have to concentrate on sports that have a massive following or are given huge exposure in order to create an effective Research Study. Minority sports, such as skateboarding or snowboarding, could provide an equally fertile area of study. You could begin by analysing the reasons why these sports are termed minority and even whether or not the term minority is accurate. Is a sport defined as minority because of the numbers of people who are interested in it or is it relegated to minority status in scheduling because of the profile of those who watch it? Gymnastics, for example, is a popular hobby and viewing preference for young girls, however it is not until the Olympics that this sport features prominently in the schedules.

Football

You could then move on to ask yourself further specific questions concerning the minority sport you have chosen to analyse. For instance, what effect do new technologies have on the coverage of that sport or what effect does sponsorship (or the lack of it) have on the way the sport is perceived? Does sponsorship-associated advertising and merchandising contribute to the perception of your 'minority' sport?

Snowboarding

The use of new media technologies in sports coverage

There is a wide range of new media technology used within the coverage of sporting events from new reception hardware, such as TV set top decoders and hard drive recorders, interactive digital programme types and internet fan sites, to new advances in 'capture' technologies, such as miniature cameras placed within the sporting event. A study of this area would have to question whether these new technologies have affected the way that sport is consumed by its audience. Does the advent of an interactive digital consumption type mean that audiences are becoming more insular in their sports viewing? Do you think the new ways in which sport can be consumed will mean a decrease in attendance at live events? Do you think that these technologies provide a greater potential of seeing a sporting event clearly and thus enhance viewing? In attempting to answer these types of questions you should use both your own response to sports that are affected by new media technologies and investigate the opinions of other target consumers.

Case Study

Sky Sports and interactive technologies

Original research

Some of the most useful original research you could do under this type of sub-topic heading would be to investigate what kinds of interactive technologies are used by Sky Sports and what kinds of sports coverage utilise them. The Sky Sports section of the Sky website (http://www.sky.com) is the most immediate and accessible source for this information and describes the use of interactive digital technologies in the provision of camera angle choice (including 'player cam'), supplies your own commentary, Ref-Link (referee's commentary), statistical data and immediate replays of sporting action. There are many possible sports contexts in which the viewer can use these interactive technologies, for example, rugby, golf, football, tennis, athletics and extreme sports. Below is an article from the Sky Sports website that describes the place of interactive technologies within the broadcasting of a rugby match.

GO INTERACTIVE WITH SKY SPORTS

The Tetley's Bitter Cup final between Harlequins and Newcastle is the latest major rugby occasion to be enhanced by Sky's revolutionary interactive technology.

Sky digital viewers can select, at the touch of button, which camera angle they want to see the action from, a stream of statistics and a continuous update of the match highlights.

And this season subscribers can get an extra angle though SKY REF-LINK. Listen to the reasoning behind the key decisions as viewers gain access to the referee's microphone throughout the game. It is a world first and allows hearing the referee to take the place of the regular commentary. When decisions are being made, our viewers will hear why.

All Sky Digital subscribers need do is tune into Sky Sports 2 and press the red button on the remote handset, once the interactive icon is showing on screen. From there the various interactive options are displayed at the bottom of the screen, simply press the associated coloured button on your remote.

Since August 1999 when Sky digital pioneered live interactive sports coverage, Sky Sports has developed and extended this innovation, broadcasting over 1000 hours of interactive sport which has been applied to seven sports, football, Rugby union, Rugby League, cricket, golf, tennis and snooker.

It was first introduced to Rugby union on Sky Digital on February 5 last year for the England v Ireland game and since then has become a regular feature of Sky Sports digital rugby coverage. England manager, Clive Woodward, used the statistics for England's successful autumn series against South Africa, Australia and Argentina and the Six Nations triumph over Italy at Twickenham.

Never one to take anything for granted, especially against ex-world champions South Africa, Woodward was constantly checking the services' essential information while masterminding the opposition's downfall.

Viewer's also have access to these statistics so can take Woodward on at his own game! To recap, the interactive world includes:

Sky Ref-Link – A world first, viewers will see the live match coverage but can opt to hear the referee's microphone in place of the regular commentary, allowing fans to be party to all the decisions, as they happen.

Cameras – There are four alternative camera angles. This year, the cameras are located in the north and south stands plus an overhead view of the stadium. The fourth is another new option. Based in the West stand, the Gain line camera which will give the viewer a constant check on territory gained or lost during play. The gain line will be re-set at each set play.

Statistics area – Screens of facts and figures are constantly updated during the match and linked up to England Manager, Clive Woodward's monitor pitch-side. These include information such as Attack and Defence Statistics showing Gain Line Success plus the lines of attack for both sides and immediate reference on team performance through ball possession, penalties conceded and handling errors.

Match highlights – An option to savour all the best moments again or catch the crucial highlights if they are missed

Source: Sky Sports website, April 2001.

Having gained the information described above, your original research should also include investigation into audience responses. Use the experiences of members of your peer group to assess what kinds of interactive technologies are used and whether they enhance viewing. Your Critical Research Project should evaluate the effectiveness of interactive viewing types as well as describe them. How might those you interview compare interactive sports viewing with standard modes of sports consumption?

Secondary textual analysis

You may be able to find academic criticism that discusses the changes in sports presentation and consumption brought about by interactive technologies, but you could also consider popular criticism when discussing the impact of interactive sports coverage. The Sky website has a link to a 'Your View' page where you can find viewers' comments on their viewing practices. You should use all of the secondary textual analysis that you find to inform your own arguments concerning the changes in viewing habits connected to the use of new media technologies. Below is a page from the Sky website which contrasts the uses of broadcast technology in the 1966 and 2000 World Cups. Although it does not constitute entirely objective secondary textual analysis (in fact it is a promotional piece), what it does do is offer explicit contrasts that you could use to extend your discussion. You could try to find someone who watched the standard terrestrial 1966 broadcast and the interactive 2000 broadcast from Sky and discuss with them how the different presentations affected their viewing.

A LOT HAS CHANGED SINCE 1966!

Posted October 7 2000

When England faced Germany in the World Cup in 1966, there were three cameras. On Saturday, there will be 66. Here we take a look at the advances in broadcasting over 34 years.

In 1966 at the World Cup Final at Wembley when the then mighty England beat the old enemy Germay 4–2 after extra time, we hoped that it would the start of something special, and it was, but not in the football circles as we would have liked.

Instead when the players run out on the pitch tomorrow, they will be surrounded by technology, British style.

It seems while England's football team may have gone backwards over the years in terms of trophy winning, the technology that is available nowadays as opposed to thirty four years ago is somewhat frightening and has put England in pole position once more.

Here we take a look at how things have changed since 1966 and what you can see:

Camera positions

In 1966 – there were eight cameras in position, but only three covering the game itself.

In 2000 – there will be sixty-six cameras covering the game in it's entirety. There will also be cameras in the airship that will be above the ground, and cameras at the German and England teams' hotels.

Cameras

In 1966 – it took four people to carry one of the cameras into its position.

In 2000 – a steadi-cam operater can move quite freely for the entire 90 minutes.

Commentators

In 1966 – the commentary team was the legendary Kenneth Wolstenholme with expert summary from Wally Barnes.

In 2000 – commentary will come from Martin Tyler and expert analysis from Andy Gray.

Technology

In 1966 – the game was shown in black and white, Colour was introduced in 1967. Saturday's game will be shown in wide screen with Dolby surround. Sky viewers will have interactive coverage, player cams and a whole host of other technical know hows.

In 1966 – the BBC had one slow motion replay machine that was based at White City and cost £68,000, as it was one of eight that existed in Britain at the time.

In 2000 – Sky Sports will have some 20 Video Tape machines at Wembley which are able to carry four different replays at any one time. To put the money thing into perspective, one of Sky Sports technical trucks costs £3 million pounds alone.

Global audience

In 1966 – the BBC provided coverage for ITV and the world with its meagre three cameras.

In 2000 – Sky will be the main broadcaster. ITV will have delayed rights and will have cameras in the stadium, as will the German TV company ZDF who will have in excess of 22 cameras inside the stadium.

Facilities

In 1966 – the BBC had approximately 20 people in attendance covering the final.

In 2000 – Sky Sports will have upwards of 150 people on site on Saturday working on the game.

Programming

In 1966 – the BBC took to the air at 10.30am and after the match they broadcast for an extra one and a half hours.

In 2000 – Sky Sports' coverage starts at 8am and continues till at least 9pm. Viewers have the chance to interact, by calling two phone ins or connect via e-mail to the interactive service.

Source: Sky Sports website, 7 October 2000.

Contextual, institutional detail and audience related research

In terms of useful contextual detail for this sub-topic, it is possible to look at three discretely different areas: Sky interactive programming within the context of the Sky Sports schedule; Sky interactive within interactive broadcasting; and interactive sports consumption within the context of attitudes towards new media technologies. For the first of these three areas, you will need to consider the place of interactive technologies within the Sky Sports programme line-up. The Sky Sports website includes a broadcast guide which would allow you to assess the balance of interactive to standard programming. You will need to ask yourself questions concerning the role of interactive programming. For example, 'to what extent does the provision of interactive technologies become a major selling point within Sky Sports marketing?'

For the second area you could look at other digital broadcasters who use interactive technologies and evaluate both audience expectations and reactions and the place of such technologies within scheduling. Is it the same kinds of sporting events that are interactive on all digital channels or do some channels have access to more events? Do exclusive rights to certain events mean that certain channels have a broader interactive potential?

The third area for contextual analysis takes interactivity into the debate concerning the way we consume new media technologies. This section of your study will also inform your discussion of audience-related issues. Does interactivity change the way in which we view sporting events? You could investigate, for example, the issue of fragmented versus linear viewing. Does stepping outside the sporting event to replay sections, peruse statistics or create your own commentary mean that the viewer approaches sporting events in 'bite-sized' chunks and therefore loses the immediacy and continuity of an unbroken viewing practice? Or does this allow for greater 'ownership' of the event through the creation of personalised viewing? How does the ability to choose what we see and hear affect the notion of a 'live' event? How has interactive viewing affected attendance at 'live' events?

For institutional detail, you could extend the points you have already made about the ways in which new media technologies are used as a unique selling point (USP) and consider the impact of interactive technologies on sales figures for the Sky Sports package. Other interactive sports providers are mentioned in your discussion of context and here you could expand your findings into a debate concerning market success and competition between the companies.

Creating your own critical response
Having gathered all of the information for your project and assessed all of the relevant areas, this section allows you to draw conclusions concerning the debates that surround your sub-topic. How important is interactive potential for the target consumer of sporting events? How important is interactive technology in the promotion of the Sky Sports channel? Has this new media technology changed our expectations and consumption of sporting events? Do you think that interactive sports broadcasting will become the norm or is it a temporary 'fad'?

PART SIX
Concept to Product

This particular topic area asks you to research a media product (from any medium) and evaluate the processes involved in production. You will need to follow your chosen product from conception, right through to consumption. Your media product can originate from Europe, the US or any other country. The style of your project will be a case study and you must make sure that you identify and evaluate all stages of the product's 'growth', as well as show understanding of the institutional contexts for production and distribution. Your study should also comment on the 'success' of the media product. Below is a list of areas that you will need to cover when studying your chosen text. Also included are questions that you may like to use in your research.

1. **Initial concept**
   How did the individual or the production team come up with the initial concept? Was there a gap in the market for a particular product? Was the initial concept a response to audience research or focus group investigation? What was the aim involved in the initial concept? To attract new audience members? To boost flagging ratings?
2. **Planning**
   What kind of planning was involved? To what extent did monetary

issues play a part in planning? Did the initial concept change during the planning stages?

3. **Personnel**

   Which members of the production team were most in evidence at different stages? Who had the most influence during the various stages of production? Did the team work as individuals who then fed back to a group or collaboratively on particular stages?

4. **Technology**

   What kind of technology was evident in connection with your media text? Did the type and amount of technology available influence the choices made concerning the text?

5. **Facilities**

   What facilities were available to the production team? Were the facilities 'on site' or hired/rented? Did the range of facilities available influence production?

6. **Time scale**

   What were the deadlines that the production team were working to? Were these externally imposed by investors, market forces and so forth? Were the deadlines met successfully?

7. **Finance**

   Where did the money come from for your chosen text? Did those who financed it have a say on the look and content of the product? Did the production team stay within budget?

8. **Marketing**

   How was the product publicised? Were there '**teaser** campaigns'? Where was the text publicised?

9. **Distribution**

   What was the range of distribution for the text? Where was it seen? Was the range of distribution controlled by target audience, budget issues or product type?

10. **Consumption**

    What is the profile of the target consumer for this product? How do they consume it? What are the contexts in which they might consume it? What is the target audience's attitude to the product? Do they consider that it is successful and fulfils their needs?

When choosing your text to study, try to be realistic. It will be much easier to access information if you either know someone connected to the text or have easy access to personnel who may be able to provide you with relevant details. Investigating a local media text, such as a new newspaper, magazine, advertising campaign, website or radio show, would be a more manageable project than deciding that you want to study a particular film and then finding that you cannot access all of the

Local listings magazine.

information you need. Of course, there is no reason why you could not investigate the production process for a film or television programme, but it would be better to check first to see whether you will be able to access sufficient research material.

Once you have identified your chosen media product and you have researched all of the necessary information, you need to evaluate the product's success. You may have begun to do this by questioning the target audience and you should also consider your own response to the product as an audience member.

Because of the personal investigation element of this particular sub-topic, it is not so useful to include a case study here. Instead, below are some examples of topic areas that could provide the basis of a research project.

A study of the processes involved in the production of a:

- Local listings magazine
- Fan site for a band
- Regional TV programme
- Broadcast live music event
- Short film
- Video game
- Advertising campaign
- A new niche or mass market magazine

7 PART SEVEN
Community Radio

Do not immediately dismiss this topic area because you think you will have to submit yourself to hours of listening and investigation into the kind of dull programming you may automatically (and stereotypically) associate with local radio stations. This topic asks you to investigate the relationship between local radio stations and their communities. You could analyse commercially or publicly-funded stations or niche programmes, and evaluate how they mirror the interests and tastes of their target consumers. There are many possible avenues you could explore as sub-topics within this area and below are some possibilities.

The nature and profile of radio communities

This sub-topic asks you to consider who the members of particular radio communities are, what their expectations might be and how their interests/lifestyles are reflected in programming. For example, you could compare two or three radio shows and consider the audience for each. As well as your own investigation, consider how the target audiences for these shows perceive themselves and their tastes; you could do this very effectively by interviewing members of the target audience. Are gender, age, race, geographical location and lifestyle common amongst those who listen to a particular show or is the diversity of the listening audience greater than you would expect? Are listening audiences 'migratory'? Do they shift listening profile en mass or is there longevity of listening? To what extent do audiences have influence over the content and format of the programmes they listen to?

The formation of radio communities

In a research study under this heading, you need to identify and assess the factors that are important in the formation of a radio community. Again, it would be much better to concentrate on two or three examples of radio programmes in order to make your comments comprehensive and specific, and to use interviews with focus groups of target audiences to gain information. Do the programmes you have chosen encourage a particular community identity? Do they use language or cultural references which are comprehensible to the target listener alone? Is any exclusivity set up by the content of the programme something that attracts the target audience? You could also consider how new radio programmes initially attract listeners. Is word of mouth a powerful publicity tool? Are new programmes advertised through other mediums or media products? Are radio personalities and individuals a factor in drawing in new listeners?

The role of community radio within community identity

You could choose a local radio station, a commercial station or one from Public Service Broadcasting in order to approach this sub-topic. This is an interesting area of investigation, because it encourages you to look at the influence and impact of community radio programmes. To what extent do the lifestyles, cultures and particular ideological positions presented through radio programmes galvanise, create or cement community identity? You could investigate whether or not the frames of cultural reference and language used within programmes, if adopted by the target listener, act to create a sense of shared community. Is the extent of potential influence affected by the profile of the audience member (i.e. their age or gender)? You could also analyse whether or not radio is an important and effective medium within community building.

Radio communities within Public Service Broadcasting

The case study below looks in more detail at how radio communities can be created within a PSB context, but here we will consider a general approach to this sub-topic. All of the BBC stations are potential sites for examples of shows that have a particular community of listener. If one of the definitions of the term community is a group of people who have cultural, ethnic or religious 'interests' in common, then you could argue that programmes as diverse as Radio 4's *Women's hour* and Radio 1's *Chris Moyles show* have listeners who share commonalities. You need to identify what these particular commonalities are in relation to your chosen shows and what the dynamic is between the content and format of the show and the listening community to which it broadcasts. Is the relationship between show and community mutually sustaining, in that one feeds off the other, or is the balance slightly skewed which suggests that one influences the other more? In other words, do listeners' lifestyles, expectations and interests influence the content of programmes or is it the programme that generates certain 'tastes' in the listener?

You do not have to limit yourself to local radio stations within this topic area and you could analyse a national show that has a specific community as its target listeners.

Case Study

Radio communities within Public Service Broadcasting
Westwood: *The Radio 1 Rap Show*

Original research

The first stage of this type of project would be to choose one or two radio shows that have a Public Service Broadcasting context. For the purposes of this case study, we will concentrate on the Tim Westwood *Radio 1 Rap Show*. Once you have chosen a show, you can begin to describe the profile of the target listener and identify their expectations of and responses to the show(s). It is much easier to research and interview within groups to which you have access, so your peer group and a show that they listen to might be a good place to begin. You could also use the 'chat boards' that are contained in many PSB websites to post questions concerning listening expectations, contexts and habits. As with any original research, your own responses to the subject matter are equally important. If you are a member of the listening audience for the show you have chosen, then why do you listen to it? What are your expectations? Are they met? Would you identify yourself as a member of a community of listeners who share common tastes, language, set of cultural references and interests? How would you define these commonalities?

Secondary textual research

You may not be able to find vast amounts of academic criticism concerning your chosen show, but there may be magazine reviews, interviews and website reviews that contain useful comment. Remember that the title of your project asks you to discuss whether Public Service shows have their own radio communities, so the secondary research that you use will need to discuss this issue. Here we are analysing the Tim Westwood *Radio 1 Rap Show* and below is an interview conducted by Danny Leigh for *The Guardian* which not only comments on the listening audience for the show, but also highlights the cultural referencing and language used by Tim Westwood in order to attract that audience. The article also addresses the issue of authenticity that is often debated around Tim Westwood and considers his role as the host for a show whose listeners are predominantly black.

The real-life Ali G

Danny Leigh

He's a middle-class white man who's the face of hip-hop to faithful fans of his Radio 1 show. But not everyone loves Tim Westwood – last summer he was shot in a London street. Danny Leigh meets him.

Tim Westwood's bright red van is parked outside Radio 1. I know this because Tim Westwood's bright red van has his name painted on it in big white letters. Inside, a courier turns to a security guard. 'What the hell is that?' Another man walks in. 'Is that Tim Westwood's bloody van outside?'

Next comes the veteran DJ Simon Mayo. 'I see Tim Westwood's here.' The first guy shakes his head. 'I'll tell you what that's about, Simon. M-O-N-E-Y.'

'And the flava,' Mayo deadpans. 'Don't forget the flava.'

As if. Because Tim Westwood has flava to burn. Two decades after making his debut as a pirate DJ, he is doing what he loves, playing the latest in US rap. To the half million British fans who listen to his weekend shows on Radio 1, he is, quite simply, Westwood: the face of hip-hop.

The white face of hip-hop. Straight outta Lowestoft, son of Bill, the late Bishop of Peterborough. No, make that the white, faintly wrinkled face of hip-hop, complete with transatlantic intonation and studied lexicon of mad skills and hot goddamn beats. Better yet, the white, faintly wrinkled, public-school-educated face of hip-hop, in his bright red van with his name painted on the side.

There. You've had the cheap shots. It's not rocket science. While he may be Westwood to his fans, to detractors he's merely the real-life Ali G, a gibberish-spouting embarrassment, guilty of being entirely the wrong colour and class for his chosen profession. To the BBC, however, he is a godsend, a proven draw for otherwise indifferent 'urban' (read black) listeners.

Which is why, alongside Radio 1 publicist Paul, he is here in spotless camouflage, talking up his employer's plans for a new 'urban' digital radio station.

'I believe in public service, man,' he declares. 'I believe in serving the audience that supports you.'

An admirably Reithian sentiment. Only I feel obliged to mention that, by fronting a project designed for, to quote the Radio 1 blurb, a black audience under 24, he (neither black, nor under 24) is playing into his critics' hands. He bristles, just slightly.

'I'm here as a DJ, man. And I really feel that I can make a strong and positive contribution to the running of the station.'

He sounds as if he is at a job interview, and that is before he gives an exhaustive rundown of his CV ('that's a lot of experience man'). Then he catches my eye. 'So ... what would these criticisms be, man?'

There is no chance to reply before Paul reminds me that the Radio 1 Rap Show is the BBC's best-performing programme with a young black audience. 'Right,' Westwood nods emphatically. 'And I think I can offer experience on-air, in production, and also in management.'

Great. After all, no one would question his commitment. When he talks hip-hop, it's almost touching. For real. 'Come on, man. There's a multimillion dollar industry comin' outta hip-hop, man, outta people who would have had no choice but be sellin' drugs on the corner, man. Come on, man. That's a revolution, man. Respect it and be part of it, man.'

Except that, despite the enthusiasm, he seems wary. Defensive. Then again, you'd be touchy if you'd been shot at point-blank range at a set of south London traffic lights, as he was last July when two men fired repeatedly through his Range Rover window. The first bullet just missed his spine. Despite various conspiracy theories, no charges were brought. 'The police got a couple of people,' he shrugs. 'Lack of evidence let 'em go. Just one of those things, man.'

No, to Westwood, the bitterest legacy of the shooting was his sniggering appropriation by the media. 'I been around forever, workin' for the hip-hop community, but before I got blasted, the press wasn't bothered, man. Then everyone wanted to know me.'

And to make a joke of him. Unkind voices even suggested that, in terms of credibility, getting shot was the best move of his career. So why does he think he provokes such hostility? 'I don't, man. I get tremendous love out there, man. Tremendous love.'

But not from the media. 'What, do you hate me?'

No, I say. I don't hate him at all.

'Then some of the media's feelin' me, man ... I don't know, man, some cats don't understand hip-hop, man. That's their issue, man.'

He's getting pricklier by the minute. Perhaps, like dogs smelling fear, the press have latched on to his reluctance to discuss his background. Take him at his word, and you would think he had come out of the womb spinning mad flavas.

'So? I'm a DJ, man. Talk to me about music, man. That's who I am, man. I'm not a '– he spits the word – 'personality.'

But he has got a van outside with his name on it in 3ft-high letters. He hesitates. 'That's just a hot truck, man. Come on man. That's a lot of flava, man. A lot of flava. Paul? Are you feelin' me, Paul?'

Paul seems ambivalent. Anyway, that doesn't explain why he won't acknowledge his early life. 'OK, man. What d'you want to know, man?'

Regrettably, I ask about his first childhood memory. Five minutes later, he's still fuming. 'Childhood memory? How is that relevant to hip-hop, man? Damn, man. My first childhood memory isn't relevant, man. Come on, man. Ask me another.'

OK. 'How old are you?'

There is a very long silence. It seems a fair point. After the shooting, his age was given as everything from 30 to 42. 'So, how old are you?'

'I'm 27.'

'Tim, you're not. How old are you?' 'I just told you my age, man. My age, right ... I'm going to tell you about my age. I don't want to be saying my age, man. My age, right ... it depends what paper you read. HAHAHA!'

I tell him I'm not trying to be funny.

'I am!'

'How old are you?'

'How old am I? Depends what newspaper you read, man.'

'No, how old are you?'

'Yeah, and my answer, for the third time, is: it depends what newspaper you read, man. Yeah, man.'

He won't look me in the eye. Why won't he tell me how old he is? 'Because I have. Come on, man. You're makin' issues at this precise moment.'

I've heard blue-rinsed old ladies being less evasive. 'I'm 27, man. I'm like Cliff Richard. Put that down. HAHAHA!'

He stares at his feet. I tell him I have no problem with him, and that knowing someone's age, even approximately, helps you get a better picture of that person.

No response. How old was he when he got into hip-hop? 'Hmm ...' What year was it? 'Probably ... '79. And I came out DJ-ing around '82.'

When he was nine? 'I don't know, man. I'll have to work it out. Next question.'

'Why won't you tell me how old you are?'

'It's not an issue, man. Paul, do I know how old you are?' Paul coughs.

'Come on, man. Let's move on.'

Does he think it's a strange question? 'No ... come on, man, I'm in showbusiness, man. Not showbusiness, but ... the music, um ... showbusiness. Showbusiness, man. Come on, man. You can understand that.' I tell him I could understand it if he was 75. 'I ain't 75, brother.'

It's hopeless. I ask more questions but he just keeps taking offence.

'So, hip-hop's become your life?' 'Yeah? And? What's your life, man?'

When I tell him we're done, he exhales, long and hard, before bemoaning at some legnth those who 'be hatin' on me.' Eventually, we – me, him, and Paul – leave.

Outside, a baffled man in Hare Krishna garb stares at the bright red van. I shake Westwood's hand, looking at a pleasant but hugely over-sensitive guy in early middle age. He looks at me as if I'm the devil. Then he heads toward the van. The last time I see him, he and the Krishna devotee are knocking fists.

'Yo, man, yo. Wha' appenin', man? Yo, man ... whassup?'

Source: *The Guardian*, 1 November 2000.

Biographical information

Biographical information within this study is a means of discussing how personalities and individuals, involved in the production of a show, either mirror or attract the target listening audience. Do these individuals have the kind of cultural credibility that can attract and retain listeners? Do they have a history of working within radio contexts that are connected to particular radio communities? Does the Public Service context in which they now work allow for a broader profile of listener or does this context restrict the potential audience? Below is a reprinted version of Tim Westwood's biography page which exists on the Radio 1 website. It includes details of his work on pirate shows, Capital FM and Radio 1. It also includes detail of awards he has been given for his *Rap Show* by the hip-hop community and work he has done to promote new artists. These biographical details could lead this study to many interesting questions. Does the radio CV identified in this biography explain why Westwood has such a large and loyal listening audience? Do you think the credibility he gained working within independent and pirate shows was lost when he joined Radio 1 or was the shift to PSB a means of gaining greater potential exposure for rap music?

Biography

Tim Westwood is regarded as the most influential figure in hip hop in Europe and as a pioneer of the UK scene.

Westwood began as a DJ on pirate radio, LWR, and then as one of the co-owners of Kiss FM during the station's pirate years. After presenting the Rap Show on Capital FM for seven years, he joined Radio 1 in December 1994. Westwood has also hosted his own television show on ITV's Night Network and has presented and co-produced several music documentaries.

Westwood is also very active as a club DJ throughout the country and organises his own Radio 1 Rap Show events. Last year, Westwood held a regular Saturday night event at the Temple Nightclub in North London. Every week the night attracted over 3,500 people and featured Hip Hop stars such as Funkmaster Flex, Busta Rhymes, Jay Z, Lil Kim, Mase, EPMD, K-Ci and Jojo, Gang Starr and the Jungle Brothers. Westwood also hosts the Main Stage at the Notting Hill Carnival, an event which attracts over a million people. Westwood organises the top UK and US acts to perform at this free open air event.

Westwood is committed to supporting UK talent on the Radio 1 Rap Show and promotes unsigned talent through open mic competitions and showcases.

Westwood has won the Sony Award for Best Specialist Music Programme in 1990, 1991 and 1994 and he has been voted the Number One Rap DJ by the readers of Hip Hop connection for the past ten years. In addition, he won the Best Radio Show at the Muzik Magazine Awards 1999.

Radio 1 Rap Show

The Rado 1 Rap Show broadcasts nationally on Radio 1 97–99FM on Fridays 11pm–2am and Saturdays 9pm–12am to over one million listeners every week. It is also available on the Astra Satellite in Europe.

The Radio 1 Rap Show is the only national rap show in the UK. It is known for breaking records into the mainstream, playing new music first and establishing new talent.

Once a month Westwood broadcasts live from New York with Funkmaster Flex for the 'New York Rap Exchange' and with Marley Marl for 'New York Live'. Once a month there is Mixmaster where local DJs have an opportunity to show their skills. Every Friday, UK artists guest in the studio and there is a NYC Update with Max Glazer. On Saturday, Westwood features hot guest DJs such as Cipher Sounds from Funkmaster Flex's Big Dawg Pitbulls. Recent guests include Method Man and Redman, Jay Z, Puff Daddy, Busta Rhymes and Eminem. The Radio 1 Rap Show is hot – so check it out.

Source: BBC Radio 1 website.

Contextual and institutional detail

There are many possible avenues of research that you could follow to investigate the contextual and institutional contexts for this kind of sub-topic. You could begin by analysing the show you have chosen alongside others in the same station's schedule. Are there similarities of listener profile? Do any of the other shows have their own listening community? Does the time that the show is aired have any connection with the potential listening community? For this case study we could place the Tim Westwood show alongside other Radio 1 shows such as *The Sara Cox Breakfast Show*, *Mark and Lard* and *The Chris Moyles Show* and investigate how the listening communities are different. How is the Westwood show advertised on Radio 1? How do the presenters of other shows discuss and introduce it? For relevant and useful institutional information, we could consider the reasons why Radio 1 decided to include the Westwood show in their scheduling. Which new listeners did radio controllers hope to gain?

Audience related research and applying critical frameworks

Here you will extend the original research conducted in your project and consider how various ideas concerning audience expectations, profiles and consumption modes are relevant to your research project. Consider how listeners consume PSB radio shows. Is this different to how they might consume local or independent shows? Is the listening context of a show with a particular listening community different from one that has a less specific community? What do listeners expect from a show like Tim Westwood's? You could consider whether or not having an ideological and cultural affinity with a particular show makes the listener less likely to challenge what they hear. Do shows with particular listening communities adopt an ideological position that distances them from the mainstream and gives them 'cult' listening status?

Creating your own critical response

Your own response within this sub-topic will have to relate back to your initial title to consider the nature of listening communities within a Public Service context. You could evaluate whether the generation of select listening communities is consistent with the philosophy of Public Service Broadcasting. Does a PSB programme like the *Radio 1 Rap Show* encourage listener loyalty or will the community it has attracted migrate at some stage when the music that was once considered underground has been placed in the mainstream?

Summary and hints

The aim of this section has been to introduce you to the main research topics outlined within your Critical Research Study unit and to describe some of the possible sub-topics you could investigate. Each section has aimed to give guidance on both content and project structure. Remember that the examiner wants to read a comprehensive, well-structured and original answer. You should bring into play all of the analytical skills and media studies knowledge that you have gained so far in your A Level course. Feel confident that your own informed and substantiated opinion will be rewarded.

Section 3
Media Issues and Debates

Introduction

This part of your Media Studies A2 Level requires you to show that you can bring together all of the various concepts and skills that you have developed and apply them to a range of topic areas which encourages you to think about issues.

Issues is a commonly used word – there are always 'issues to consider', people have 'issues' they need to resolve. We rarely stop to think what the word means when used in this way. Media Issues are the concerns that people argue about, the discussions we have as a society about the role of the media and the relationship between individual people, media organisations, producers and governments.

Some examples of these issues are:

- Should violent films be censored?
- Should we have to pay a licence fee if we only want to watch Sky Sports?
- Why are 90 per cent of the films shown at our local multiplexes American?
- Should journalists be able to intrude on people's privacy?

These questions have one thing in common. There are no right answers, but instead a whole range of facts, opinions and different areas of debate. Your job is to understand the subject matter, the factual, historical and political context so that you can make your own conclusions in an intelligent way. You need to show personal engagement – that you care and have a view, but only after you have explained each point of view.

The interesting thing about Media Issues is that they involve you as a citizen. It is not just a case of gaining knowledge. Instead, it is about discussing how the media represent you, take profit from you, serve you, provide for you, include you and exclude you.

Some of the topics are about the government's role in regulating the media. Broadcasting since 1990 involves knowing about some legislation that changed things for television and radio producers and also for us as the audience. At the same time that technology has changed, so too has the playing field for the BBC and its competitors. We are in the midst of

141

great historical change and this topic puts you in the centre of it, deciding which point of view you support. Should Public Service Broadcasting be protected in the national interest, or have Sky and its rivals increased the quality and choice of TV in Britain? The process of learning about the British press gives you insight into the rules and regulations that journalists work to, so that you can understand the debates about press intrusion, libel and disregard for the truth from an informed angle. Film censorship is also a rich topic for discussion. Who has the right to judge what we can and cannot see, and what is offensive? You probably have your own opinion on this, now you can weigh it up against others.

Other topics ask you to consider issues of quality, representation and labelling. For example:

- Are soap operas worthless fodder for couch potatoes or vital **social realist** texts documenting our culture?
- Does our national cinema represent Britain as it is in the twenty-first century, or as the Americans like to think it is?
- Do magazines aimed at men and women serve to reinforce damaging gender stereotypes?
- Why are so many of the films we see using the same genre formulas over and over again?

Some topics ask you to consider the role the media plays in gatekeeping our understanding of local, national and global events. If you study the local press, you will be asked to think about your own local community and the news service the press provide for you. At the other end of the spectrum, a study of TV and radio news cannot avoid a high degree of immediate relevance. At the time of writing, the events of 11 September 2001 and the aftermath in Afghanistan represent a hugely significant chain of events for the future of international relations that we only understand through the media images provided for us.

Since Media Studies was introduced in schools, colleges and universities, there has been much debate about its academic status. The thousands of students who have opted for it have provided evidence of its relevance to their lives. This part of the course offers opportunities for you to think about the relationship between the mass media and your own citizenship.

This section contains starting points for each of the nine topics on the OCR specification. For it to be most effective you should work through the activities and use the content as a springboard for your own work, finding your own examples to integrate into your exam responses.

Within each area there are hints for synoptic links with other units and at the end of each topic there is a practice exam question and an extension activity designed to take your understanding to beyond A Level. This is ideal for those who want to pursue Media Studies in higher education or for those who want the best possible exam grade!

PART ONE

British Television Soap Opera

Synoptic links

In other units, you could:

- *Make* a soap opera sequence or trailer (for TV or radio)
- *Produce* a soap magazine
- *Design* some DTP promotional materials for a soap
- *Research* children's consumption of soaps and other television
- *Research* the making of a new soap from concept to product

The key synoptic concepts (ones you will be familiar with from your studies so far, and which link across all the different units and topics) for this topic are:

- *Genre*: Soap opera has a clear set of conventions, it follows a formula. British soaps have different 'sub-generic elements' with which you will need to be familiar
- *Narrative*: Soap opera has a narrative formula that involves interweaving storylines and methods for making sure the audience can 'catch up' quickly if they have missed episodes
- *Realism*: Soap opera has to make us believe that what is happening is taking place in real time, continually, to ordinary people in an ordinary location in a close community
- *Representation*: Soap opera tries to reflect the real world by representing gender, ethnicity, age, occupation, and a range of social issues. However, you need to consider whether soap operas reflect or *construct* our ideas about people and issues, and whether they have a responsibility to challenge ideas. This requires you to think about ideology
- *Audience and popular culture*: People are very critical of those who watch soaps, saying it is a genre for 'couch potatoes', fed on a diet of junk TV. You will need to be aware of the audiences for different British

soaps and consider the pleasures soap offers and how you feel about criticisms of the genre and its fans. This might lead you to think more generally about popular culture (texts that appeal to 'the masses' rather than the educated élite) and the way it is presented and received compared to products that are traditionally considered to be 'high culture', like theatre and the opera.

Does this topic relate to other work?

Studying British soap opera will require textual analysis of conventions, meanings, technical and symbolic codes, consideration of audience and analysis of narrative and genre. One of the most important concepts for understanding how soaps attract audiences and deal with society's issues is **realism**, which is a kind of representation.

Each British soap opera is broadcast by a particular channel and plays a significant role in earning ratings. Some soaps are their channel's 'flagship', some are talked about as institutions in their own rights, and some are criticised as examples of low cultural worth and the channel that shows them accused of 'dumbing down'. This relates to institutions and audiences and media ownership.

Soaps have their own websites, in some cases it is possible for the viewer to watch the set at their leisure as though it were a real place! Here the 'soap experience' can be enhanced by new technology.

You might be producing or have produced a soap or another kind of television programme for your production work, you may be studying British broadcasting and regulation/deregulation or you may be looking at the concept of genre in film. All of these activities would share some common ground with this topic.

The origins of soap opera

The name, soap opera, dates back to the 1930s when daytime drama programmes were broadcast on radio in the US. They were targeted directly at a female audience (presumed to be housewives) and so soap manufacturers sponsored the programmes to advertise their brands to their primary consumers. Using the word opera was a way of mocking the programmes that were considered to be trivial and domestic.

Soaps were also, and have remained, melodramatic with high emotional content, exploring the domestic and personal worlds of their characters. Arguably, we are more fascinated with the everyday drama of relationships and communities than with seemingly 'serious' events like politics or current affairs.

In Britain, early radio soaps included *Mrs Dale's Diary* and *The Archers*, the latter first broadcast in 1951 and still achieving a regular audience of over 7 million. *The Grove Family* was the BBC's first domestic soap opera and ITV's first soap was *Emergency Ward 10*, which ran for ten years. *Coronation Street* was first screened in 1960 and is Britain's longest running television soap. You can visit Granada Studios in Manchester and walk down the famous street.

ACTIVITIES

To get you started, make a list of all the British programmes that you think of as soap operas. Use a TV listings guide to do this. Then, in a group, see if your lists are the same or whether there are some programmes that might or might not be soaps.

● What conventions determine what you consider a soap opera to be?

Some of the key conventions are listed below:

Location, characters and subject matter

There is an established location (a street, a close, a square, an area, a workplace). Some programmes such as *The Bill* and *Casualty* are considered to be **occupational soaps**.

Community – everyone knows each other (much more so than in real life). Characters ask each other about personal matters when they meet in the launderette, in the pub or even by the postbox.

There are a few *meeting places* where characters can mingle and spread gossip and information. The local pub, for example, is a place where nothing is kept a secret for very long and where enemies cannot avoid one another.

Proximity – nobody ever goes very far away, either to work or for an evening out. For example, characters work in the newsagents all day and then go to the local for a night out.

There is a set of *established characters* in a close-knit community. New characters come in, some characters leave, old characters return. Leaving, arriving and returning provide a major narrative focus.

Family – extended family and rivalry between families dominates proceedings.

Different characters and families live in different environments that remind us through the use of 'signs' what class or type of people they are. The use of costume and cars and possessions are elements of signification.

Characters often have 'skeletons in their cupboards' – secrets to be gradually revealed. Sometimes the audience is allowed to discover parts of the secret, but are also left guessing. This combination of discovery and frustration constructs much of the pleasure of soap watching for the audience.

Narrative conventions

Ongoing – soaps, in terms of narrative, have no beginning and no end. There is the illusion that they have always existed. There are normally several *interweaving storylines*, narrative threads and strands. The programme usually begins with an *establishing sequence* that reminds us of the location and often begins at the start of the day. There is normally a *cliff-hanger* or tease device at the end. The episode normally offers a combination of *enigma* (questions raised) and *action* (questions answered) for the audience.

The audience is often given information that the characters do not have (we know things they do not). This can produce *dramatic irony*.

Sometimes storylines in an episode can be arranged around a *theme*. In any given week, some new storylines will be introduced (and are then gradually developed over a period of time) and others will come to *resolution* (an end) or *partial closure* (with something left open for future development).

Camera, editing and sound conventions

Soaps are rarely action-driven, they are mostly *dialogue-driven*. Therefore, the vast majority of soap opera time is taken up by people talking to each other. Although, this does not necessarily mean communicating.

The camera needs to be as invisible as possible because it is supposed to represent the eye witness. It is as if you, the viewer, are a member of the community or a fly on the wall. This is achieved through an economical distribution of **establishing shots**, over-the-shoulder shots, **two-shots**, mid close ups and extreme close ups. The movement of the camera is very important and takes us from one conversation to another, moving the narrative on from one to another of the interweaving storylines. Storylines interweave in terms of subject matter, but also visually.

Establishing sequences or linking sequences remind us of the spatial context by providing an overview of the location. They take us from one storyline to another when this is impossible to do seamlessly with narrative.

Editing looks very simple (no dissolves or fades, purely hard cuts) but is in fact very sophisticated because it takes us from one storyline to another 'naturally'.

Sound is always **diegetic** (this means that if you were really there you would hear it, unlike in a horror film where disturbing music is added for the audience). This is a key difference between British, American and Australian soaps. Sound is normally conversation, background noise, music being played in the background (but not added as a soundtrack).

The theme music plays a major role in signalling the start of the programme (soaps are usually on at scheduled times and you can set your watch by the theme tune) and the cliff-hanger/suspense at the end. Usually the first bar or drum beat of the theme tune overlaps the final frames of the programme – this is the only non-diegetic device.

Lighting and mise-en-scène conventions

The lighting is usually **naturalistic** to represent the real world. It is rarely symbolic or expressive.

Mise-en-scène is crucial – every decision about costume, interior and exterior design, props and layout of shot reminds us about the types of people the characters are.

Representation

The characters represent different genders, ethnic backgrounds, sexual preferences, ages, occupations, opinions, incomes and family backgrounds. They are supposed to represent our society, usually focused on the working classes (although how people fit into different class groups is no longer as clear-cut as it used to be).

The storylines often reflect contemporary social issues and these often create differences of opinion. Hence, soaps try to be topical. Sometimes soaps are criticised for the role they play in reinforcing or challenging our ideas. When the social issues are those that can affect people negatively, the programme often ends with an advice telephone line number that members of the audience can ring. This shows us the power of soaps to relate to real-life issues.

Soaps mostly rely on conflict between people. One of the main pleasures for the audience is taking sides. For the audience, different characters attract more sympathy or respect than others and often people disagree about these issues, depending on their own backgrounds and opinions. In this way, soaps can be thought-provoking.

ACTIVITIES

In a group of five, each choose one of the following choices to work on:

- Location, characters and subject matter
- Camera, editing and sound
- Lighting and mise-en-scène
- Narrative
- Representation

Watch the first 10 minutes of one soap and the last 10 minutes of another. Remember they must be British soaps! Analyse the two 10-minute sequences using the content of this section that relates to your focal starting point.

Next, present and share your notes with the rest of the group so that you each have a complete set of notes.

You will realise how much there is to analyse in such a short extract. Your task for the exam is to relate all of this specific analytical information to the specific issues and debates. Remember to be analytical. Do not offer simple descriptions. Understand the programme as a constructed text and use the appropriate theoretical terminology to analyse or deconstruct it.

Combine the five sets of notes, presenting the information to one another. Now work on this and give your individual response.

Write a 500-word textual analysis of either of the two sequences. You should find that you are struggling to keep this down to the word limit.

Next, you need to consider some of the wider issues about British soaps, their appeal and their role in British broadcasting, television and contemporary popular culture.

Can we read soaps as social documents?

There is disagreement about the 'value' of soap opera. For some, soaps are 'junk TV', easy to follow and limited in stimulation of the mind. For others, they are examples of realism, reflecting the society they depict by tackling social issues head on in a dramatic form. You need to come to your own conclusions.

The negative **discourse** on soap operas tends to rest upon the following notions:

- Because soaps are 'easy viewing', they do not demand any intellectual activity on the part of the viewer
- Soaps trivialise social issues
- Soaps are ridiculously far-fetched, with an incredible number of incidents constantly happening to a small number of people within a small community
- Soaps encourage us to see life in very simple, black and white ways
- Soap acting and scriptwriting is poor
- Because soaps are on several times a week and there are many of them, they encourage TV addiction. People should be doing more worthwhile things with their spare time
- The tabloid press focus so heavily on events in soaps that people lose sight of the distinction between reality and television, characters and actors/actresses

You should be able to think of more aspects of this criticism.

The defence of soap operas contains the following ideas:

- Soaps reflect the society in which we live and encourage us to reflect on our own lives and attitudes
- We can understand soaps as social documents. Watching a soap from

an earlier time period (e.g. *Coronation Street* in the 1960s) can serve as an historical document

- Soaps are hugely popular because they are relevant to the lives of the audience
- Soap scriptwriting is very skilled, gripping audiences and leading to conversations about soap events in our daily lives
- Soaps reflect social issues in a topical, challenging and responsible way, maintaining a balance between drama and realism
- Soaps depict ordinary people, different genders, and people from different ethnic backgrounds in positive ways
- Soaps deal with issues such as euthanasia and homosexuality in a responsible and positive way, leading us to be more enlightened in our views
- Soap acting is at times very good, and some of the best television drama can be found in this genre

Again, you should be able to think of more positive ideas about soaps.

Realism and social issues

What British soaps often tend to do, for better or worse, is reflect social issues. These are things (usually negative) that are significant in society and in the news at any one time, and they produce conflicting responses. Some issues are long-standing such as alcoholism, teenage pregnancy and abortion, drugs, crime, single-parent families, domestic violence, rape, child abuse, bullying, and depression and mental illness, AIDS, internet pornography, asylum seekers, cloning, illegal adoption and 'Girl Power'. Soap operas tend to try to reflect as many of these issues in their storylines as they can.

Soaps are following a tradition of British realist television and cinema that is said to have started with the social realist dramas of the 1950s and 1960s, such as the films *Saturday Night and Sunday Morning* (1960) and *A Taste of Honey* (1961) and the television programme *Cathy Come Home*. More recently there have been films like *Brassed Off* (1996), *Billy Elliot* (2000), *The Full Monty* (1997) and *East is East* (1999). All of these films and programmes are said to have, to a lesser or greater degree, a 'realist aesthetic' which means that they portray the 'reality' of working-class life in a dramatic form. Although they are fictional and produced for entertainment, they are sometimes described as having a 'documentary style'. Two film directors, Mike Leigh and Ken Loach are particularly famous for this.

Are soaps for women?

There is strong evidence that soaps do appeal to women more than men and it has been argued that it is easier for women to predict the outcomes of domestically focused storylines. However, it is crucial to understand that soap operas are **polysemic** – that is, they offer a variety of interpretations or meanings and are understood and enjoyed differently by different viewers. It is too simplistic to suggest that soap opera is merely a female genre. It may be that women are socially conditioned to take part in more day-to-day discussions about the fictional world of television and one of the key pleasures of the soap genre is its mirroring of real time. Thus its pace is suited to daily gossip and speculation.

Soaps as sites of conflict

The classic realist text is organised so that a dominant voice (or discourse) is set up which the audience can relate to. Oppositional voices in the text are interpreted from the position of this dominant discourse. This is as true of documentaries as it is of feature films; the voice-over serves the same function as a lead character's viewpoint. Soaps are organised differently because it is possible for different viewers to empathise with different characters. In any one episode, it is possible to take on any number of positions as no one voice is dominant. Hence, soaps are always sites of conflict.

ACTIVITIES

Try to invent a new BBC soap opera that will both conform to the conventions of the genre whilst offering something new to the British audience. As the programme is for the BBC, it should not be competing with *EastEnders*. Consider setting, community, audience and scheduling. Then plan the content of the first half-hour episode, including:

- Characters
- Four interweaving storylines
- Two current social issues
- Representation of gender, ethnicity, class etc.
- A cliffhanger

It may be possible to expand this into a sequence or trailer for your production unit.

Next, write two different TV reviews, one arguing that your new soap is guilty of further 'dumbing down' our television diet, and the other celebrating the way your soap is dealing with serious social issues in a responsible manner. Try and be as negative and positive as possible, while using the same examples of storylines, characters and issues.

Practical activity: Plan a website for the new soap that will offer something the *EastEnders*, *Coronation Street* and *Brookside* sites do not. Try, as far as it is possible, to create the illusion that the soap is real.

Night and Day

At the time of writing, ITV had just released a new 'cutting-edge' soap called *Night and Day*. What differentiates this new soap is its departure from the usual conventions through the use of flashback, fantasy sequences, slow motion and split screen. Another innovation is the target audience, assumed to be younger and more middle class than the usual soap consumer. The mise-en-scène is constructed to be lusher and warmer than the conventional 'drab, everyday' aesthetic of *EastEnders*, for instance. Non-diegetic music is another crucial departure. Scenes are cut to fit the music and the music is used to **anchor** meanings about the characters. This soap opera is defined by a deliberate breaking of all the usual rules of the genre.

A still from Night and Day. *See figure 30.*

DISCUSSION

At the time of reading, *Night and Day* should be a well-established programme.

How successful has it been, compared with the older soaps, and what do you think are the reasons for its success or failure?

Exam practice question

Are British soaps the ultimate examples of dumbing down or valuable documents of social realism?

PART TWO

British Radio and Television News

Synoptic links

In other units, you could:

- *Produce* a TV or radio news broadcast
- *Research* the relationship between politics and news media

This section deals specifically with television and radio news. However, you can benefit from studying news as a whole, including the press, broadcast news and the role of the internet. Awareness of how these other media provide news will yield useful comparative understanding.

This topic relates to the key conceptual framework of Media Studies as follows:

- *Genre*: News itself is a genre. Nevertheless, it is possible to break news down into several sub-genres. There is not only TV news or radio news, but local, national, international and global news and then the different styles of news within even those categories. You will need to look into how different news programmes offer different types of news with varying conventions.
- *Narrative*: Although news is not fiction, it still involves a high degree of storytelling. Investigating how one story is treated and constructed differently for different purposes is essential to this topic. News has characters, conflict, disequilibrium and various stages of resolution and so theories of narrative will be just as relevant to the analysis of news broadcasts as they are for soap opera or action films.
- *Representation*: How people are represented in news tells us much about our culture and society. As news and entertainment merge, the portrayal of individuals, groups and issues becomes an increasingly contested areas of debate. There will be interesting differences between local and national representations.
- *Audience*: The way news stories are selected, constructed and presented varies, depending on the broadcasters' assumptions about the audience they are informing. News is seen by some as an essential public service, at the heart of state-supported media, while for others there are new, innovative ways of delivering news to audiences.
- *Ideology*: News values inform the process by which events are reported.

These values relate to the dominant ideas of the culture in which they circulate. News changes over time and its presentation varies from culture to culture. Issues of freedom, control, bias and public interest lie behind the study of news.

News values

Before we deal with TV and radio news specifically, it is helpful to consider some models and theories that have become conventional in discussions about how news is selected and constructed. These theoretical offerings all provide useful ways of understanding a very simple concept. This is that we only get to see or hear about things people choose to tell us, and that we only ever hear versions of events as seen by journalists. In other words, the news is not fact, it is not a transparent 'window on the world'. Instead, it is a collection of stories, chosen for their 'newsworthiness' according to a set of values, relating to ideas the journalists have about their audience.

An obvious example in print news is the difference between the reporting of stories in *The Sun* and *The Guardian*. In broadcast news, the comparison tends to be less extreme.

Galtung and Ruge's famous (and overused) description in 1965 offers us the characteristics of news values. For a detailed reference to news values, see pages 27–8 in Advanced Practical Production.

Journalists tend to think that stories are newsworthy when they offer recency, currency, continuity and simplicity. Alongside these are the benefits of stories that are close to home, feature celebrities or élite and powerful people, relate to human interest and, more often than not, are negative. We get to know about events that can be made into stories relating to where we live, involving people who are famous, offering us things with which to relate or empathise, and involving bad news which tends to be more interesting than good news.

Galtung and Ruge arrived at these values of news by analysing news stories over a period of time. It is useful to look at a news event that features all of the values listed here first.

The terrible attacks on the World Trade Center in New York and the Pentagon in Washington on 11 September 2001 and their aftermath dominated the British news for a long time and led to extended news coverage replacing scheduled TV and radio programmes. The values offered by the events themselves and those that followed readily relate to specific news values.

Recency, currency and continuity

The enormity of these terrible events and their implications for world security, financial markets and our fears of war ensured that the story would be long running. And while the actual attacks would become further in the past from day to day, responses to the attacks, the attempts of rescuers and the investigations into the events and their perpetrators were guaranteed to offer long-term, day-to-day interest across the globe.

Simplicity

While there are complex undercurrents underlying the events (political and historical details), the atrocities of such terrorism could not be simpler in terms of villains and victims. Unlike many political stories where news offers a simplified version in order to intrigue and involve the audience, this story offers total unambiguity in the form of universal horror, outrage, shock and anxiety.

Closeness to home

The British news broadcasters, in the aftermath, were able to focus upon British victims, the political alliance of Britain and the US, the possible deployment of British troops and the increase in security at British airports. Furthermore, Britain's own experiences of terrorism offered comparison and context. Local bulletins focused on victims from specific areas and regions of Britain.

Negativity and human interest

The events were clearly terrible and nobody could fail to be horrified by the amount of casualties and the scenes of chaos. The most resonant human interest aspects were offered by eye-witness accounts and the stories of people searching for their lost relatives.

Celebrity and powerful people

World leaders were involved at every stage and the aftermath centred on the reaction of President Bush and the threat of war. The US is the world's most powerful nation and much of the devastation arose from the shock that such a dominant country could be attacked in such a way.

Television news in Britain

History

*11 September 2001.
See figure 31.*

Radio dominated news broadcasting until the 1950s, when the BBC started producing its own visual news material. The 1953 coronation of Elizabeth II was probably the first event to be covered in the way we expect today, with the nation watching a major event in the comfort of their living rooms. Soon after, the BBC was rivalled by ITN's *News at Ten*, first broadcast in May 1955. ITN's style was slightly less formal than the BBC's, and to this day the BBC have been more reluctant to consider news as a form of entertainment. Since the 1950s, the two institutions have consistently offered slightly different news styles.

Conventions

News is increasingly gathered, produced and transmitted with the benefits of digital technology. Our appetite for instant information has accelerated the haste with which news is communicated across local, national and global boundaries. There is an increase in anchor footage recorded by members of the public and some of the traditional practices of the broadcast journalist are ever-changing. However, while the means of gathering and transmitting footage might be evolving at a rapid pace, the style of presentation, in the main, has remained very traditional. Broadcasters are apparently reluctant to challenge the conventions of the formal bulletin for risk of being accused of 'dumbing down' or offending their audience.

As with all moving image analysis, deconstruction of camera angle, movement and position is important, not only in the studio but also when considering the construction of footage or location/outside broadcast material. Depending on the events being covered, you will see different choices of shot type, varieties of editing and decisions about camera position that can manipulate the way we understand news events.

Pictures are selected for the bulletin when they complement the narrative and conform to the news value of simplicity. **Semiotically** speaking, pictures must instantly provide the viewer with a clear range of signifiers.

Colour Plates

Figure 1

Figure 2

Figure 3

Figure 4

Figure 5

Figure 6

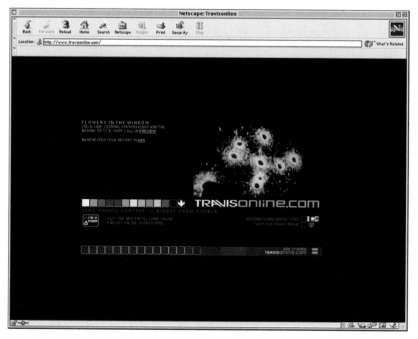

Figure 7

Figure 8

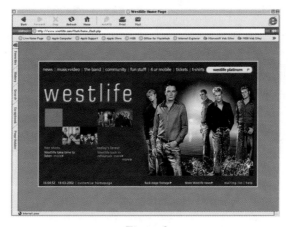

Figure 9

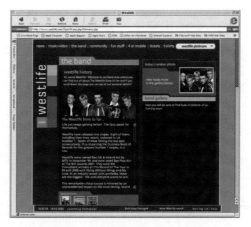

Figure 10

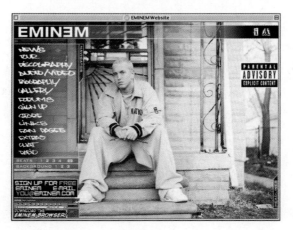

Figure 11

Figure 12

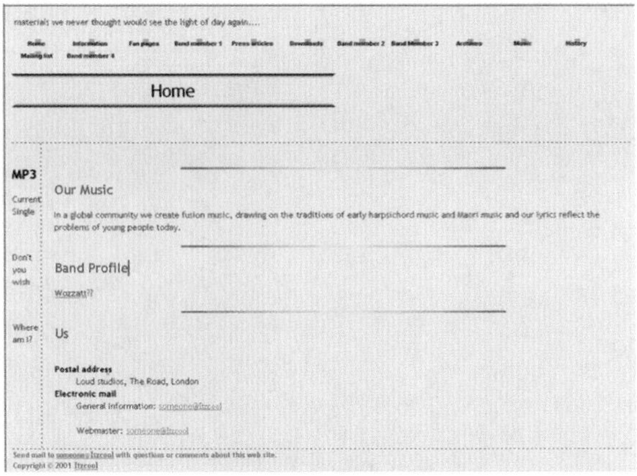

Figure 13

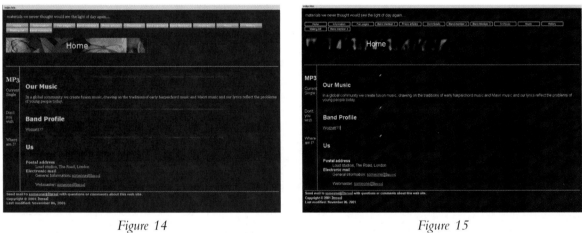

Figure 14

Figure 15

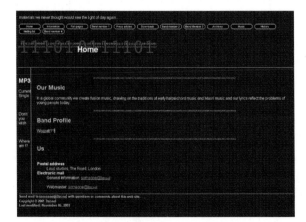

Figure 16

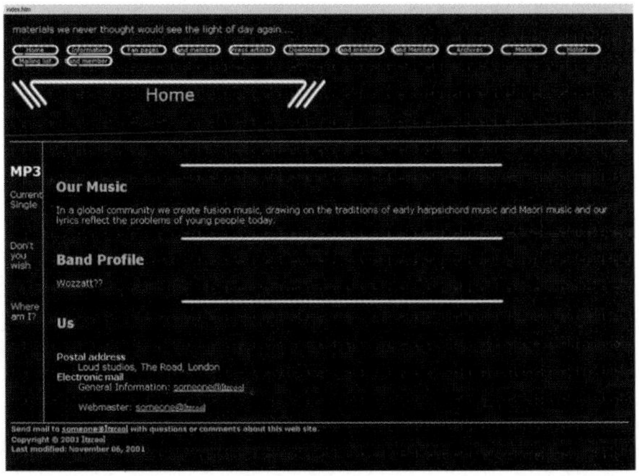

Figure 17

Figure 18

Figure 19

Figure 20

Figure 21

Figure 22

Figure 23

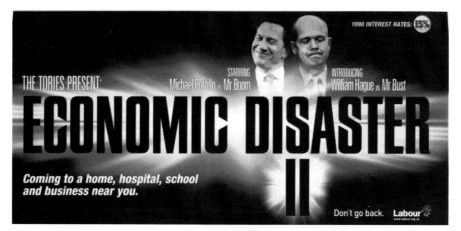

Figure 24

Figure 25

Figure 26

Figure 27

Figure 28

Figure 29

Figure 30

Figure 31

Figure 32

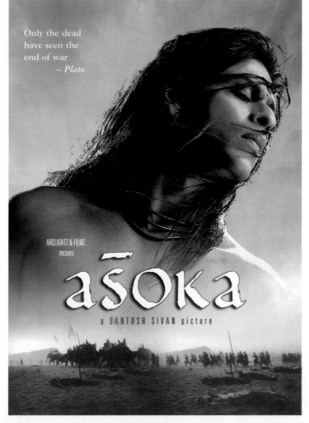

Figure 33

Figure 34

Figure 35

Narration or voice-over is only used alongside when it can meaningfully add to these self-explanatory images.

News relies on experts or eye-witnesses being interviewed. The conventions for this are clear – the interviewee is profiled in three-quarter style, looking slightly to one side of the camera, where the questioner's shoulder might be seen. If you set this type of interview up yourself, you will see how forced and unnatural it actually is, emphasising the power of conventions that have become commonplace or 'natural'.

When there is a break in continuity, news broadcasters use cutaways, such as the questioner nodding or images that relate to what is being discussed. They are used to link sequences, break up the tedium of talking heads or anchor the subject matter. For example, most news items on the NHS feature shots of ambulances, waiting rooms, patients and the outsides of hospitals.

It is important to remember that seemingly trivial factors like the use of cutaways, 'noddy' shots or edits of interviews can cause conflict between broadcasters and the subjects of news items, since these techniques mediate our understanding of events.

The most classic of all TV news conventions is the 'piece to camera' where a reporter stands in front of a news location (sometimes the scene of dramatic events, like military conflict or a disaster, sometimes a building where political talks have taken place) and speaks directly into the camera, summarising the story or concluding the item (having the final say).

DISCUSSION

In a group, consider what difference it would make if interviewees could also speak directly into the camera. Why is it that the newsreader and reporters speak to us directly, while the subjects of items speak to the side of us? This should raise issues of control, authority and trust.

Agendas

Those who select, construct and present the news we receive have enormous power to control the flow of information in our democracy (one of the reasons why Media Studies is so important for citizenship). The combination of the news values a particular news broadcaster holds, the conventions they use for the delivery of their stories and the political or ideological positions they inhabit are described as the broadcaster's news agenda.

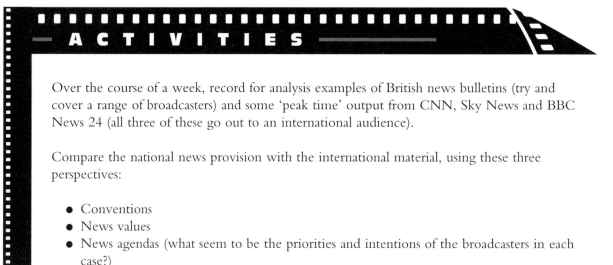

ACTIVITIES

Over the course of a week, record for analysis examples of British news bulletins (try and cover a range of broadcasters) and some 'peak time' output from CNN, Sky News and BBC News 24 (all three of these go out to an international audience).

Compare the national news provision with the international material, using these three perspectives:

- Conventions
- News values
- News agendas (what seem to be the priorities and intentions of the broadcasters in each case?)

Radio news in Britain

As we have seen, it was not until the royal coronation in 1953 that television began to emerge as the 'natural' outlet for news information (alongside newspapers). However, television has not reduced the power of radio news. This is due largely to its portability (whether that means commuters receiving live updates on the way to work, or travellers tuning in to the BBC World Service on tiny radios all over the world). In the absence of the raw images we have come to expect, radio news has to have its own conventions that compensate and offer alternative benefits.

Nowadays, digital technology allows for ever-smaller recording equipment, and ISDN lines offer the journalist instant transmission to the studio. Although this new wave of technology has made lives easier in terms of carrying equipment and communicating quickly, the radio journalist still has to observe the same conventions of sound, ethics and presentation. Sue MacGregor of Radio 4, when asked about the differences digital radio would make, remarked:

'The pressure is on for quantity, not quality. We may even be the last generation to know and appreciate the excellence of good radio; to realize that the best of good radio produces unforgettable pictures in the head.'

Local radio is an interesting area to explore in order to understand both radio news conventions and to approach issues of access, democracy and equality. Together with the local paper, these broadcasters offer information to small local areas that television cannot. Carrying out a small case study on radio news provision in your local area will raise some useful issues about the function of news as a public service.

NB: Public Service Broadcasting as a concept was mentioned in the introduction to this section (p. 141) and features in detail in the next topic, British Broadcasting since 1990 (p. 161). A glance at that area would also help you with this topic.

Major events

In the main, this topic requires you to understand the conventions of daily news bulletins on various kinds of television and radio channels. However, it is also essential to consider how broadcasters react and deal with events that transcend the boundaries of the half-hour summary and also to examine the role of 24-hour news channels like CNN and BBC News 24, not only in reporting events but also in shaping them.

Again, the attacks on the World Trade Center and the Pentagon demand our attention. Many commentators observed that the televisual nature of the events (the pictures of the attacks were beamed across the globe constantly in the days that followed) actually served as a premeditated aspect of the operation itself. The timing of the planes' impacts seemed to maximise world television exposure. The power of broadcast news is such that we can sensibly consider the terrorist attack on America as a terrible kind of PR event. It was said that the attackers gained themselves the live television publicity coverage for the terrible infernos at the World Trade Center and the Pentagon and that the world was both powerless to stop the attack and unable to switch off and stop watching.

Residents of Manhattan spoke of simultaneously watching the horrific moments from their apartment windows and on the TV screen. After the initial shock and trauma, people started to discuss the way that the intensity of the images amplified the horror – many saying that the terrible moments looked like 'a science-fiction film'.

Images of Palestinians celebrating the attack ceased to appear soon afterwards and it was later claimed that reporters' cameras had been confiscated by authorities, attempting to censor the circulation to America of this footage.

BBC Radio Five Live offered virtually constant coverage of the events and delivered an alternative diet to the intense images on screens by broadcasting public debate phone-ins, allowing the people of Britain and the US to respond live. The combination of raw images and public debate created a feeling of a huge community reacting through the media.

We accept today that, as well as getting camera operators to the scene and beaming live sound and pictures around the world, broadcasting organisations also frame the news, making decisions on which pictures to use, which speeches to focus upon, which interviews to continue (with or without interruptions) and what questions to ask the expert commentators. All these decisions define the nature of TV and radio coverage. After events like those of 11 September 2001, while the public are trying to piece together the reality behind the TV images and work out their own attitudes to political and military retaliation, the nature of broadcast coverage has had enormous influence in shaping the public mood.

ACTIVITY

Gather broadcast examples of news coverage of a major event that occurs during your work on this unit (one national TV bulletin, an extract from an international 24-hour news channel, one national radio bulletin and either a local radio bulletin or a phone-in on the topic). In addition, research TV or radio news coverage of an event from at least ten years ago. There are some famous accounts of news coverage available, produced by organisations like The Glasgow Media Group. Use of the internet should help.

When you have gathered your material (primary material for the current event, secondary research evidence from the historical one), prepare a presentation about the way that broadcast news has or has not changed, based on the examples you have chosen.

Exam practice question

Both radio and TV news offer a constructed, mediated version of events, while claiming to provide objective, transparent reports. Using examples, explain whether the level of mediation is equal for both broadcast news media.

ACTIVITIES

Arrange an interview with a local radio news journalist and find out about their working practices and how the format of the radio programme they are working for determines the way they gather news. Focus in particular on the unique qualities of radio news as opposed to newspaper or television journalism.

PART THREE

British Broadcasting since 1990

Synoptic links

In other units, you could:

- *Produce* a documentary, magazine feature, newspaper supplement or website covering audience responses to new broadcasting technologies and delivery methods (e.g. subscription TV)
- *Design* promotional materials for a new subscription TV channel
- *Research* the impact of new technologies in sports coverage and the response of armchair viewers to new arrivals like pay-per-view
- *Research* the relationship between football television, fans and players, focusing on conflicts and disputes over the allocation of money

Essentially this topic requires you to understand factual detail, historical developments and political issues, and there is a body of knowledge that you must have at your disposal. However, in order to engage personally with the issues and debates that surround the current broadcasting scene in Britain and to understand the future possibilities, you will need to develop your own point of view on the topic, ideally through some personal audience research. To this end, this section will introduce you to:

- The Peacock Report, the Broadcasting Act and Deregulation (the facts)
- Issues and debates surrounding deregulation
- The future of broadcasting in Britain
- Possibilities for audience research

This section will focus on television, but take into account that broadcasting includes radio and there is interesting work to be done on that medium also.

In 1986, the Peacock Report was published and paved the way for the Broadcasting Act of 1990 which changed the institutional context of TV and the ways in which we consume it. This topic is about the changes the Broadcasting Act has brought about since 1990. However, it is necessary to go back to Peacock to understand the changes and the motives behind them.

Margaret Thatcher's Conservative Government wanted to increase competition in broadcasting and to decrease the control the state held over TV. As part of Thatcher's wholesale privatisation, it was decided preferable for companies to bid for transmission rights (called franchises) and for the government to stop seeing television as a part of the public sector (like education or the NHS).

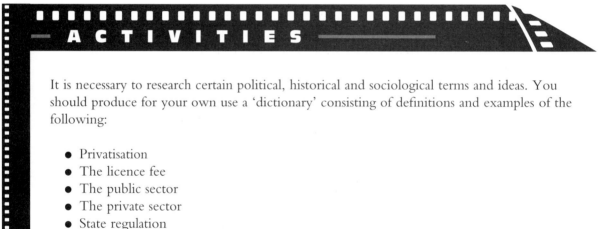

ACTIVITIES

It is necessary to research certain political, historical and sociological terms and ideas. You should produce for your own use a 'dictionary' consisting of definitions and examples of the following:

- Privatisation
- The licence fee
- The public sector
- The private sector
- State regulation

DISCUSSION

What difference would it make if the BBC took advertising?

Why do we have to pay a licence fee to fund the BBC if we want to watch mostly Sky Sports, for instance?

The answers to these questions may not spring to mind as readily as you expect.

Public Service Broadcasting and the licence fee

For over 80 years, British broadcasting has operated under the state-imposed ethos of Public Service Broadcasting. This means that, although commercial and subscription channels are on the increase, there still has to be material which serves the public by educating, entertaining and informing us. These three criteria were put in place by Lord Reith, who was in charge of the BBC (which is still 100 per cent PSB-driven) in the 1920s.

The difference between the BBC and BSkyB is clear – the BBC exists to provide the nation with programmes that fit those three categories in equal measure. We own the BBC, paying for it to exist through the licence fee. Therefore, we have a legitimate right to be represented in its programming. There must, quite literally, be something for everyone on offer. BSkyB, however, exists as a profit-making organisation, funded by the considerable capital of Rupert Murdoch and by advertising and sponsorship. The reason that the BBC does not carry advertising is not just because it does not need to create revenue in this way. It is also because it was felt that commercial interests, such as those of advertisers, would compromise the BBC's ethos in the race for bigger ratings.

The key point is that Reith, and many since him, believed in the fundamental principle that what is popular does not appeal to everyone and that minority audience groups deserve a share of transmission time. Hence, Public Service Broadcasting can be seen as a democratic right.

Commercial TV has to reflect the interests of those who own and fund it and so it needs to make money. In this case what serves the public might be secondary to what attracts audiences. Therefore, competition does not necessarily lead to an increase in quality. In fact, Reith and the subsequent directors of the BBC have believed the opposite – that it is precisely the lack of competition and the BBC's status as a neutral, public utility that has allowed for its quality programming.

Those who believe in PSB think that choice is created through the avoidance of commercial imperatives. Those who subscribe (literally) to the principles of the free market and paid-for TV think that more channels with more specialist output (e.g. Sky Sports or the Sci-Fi channel) create more choice.

This topic looks at the situation post-1990 for a good reason. An act passed in that year changed the relationship between the state, the BBC and commercial broadcasters forever.

The 1990 Broadcasting Act

To summarise, this government white paper put forward the following changes:

- Government intervention into broadcasting content to be reduced, providing that taste, decency and 'quality' are maintained
- Subscription television to increase, with new methods of transmission encouraged
- Advertising and sponsorship of programming to be allowed in new ways and advertising rates to be kept in check by increased competition
- Competition between broadcasters to be encouraged (moving away from the BBC/ITV duopoly)
- The introduction of a fifth terrestrial channel and more satellite services

What this meant in real terms was good news for Rupert Murdoch's BSkyB and a wake-up call to the BBC and ITV.

Deregulation

There are two kinds of regulation that were attacked by the government at the beginning of the 1990s: editorial regulation (over content – the PSB ethos) and economic regulation (control over how many channels there can be, who owns them and what other institutions they own – in other words, regulation that protects the BBC's existence from commercial competition).

We saw earlier how Margaret Thatcher's government were anxious to 'privatise' the air waves in order to increase free market ideologies in broadcasting. In this way, Thatcher viewed broadcasting as a service no different from any other; different providers of the service should compete for audiences. The key debate rests on the question of whether competition increases quality or minimises risk-taking.

Channel 5 was launched as a new commercial channel in 1997. There was a great deal of early transmission problems (many viewers could not receive the signal), but the channel promised to push back boundaries and offer new, innovative kinds of television. Many sceptics saw Channels 5's ideas of innovation as indicative of the inevitable 'dumbing down' brought about by the 1990 Act.

After the revolution of the Broadcasting Act, it was necessary for the government to consider the future development of the BBC. What place was there for a public service institution funded by the taxpayer through the licence fee in the face of the free market, satellite and subscription services? The government proposed that the BBC should continue to exist as a public service, with the licence fee maintained, but that the organisation should become 'more efficient'. What this meant in reality was that the BBC would have to develop cable and satellite methods of transmission alongside their terrestrial provision. The outcome of such a proviso has been the introduction of BBC News 24, BBC Choice, BBC Knowledge and BBC Online. These might seem fairly innocuous projects in the current climate, but they have been very controversial. Critics have questioned the value of these as licence fee funded channels. Again, where you stand on this depends on how you feel about PSB, populism and notions of 'quality'.

Interactive TV

The possibilities brought about by the advent of digital broadcasting, combined with the freedom of the market following the 1990 Act are already in effect with pay-per-view, interactive TV and internet TV growing in popularity.

The Tivo box, currently in use in American households, has a large hard drive to store huge amounts of TV digitally without the use of tape or disc. It even suggests programmes you might like by 'learning' from your viewing habits over a period of time. The catch is that this memory facility is not just used for your convenience. Shortly after installing Tivo, viewers start to receive information about products and services that are targeted at the groups to which Tivo thinks they belong. Perhaps the most attractive feature of Tivo is its ability to pause live TV.

It is now possible to pay for films to be downloaded via your phone line and the technology is under development that will allow viewers to decide exactly when they want *EastEnders* to be transmitted to them.

These innovations do not just mean that the technology is different. They may revolutionise our viewing habits to the extent that we will look back in affectionate amusement to the days when we all used to sit down and watch the television at the same time – a context for broadcasting that has been commonplace since the coronation!

What about PSB?

A good way to understand the issues and debates about current broadcasting and its future arises from looking at how the BBC has reacted to the challenges described earlier. Financially, the BBC is still sustained principally by the licence fee. This is justified by the view that, free from commercial imperatives the company can guarantee the preservation of quality and programming diversity (rather than relying on successful formulas or 'dumbing down' to attract the mass audience). It is also argued that the BBC sets the standard for others to follow and as a result, commercial broadcasting offers higher quality than would be the case without the BBC as it is currently funded (this is referred to as a 'virtuous circle').

However, the BBC is divided internally between two kinds of activities – those funded by the licence fee and its commercial activities. The latter tend to be internationally or globally driven.

Since the 1990 Act, the BBC has changed. Under the leadership of Sir John Birt it has restructured to become more efficient (in the economic sense) and now broadcasts a range of programmes produced by independent companies (these can only be non-news programmes). The BBC has also embraced the internet, creating successful sites for news and education within BBC online. Importantly, the BBC has worked in partnership with private sector companies on its new media initiatives. Whereas BBC online exists as a public service website, beeb.com is a commercial venture that controversially showcases material funded by the licence fee.

The BBC has invested heavily in its online activities and alongside the News 24 channel, this represents considerable investment in activities either peripheral to or outside of its traditional remit. The decision to commit a 'strategic investment of public service assets online' would, according to many commentators, substantially diminish the original Reithian Principles of Public Service Broadcasting.

The BBC has ventured into new areas editorially, financially and technologically since the 1990 Act, to the extent that Birt declared the institution a 'major media global player' in 1999. The impulse to explore new areas has arisen due to outside pressure exerted on the BBC since Thatcher's attacks on the fundamental validity of the licence fee structure.

In 1999 the Davies Committee published 'The Future Funding of the BBC'. This suggested that the BBC's request for increased revenue from government for its online projects was unrealistic and that it should be operating with roughly one-third of the suggested budget.

The situation will have changed since this section was written. You will need to keep up to date with the operations of the BBC and commercial/digital broadcasters. Although the internet is not broadcasting in the traditional context, the BBC's embracing of the medium will yield some interesting ideas related to the concept of PSB.

The internet is said to have 'destabilised' the boundary between the BBC and commercial media. In this sense, the internet has broken down and made meaningless the traditional boundaries between different media and also between the Corporation's commercial and publicly-funded activities. Furthermore, the web has confused the link between the licence fee and the national audience.

ACTIVITIES

Research
What significant changes have occurred within the organisation of the BBC since January 2001?

Audience research
The best way to gain an insight into how all of these developments might affect people's lives is to carry out two kinds of research with people you know or with members of your local community. These will be quantitative and qualitative types of research. The first research method is concerned with gathering data or figures to demonstrate trends or changes in order to measure audience behaviour. The second method is to get a sense of what people think by researching their attitudes and feelings about the future of television. Here are four activities to get you started:

Decide on a community or sector of the population that you can easily work with – you may decide on a small local area or an age group in the area, a gender or college students. Work with your teacher to construct a suitable 'focus group'. Then conduct the following research activities with the same group:

1. A survey to find out how many of the group subscribe to either Sky or ITV Digital or a cable provider and how many of these people object strongly to paying the licence fee in addition
2. Consumption 'tracking' to acquire the following data. Of those above that do subscribe to digital, satellite or cable providers, find out the percentages of their average weekly viewing that is broadcast by:

- The BBC
- Commercial terrestrial channels
- Subscription channels

3. Interviews/attitude tests to find out how much people know about the reasons for the licence fee and how the money is used (this should be with a cross-section of the original sample, not just subscribers)
4. Interviews to find out how people feel about the BBC's online and international/global activities, some of the funding for which is generated through the licence fee

The first two activities are quantitative, the latter two qualitative. Hence, 3 and 4 will need some organising and serious thought about research methodology (covered in the section on Critical Research (p. 81)). You must remember not to 'lead' your respondents into the answers, and bear in mind that no research can be 100 per cent objective – you will inevitably interpret the answers through your own critical perspective.

Exam practice question

Explain how broadcasting in a deregulated Britain offers more or less choice, depending on your point of view.

PART FOUR
British Cinema since 1990

Synoptic links

In other units, you could:

- *Produce* a trailer or sequence for a new British film
- *Design* a DTP promotional campaign (film posters, stills, video sleeve, magazine cover, reviews and features, soundtrack cover and so on) for a new British film
- *Research* women in the British film industry or the representation of women in British films, or women as an audience in Britain (or perhaps a tighter focus, like Asian women and Bollywood in Britain?)

The key areas of knowledge and understanding for this topic are:

- The current state of the British film industry
- The relationship between British film and European cinema/Hollywood

- The representation of contemporary Britain in films

This topic requires careful selection of material (you cannot cover every kind of film since 1990, so you have to work out what is important and significant). To get the most from this work, you must not merely describe the industry and the films it makes, but consider issues and debates in relation to British film since 1990.

This section covers the major areas of enquiry and offers a framework within which you can study selected films. It is useful to recognise that the majority of films most of us see at the cinema or on video or DVD are from Hollywood. However, there are a notable number of films which portray British life and, because our society is diverse and multicultural, Bollywood cinema and other national cinemas draw large audiences in many of our major cities. You may consider whether Hollywood films manage to be 'universal' or whether it is important that a nation has a cinema which reflects its specific social issues and its people more 'locally'. The question of what is 'Britishness' and how does cinema reflect such diversity arises in the twenty-first century.

Context: some facts

- In 1989, US films enjoyed 84 per cent of market share in Britain. In 1999, 86 per cent.
- In 1945, 1585 people attended a cinema in Britain, in 1985, 72 million and in 1999, 140 million.
- In 2000, 39 per cent of the cinema audience in Britain were between the ages of 16 and 24, and 29 per cent between 25 and 34.
- In 1998, the average number of visits per person to the cinema in Britain was two.

(Source: *The BFI Global Media Atlas*, BFI, 2001)

Combine the above information to produce a short paragraph describing recent trends in British cinema audiences and the films they see.

Context: a period in time

Thinking in terms of periods in British Cinema history helps us to understand the workings of historians more than the role of cinema in society. For example, if this topic covered the 1960s, we would immediately think of **Kitchen Sink Drama**, realism, Swinging London, Bond and *Carry on*, and a whole host of ways in which Britain represented itself anew. However, this would be to see that decade through the filtering effect of a particular retrospective 'spin'. The advantage of studying British cinema since 1990 is that you are immersed in such cinema as you study it. Hence, any labels used or grand claims made for the impact of specific films or groups of films and their authenticity of representation (or not) will be of your own making and negotiation. As you study films like *East is East* (1999), *The Full Monty* (1997), *Billy Elliot* (2000) and *Brassed Off* (1996), you need to reflect on how those films portray the Britain you live in.

A still from East is East *(1999). See figure 32.*

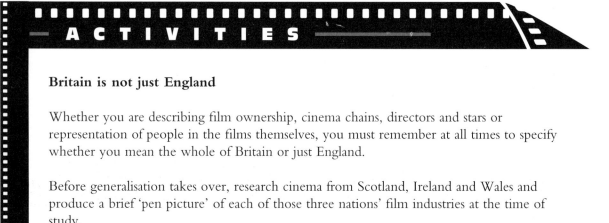

ACTIVITIES

Britain is not just England

Whether you are describing film ownership, cinema chains, directors and stars or representation of people in the films themselves, you must remember at all times to specify whether you mean the whole of Britain or just England.

Before generalisation takes over, research cinema from Scotland, Ireland and Wales and produce a brief 'pen picture' of each of those three nations' film industries at the time of study.

Multicultural Britain

Themes

It is important that you think thematically about a time period. It is neither possible nor desirable for you to cover the output of British filmmakers or the manoeuvres of the British film industry chronologically from 1990. You need to address the way British films have depicted changes to society in diverse ways, consider the major funding and institutional contexts and look at the film audience in Britain to reflect on demographic factors. An interesting strategy is to project yourself forward in time to 2050 and think about how the 1990s and 2000s will be written about by film historians and theorists in retrospect. What will have been the main movements? Who are/were the key industry players? What changed, and for whom?

Before any study of British film can begin, we have to return to the timeless question of what is a British film? The industry is increasingly fragmented, many films are co-funded across national boundaries and many British directors are working abroad. Equally, there is the issue of whether we can any longer (or ever could with accuracy) group films together under the British banner. Films like *The English Patient* (1996) and *Shakespeare in Love* (1998) have little in common either institutionally or representationally with *Nil by Mouth* (1997) or *The War Zone* (1999).

The idea of representing Britain cannot be understood in isolation from an understanding of context and purpose – who is being represented by whom and to whom? Hugh Grant's awkward upper-class charm in *Notting Hill* (1999) may appeal to an American audience who would struggle to understand Peter Mullen's dilemmas in *My Name is Joe* (1998).

Therefore, it is useful to begin with an attempt at categorisation by institution, funding, director, audience and genre, in order to get a broad view of the texts in question and how they relate to the exam question further down the line. Research into the following areas can act as starting points:

ACTIVITIES

Interview a relative or family friend who was a regular cinema-goer in either the 1940s, 1950s, 1960s or 1970s. The further back the better! Ask them to recall their experiences, not just of the films, but of the social experience, who they went with, where they went, what the cinema was like, how they chose the films. Let them speak uninterrupted for as long as possible (record their memories if you can).

Compare their experiences to your own.

1990s Britain: politics and culture

There have been many changes to British society that will have formed the backdrop to your own childhood – new technology, the post-Thatcher and New Labour eras, globalisation, changes to popular culture consumption (or the privatisation of culture) and arguments about 'dumbing-down'.

Think about Britain as an advanced multicultural society, linked to questions about national identity in the face of globalisation, American dominance of culture and its exhibition and arguments over Europe. In sociological terms, the post-Thatcher era can also be understood as a post-industry era, with the dominance of the service economy and claims of a leisure society.

Contemporary ownership and institution

In terms of production, most film companies in Britain are either small scale, working on a film-by-film basis, or subsidiaries of larger companies. British broadcasters moved into film in significant ways in the 1990s, with Channel 4, Granada and the BBC all involved. In distribution, Film Four are a major player, but the majority of distributors sharing the market in Britain are still American. In exhibition, those who yearn for diversity have been dismayed by the fact that the increase in the number of screens with the rise of the multiplex has done little to increase the range of films shown. Equally, the visible increase in cinemas and screens has failed to help film producers in Britain get their films shown.

The 1990s was a period in which the internet emerged, along with other technological developments, and changed the face of all media production and consumption, not least in cinema. Film-related websites, DVD, IMAX and pay-per-view movies were all introduced.

Alongside the technological fervour, Britain had a new government with a minister devoted to film. In 1998, Chris Smith, the Minister for Culture, Media and Sport commissioned a review called 'A Bigger Picture', which investigated national film policy and made recommendations for the future. The outcome of this was that film distribution (essentially marketing) was recognised as the most significant area for attention, not production.

The Arts Council and the National Lottery shared out nearly £100 million to film producers who had successfully applied.

However, it still remains the case that there are no large companies producing films in Britain, and thus one disaster release can bankrupt our studios. The medium-sized companies that operate in Britain tend to be parts of bigger international corporations. These companies mainly concentrate on one film at a time. This means that there may be almost as many production companies as there are films produced in Britain (one or two films each, essentially) at any one time.

Traditionally, countries have chosen between two types of film industry. A studio system like Hollywood – a 'factory' system with huge capital, exporting its products worldwide and where all the 'major players' operate from. Or a state-funded system where the government provides money for films that will reflect domestic life, in order to preserve national identity and resist the pull towards a 'universal' American culture. In Britain, neither system operates and our filmmakers have neither the corporate system of Hollywood or government money to support them. This is the reason why so many 'British films' are only British in terms of either filmmakers, artists or part-finance, and why for decades many of our most talented directors and stars have gone to Hollywood.

An additional problem is created within the areas of distribution and exhibition. Because our cinema screens are mostly owned by large American corporations, who tend to 'play it safe' when booking films for exhibition, British filmmakers have trouble getting their films shown in Britain.

In 1996, for instance, only 19 per cent of British films were released on over 30 screens, 13 per cent had limited release and the remainder were never screened! We also struggle to see foreign, non-American films which tend to be shown at independent or 'art-house' cinemas only. This is where most of our own famous 'realist' directors like Mike Leigh and Ken Loach have their films shown as well. Many British films have been more successful abroad than at home and they then become popular in Britain once reputation is established through award-winning and critical acclaim elsewhere.

When looking at the British film industry since 1990, you will realise how difficult it is to find a 'purely' British film institutionally, and to distinguish between those that are funded and created through British creativity and money, those that are co-funded with European or international partner companies but feature 'British content' and those which are really foreign films with some British investment. It is useful to look at films from these institutional backgrounds and to bear in mind these factors when dealing with representational issues.

Consider the example of *The Man Who Killed Don Quixote*. The National Lottery provided £2.3 million for this recent film by Terry Gilliam, through the new Film Council, a government organisation. This was an example of state-sponsored domestic filmmaking. However, this lavishly expensive film was set in Spain and featured largely foreign talent. Moreover, the rest of the money for the film came from Pathé Pictures (France), Le Studio Canal Plus (France) and KC Medien (Germany). Here we have a truly international co-production.

The fall and rise of cinema in Britain

Cinema-going (as opposed to watching films at home) has survived some major setbacks over the last 60 years. Cinemas have survived the advent of television, the VCR, digital subscription services and DVD.

Part of the reason for American dominance is that, in order to fend off these 'home comforts' and tempt people back to the cinemas, exhibitors had to create new kinds of spectacle and lure us to a 'cinematic experience'. Bigger screens (and more of them), comfortable seats, lavish foyers, surround sound and special FX help this cause. Arguably, British films that are traditionally more narrative-driven are less tempting to a new audience seeking spectacle. New IMAX developments could be seen to take cinema back to its origins, when the audience cowered at the sight of an approaching train on the screen and marvelled at images moving for the first time. Stories were secondary to spectacle when cinema began, and it might be argued that the 'multiplex age' has a lot in common with the dawn of film in this sense.

The British film industry is enjoying a boom period, but it is important to think about exactly what this means. You will probably find that at the time of reading this, most of the top box-office hits in Britain are American. It is likely that even successful British films will be partially financed by American companies, and that the cinemas where tickets are sold will be mostly American owned.

It is important that you find out about films that you do not normally get to see. We only know about a minority of the films that are produced. Some do not even get to cinema screens and those that do are ones purchased by distributors who are confident of a profit (there are exceptions to this, but this is the norm). While the British film industry is enjoying a boom period at the time of writing, this does not mean that there is a growth in choice or diversity. If you look at what is on offer at multiplexes in your local area, you will probably find that they offer a very similar range of titles.

You will need to find out about local independent or 'art-house' cinemas and examine their film listings. Consider why these films are not exhibited at the major chains.

Framework

Select three films released since 1990.

Criteria a)

- One film must be 'purely' British in the sense that both the money and talent come from Britain
- One film must be co-funded with both British and foreign investment
- One film must have mostly foreign investment, with a small British input in either money or creativity

Criteria b)

In one of the films chosen, the subject matter shall be related to contemporary British life or an aspect of it. Preferably this should be a film which represents either a 'minority' group, one of the other home nations (Scotland, Wales or Ireland) or portrays a representative cross-section of our society.

In another of the films, Britain should be represented in a way that is highly specific to a majority group (e.g. white working-class males or the aristocracy). In one of your films, it should be clear that a traditional, stereotypical portrayal of Britain is being employed to appeal to an international audience.

ACTIVITIES

Compare the three films in terms of their production contexts, levels of success, representational elements and social themes. What view of Britain does each present and in what ways is this linked to the film's funding and creative personnel? Research background to the films in order to trace publicity and critical reception in each case.

You will then be able to draw conclusions from this close analysis which will help you to discuss wider issues in an exam context. Moving from the specific to the general in this way is the most fruitful strategy for covering such a broad area.

Time-constraints

You will not have time to cover all three films in great depth and so you should have a 'hierarchy' of detail. One film should be analysed in depth, one used for meaningful comparison, but in less detail, and the third should be for reference only.

Exam practice question

'The British film industry has enjoyed a revival since 1990, and yet it is increasingly difficult to define a British film'. With particular reference to the way that films are funded and the representation of Britain in recent cinema, discuss this point of view.

ACTIVITIES

Arrange an interview with representatives of your nearest independent cinema and your nearest multiplex on the subject of the current state of British cinema.

PART FIVE
Film Genre

Synoptic links

In other units, you could:

- *Produce* a film trailer or sequence in a particular genre
- *Create* a new magazine aimed at fans of one film genre
- *Research* the relationship between genre and gender

This topic requires you to understand how genre works as a concept and a theory. You will already be familiar with genre from your AS work, but because this is one of the 'Issues and Debates' areas, you now need to evaluate how useful genre is as an analytical tool.

Essentially this area of investigation is about formula and pleasure. However, genres do not comprise an unchanging set of 'rules', rather they are templates from which directors and studios may deviate.

Many established film genres have been 'parodied' by directors, who take the classic conventions and revisit them and exaggerate the conventions to humorous effect. Directors are able to give the genre a twist (new kinds of Westerns have sprung up in recent years that return to the 'wild west' and examine it from different points of view, and horror films have arrived that 'play' with the history of the genre).

Ultimately it can be argued that we are now in a 'post-modern' era of filmmaking where films do not just offer representations of the world, but take a filmic reality as their starting point.

Most importantly, you need to challenge the idea of genre and adopt a sceptical approach. This means thinking seriously about whether it is the films themselves that are formulaic and predictable in the pleasures they offer and the conventions they adhere to, or whether it is actually our way of thinking about films in genre terms that is formulaic.

ACTIVITIES

Working in pairs decide on two genres that you want to consider. One should be a genre that has enduring appeal and the other should be a newer genre or a sub-genre. An example would be to consider the Western and the 'Serial Killer horror film' or the Hollywood musical and the '**Masala** movie' from Bollywood.

From your existing knowledge of these kinds of films, list the classic conventions that might include:

- Narrative (subject matter, storyline conventions)
- Representation (who are these films usually about and who is represented in a positive or negative light?)
- Iconographic (mise-en-scène, settings, lighting, visual style)
- Technical (use of camera and editing, FX etc)
- Sound (kinds of music, sound FX, dialogue)
- Ideological (what kinds of messages do these films tend to offer?)

Imagine you are writing a genre guide that offers an explanation of the pleasures of each film genre. Write a three sentence statement for each of your genres. These can then be accumulated and copied for everyone as a quick-reference guide to film genre pleasures.

Looking at the guide as a whole, can you find any pleasures that may be said to be 'universal' pleasures, that all the classic film genres offer?

Finally, consider the reasons why some genres have lasted so long and whether the fact that they have tells us anything about our society.

Genre theory

The word genre relates not only to film, as you will know from your other work in Media Studies. It does not just belong to the subject of Media Studies either, nor indeed to the study of texts in general (there are literary genres and musical genres). Genre comes from the Latin *genus* and means kind or type – it was used to classify biological phenomena, for instance. Since the nineteenth century, it has been used mostly to define texts.

One important difference between film and TV genres and those of literature is that in written fiction, genre labels were used by theorists and critics to compartmentalise literary output long after poems, plays and novels were in existence, whereas in moving image production genres were in the minds of producers and directors as well as audiences, critics and academics from the start.

Genre relates to the three 'phases' of the film industry in different ways. To the producer, the genre acts as a template for the film; to the distributor/promoter it provides assumptions about who the audience is and how to market the film to that audience; and to the viewer (at the point of exhibition) genre acts as a label that identifies a liked or disliked formula and thus gatekeeps and filters our tastes. Genre regulates our consumption, but it also provides 'rules of engagement' for the spectator in terms of the anticipation of pleasure.

In this way, as genres become 'classic', they exert great influence over all of the areas of cinema. Production can be quicker and more confident, screenwriters follow tried and tested formulas and create characters that fit standard 'types', appropriate to the genre in question. Actors and actresses can be filtered into genres, their 'raw material' (acting ability) transformed into star quality at the point when their mannerisms, physical attributes, ways of speaking and acting fit a particular style. Directors, cinematographers, sound people, costume designers all have a ready shorthand to work with. Films can be produced as products on an assembly line. As viewers, we become 'generic spectators'.

The generic audience knows what to expect from a horror film or a comedy and judges it according to prior experience of the genre – in this sense we do not consume films as individual entities but in a fundamentally intertextual way. Films make sense in relation to other films, not reality (film can be described as a post-modern medium in this way).

Genres have rules (conventions) which should already be clear to you from your textual analysis work for AS Level. Genre can be understood as a 'contract' between producers and consumers, the assumed pleasure of the latter determining the creative output of the former in a cyclical manner.

However, genre texts do not work by simply copying other texts in the genre but by adding their own contribution which strays more or less from the norm, depending on the director's intentions. Sometimes directors deliberately frustrate the audience by leading them down blind genre alleys. This frustration is not negative, usually it leads to a more interesting experience for the viewer, but for it to work, it depends entirely on whether the generic template is firmly entrenched in the audience.

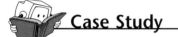

Case Study

Science fiction

The science fiction genre can be traced back to the beginnings of cinema itself. The Lumière Brothers, who are credited with the invention of moving images, created an early film sequence in which a pig was fed into a machine and sausages were produced at the other end. This machine was not real, but it was considered scientifically possible. In 1902, Georges Melies made a surreal film about a trip to the moon and in 1910 the first adaptation of the novel *Frankenstein* was made. So, in the first 15 years the three central narrative themes – scientific/technological discovery, space travel and other worlds/life-forms and creation/existence – were already in place.

Here are some important questions to ask about any genre that has survived for such a long period of time:

- What are the common themes that underpin the narratives of individual films?
- How do these themes relate to our society's concerns and preoccupations?
- Science fiction is a genre that has centred on three central themes since it began as a literary genre:

    1. What are the limits of science (how far can or ought we go in the desire for progress)?
    2. What is the relationship between science, nature and religion?
    3. What do we consider to be the future for the human race?

These themes have been explored through a number of story types, involving space exploration, alien invasion, terrors of technology or **dystopian** visions of the future. Many of the narratives relate to what is known as the 'Frankenstein myth'. In Mary Shelley's novel, Dr Frankenstein creates a man he cannot control, with disastrous consequences. Films like *Terminator* (1984), *Blade Runner* (1982), *Jurassic Park* (1993) and *The Matrix* (1999) all deal with the same theme – humans using science and/or technology to 'play God' with nature.

At the heart of the genre, which may seem to be completely fantastical and escapist on the surface, lies a number of serious, political philosophical, existential and metaphysical questions. In some ways science fiction relates to the important questions about humanity, namely why are we here and where are we heading?

ACTIVITIES

Research the history of the science fiction film genre, making notes as you work on the following:

- Science fiction conventions
- Hybrids such as the Sci-Fi/horror *Alien*
- Common themes
- Pleasures

Keep a list of examples of key films under each heading.

Choose another 'classic' film genre and consider the issues that are addressed within the genre, for example the representation of women in horror films. You will be able to do this for horror, romantic comedy, action films, musicals and Westerns.

Build a 'genre file': in a small group, each choose another genre and, having done some basic research, present a short genre history for one another.

Case Study

Bollywood

Bollywood itself is not a film genre, but an industry rivalling Hollywood in terms of worldwide appeal. It produces an average of 800 films a year with global appeal. 'Bollywood' describes popular Indian cinema from Bombay. In Britain today, several cities and towns have a Bollywood cinema showing Indian films. Bollywood cinema is interesting for this section because it has been argued that its treatment of genre is very different to films made in the West.

If you do an internet search for Bollywood, you will immediately see the massive scale of this kind of cinema. Bollywood films often revolve around spectacular song and dance routines which carry the narrative; central ideological themes that relate to cultural issues and conflicts such as East and West; tradition and modernism; family and individual desire. For our purposes, the most interesting comparison between Hollywood and Bollywood is the fact that while the former employs a range of classic stock genres, Bollywood cinema offers the 'Masala movie'. This is where any one film offers something for everyone, a blend of different generic elements, including the themes of love and romance, thriller, crime, family drama, social realism and musical. Thus, strict adherence to a single genre does not occur in Indian cinema. This is more complex than merely a genre hybrid. The reasons for this vary from the legacy of mythological epics to the idea that cinema-going in India and Bollywood cinemas in Britain is more of a whole family experience. Audiences expect to see favourite elements of individual films, rather than favourite types of films. Whatever the reason for this different approach, it provides an interesting perspective on 'the norm' that we have come to expect from Hollywood genre films.

Fandom

For genres like science fiction and horror in particular, there are groups of fans associated with each sub-genre that develop a deep interest in certain kinds of films within the genre (e.g. Japanese manga animations) or a particular series of films such as the *Star Wars* films. When the latter happens you might come to the conclusion that a series of films becomes a sub-genre in itself.

Some interesting sociological and media research has been carried out into fans and their interests in certain kinds of films. This research has looked at the ways in which people identify with certain kinds of films and the psychological reasons for this. It has looked at fans in terms of subcultures – groups of people who adopt whole lifestyle traits around film types. This is more common for popular music than film, but particular kinds of science fiction attract people who collect all kinds of memorabilia and clothing or videos and DVDs and attend conventions and social events. An hour on the internet searching for sites related to *Star Wars*, *Star Trek*, *Planet of the Apes* and *Blade Runner* will introduce you to this world.

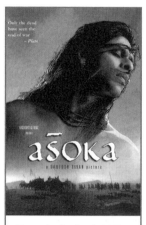

Poster for Asoka *(2002) See figure 33.*

So how useful is genre?

We have looked at how genres stay popular, we have researched some classic genres, looked into sub-genres and fandom, and compared Hollywood genre films with Masala movies that operate in a different way. Lastly, but crucially, we need to 'problematise' the concept of genre. This means that we need to consider whether it is a useful way to think about films, or whether it is simplistic and reductive. A good way to start is to think about pop music.

ACTIVITIES

Get as many of your class together as you can and draw up a list of pop music genres. When you cannot think of any more, decide which are actually genres, and which are styles that cut across a whole range of genres (e.g. is dance music really a genre?).

Next, break down each genre into sub-genres, and then each sub-genre into further sub-genres and so on until you can go no smaller.

Finally, each person should list their top five CDs of all time and then identify which genre they are in.

Was this an easy task? Did everyone agree? Usually the answer is no. This is because if you have a keen interest in something, it is harder to use a blunt tool like genre to define it since you are more aware of the nuances and individual features of each item.

So why should we think of film in terms of genre? Could it be that every film has individual features that defy any one simple act of labelling? If so, why does genre exist and whose interests does it serve? Perhaps it serves our lazy nature – efficient packaging saves time when making choices. Certainly it serves marketing people and their ideas about audience appeal and targeting strategies. Some say that it serves an overly commercial view of cinema. In other words, we are denied access to a rich variety of unique films which never get made because the studio executives prefer funding safe bets – films which can be packaged and sold because they adhere to tried and tested formulas.

Adopting a sceptical approach to genre works by simply starting the other way around, i.e. with the film, not the genre. Rather than saying that there is a romantic comedy genre and films within it look like this, you ask the following questions:

- Is it possible to categorise films in different ways, and if it is possible, why is it useful – how does it help us?
- If we can come up with categories, how are these best defined – are they related to themes and issues, narrative and characters, or content, the visual style or 'look' (i.e. mise-en-scène)?

Most importantly, you need to examine the ownership of genre definitions. Think about who labels films and why; whether the label is 'fixed' (i.e. we all agree) or open to debate; and whether it has changed over time or remained fixed as a label.

Consider how elusive a genre is. Do texts from within it cross over into other genres? Are there sub-genres within the genre, and is it possible to come to a clear, final categorisation of any film within this group?

Do we come to the ultimate conclusion that all films are Masala movies? Does every film tend to contain elements from several genres in a hierarchical fashion, which means that one genre becomes dominant and this is the one we use for our simplistic desire to label?

183

ACTIVITIES

Find a film which is ambiguous in generic terms. Research different viewpoints on the film using promotional materials, academic responses and critical reviews. You may find that the same film takes on a variety of different genre elements depending on what audience the poster, review, feature, website or article is for.

My Name is Joe, the Ken Loach film released in 1998, was a 'social realist' drama about a recovering alcoholic. However, it contained comic scenes, scenes of violence and action and the plot revolved around a romantic melodrama. A film like this is open to any number of generic definitions. When first promoted, the distributors targeted the film towards those who have seen Ken Loach films before, stressing the social realist elements and the critical acclaim that this 'serious' film had attracted. When the video was released, to cross over to the more mainstream video renter, the sleeve boldly shouted 'Take that John Woo' and adopted the promotional conventions of the classic action movie.

Your own examples of such films will lead you into some interesting findings about the way that genre can serve the interests of the industry and lead the audience down blind alleys. In this sense it is a profoundly restrictive tool.

Exam practice question

How useful is genre as a way of understanding films?

ACTIVITIES

Interview the editor of a fanzine/magazine or the creator of a fans' website (you could carry out an electronic interview) about the pleasures offered by a particular film genre.

6 PART SIX
Censorship and Film

Synoptic links

In other units, you could:

- *Produce* a documentary on film censorship and public views or a newspaper/magazine supplement feature, or radio discussion programme or either a pro or anti-censorship website
- *Research* women's responses to films that contain violent and sexual imagery to see whether our responses to 'shocking' texts are gendered
- *Research* the effects model in relation to a research project on children and television

When you think of film censorship, the examples that spring to mind tend to be of violent or sexual content that has led to outrage and claims that the fabric of society has broken down. However, there are a great many films that may not have been banned, but either by a process of self-regulation on the part of the director or studio, or through some cuts on the part of the censor or, and far more commonly, through classification are either released in a form different to the original, or are only released for some of us to see.

A Still from Harry Potter and the Philosopher's Stone *(2001). See figure 34.*

Even the recent record-breaking success of *Harry Potter and the Philosopher's Stone* (2001), though not censored, raised concerns. In this case it was teachers who warned that a dangerous interest in the occult could be a possible outcome of the film's huge influence over children. As is often the case, it was only the film release that raised any concern (the same was true of *A Clockwork Orange* and *Crash*, both apparently perfectly acceptable in novel form).

DISCUSSION

Why is it that many texts that start their life as novels only provoke calls for censorship when they are made into films?

Below we list the areas of concern that must be addressed by the British Board of Film Classification when judging whether film content is acceptable (and acceptable to what age groups) or whether it needs to be cut or censored. The BBFC is neutral and independent (although there are suggestions that, despite this claim, it is accountable to government).

- Sexual violence
- Emphasis on the process of violence and sadism
- Glamorisation of weapons that are both particularly dangerous and not already well-known in Britain
- Ill-treatment of animals or child actors
- Details of imitable, dangerous or criminal techniques
- Blasphemous images or dialogue

The question that needs to be considered at the beginning of this topic and throughout is simply, who decides?

All of the Media Debates and Issues demand an opinion and personal engagement to the degree where you have your own informed view to argue in an intelligent and balanced manner. For instance, what is the cultural value of soap opera, has deregulation provided more choice for consumers, is the press free from bias and is Hollywood domination imposing cultural imperialism upon the British film industry?

The difference with the topic of film censorship is that you probably have your own opinion already, before you learn about the academic perspectives.

ACTIVITIES

Before formal study begins, debate the following issues with your group and gauge the degree to which there is consensus amongst your peers:

- What is censorship and why does it happen?
- What are the different kinds of censorship or what different kinds of material get censored?
- Is censorship necessary (and reasons for responses)?
- If it is necessary, are there some kinds of material that need to be censored more than others?
- Which kinds of material should be censored to certain groups of people and which banned altogether?

The key issues for this topic are:

- History of film censorship
- Different motives for censorship
- Arguments for and against censorship
- Debates concerning effects theories

You will need to relate these issues to contemporary examples. This section will point you towards some famous examples, but at the time of reading there will be new, 'present-tense' films that are either being censored, banned or are causing certain sections of the public to call for their withdrawal from circulation.

The British Board of Film Censors/Classification

From 1912, this body came into being in order to ensure that the Cinematagraph Act of 1909 was enforced. This meant that cinemas were licensed by local authorities and that films were classed as either suitable for everyone or for just adults. In the 1920s, a 'middle ground' was introduced, involving films that children could see under the supervision of parents, and in the 1930s horror films were classified separately as 'H'. Shortly afterwards the **'X' rating** was introduced for any film seen as entirely unsuitable for under 16s. In the 1970s, the age for 'X' went up to 18, and 'AA' was introduced for age 14 plus only. In the 1980s, the framework became U, PG, 12, 15 and 18 and was also applicable to video retail and rental. In 1982, the board changed its title from Censors to Classification to acknowledge the fact that, in the vast majority of cases, their role was not to prevent the exhibition of films, but to control the audience.

ACTIVITIES

Try to produce a short statement explaining what changes occur in a person's life at each of the key ages defined by film classifiers (i.e. 12, 15, 18). How do these changes make them able to respond safely to different kinds of films? Given that most A Level students are under 18, you may find this difficult, but put yourself in the mind-set of the censor if you can.

Before the 1909 Act, censorship was voluntary in the sense that filmmakers wanted their new medium to be established as a respectable art form. The Act led to the establishment of the BBFC and then films were either cut or banned fairly frequently when they were deemed unsuitable for the public. This notion of unsuitability has always been fiercely contested. Who can say what is suitable, who has the right to judge? Censorship has tended to operate around the following key kinds of examples:

Sexual content – in 1919 *Damaged Goods* was not given a certificate (the story of a solider with a sexually-transmitted disease)

Violence – in more recent years both *Reservoir Dogs* (1992) and *Natural Born Killers* (1992) have fallen foul of the censor at the video release stage

Taste – a much harder category to define, many films have been controversially censored for this reason. In 1959, *Night and Fog*, a film containing real footage of corpses found in Nazi concentration camps, was cut before release

Politics – an even more controversial area, censors have refused to classify films for release if it was felt that their political content could lead to public unrest. *Battleship Potemkin* (1926), a famous Russian film with a socialist/communist slant was banned in Britain because the BBFC were concerned about a possible revolution

Blasphemy – the Monty Python film *The Life of Brian* (1979) was banned in some areas of Britain (local councils reserved the right to make local decisions) because of its comic treatment of the story of Jesus

Moral panic – this term describes the hysterical reaction that mainstream society sometimes has to groups of people who challenge conventions and behave in ways that threaten the status quo. Films that offer an insight into such subcultures are often banned or edited lest they serve to encourage people to participate. For example, *The Wild One* (1954) starring Marlon Brando is a film about Hells Angels that was banned in Britain because it was seen to set a bad example to the young

ACTIVITIES

Above there is just one example of each of the most common different kinds of censorship. Research others – try to find at least three more of each type (some you will already know about). Try to get an old example from the early days of censorship, an example from the 1960s or 1970s, and a current or recent example. For each film, answer the all important question, who was being protected, and from what?

Examining the discourses of censorship and outrage is a useful way to understand and discuss its functions. The following are all quotes from either censors or other groups who have chosen to publicly express their shock at the content of films, ranging from the 1920s to recent years.

The Exorcist (1973): 'the most shocking, sick-making and soul-destroying work ever to emerge from filmland' – *The Daily Mail*

Battleship Potemkin (1926): 'damaging references to controversial politics' – the BBFC

The Wild One (1954): 'the police were shown as weak and characters and the teenagers did not get the punishment they deserve' – the BBFC

Straw Dogs (1971): this film features a controversial rape scene – 'if anyone tries to reenact this, god help Britain.' – *The Sunday Times*

Crash (1996): this film is about sexual autoeroticism – 'a movie beyond the bounds of depravity' – *The Evening Standard*

ACTIVITIES

Examine the statements above. What do they have in common? What do they all assume about the viewers and the effects of films on them?

Arguments for film censorship

Those that believe in some form of film censorship hold the view that censorship protects the moral values that are prevalent in society, thus it reflects our values. The counter-argument is that censorship imposes the values of certain people, who do not necessarily represent the rest of us, and it assumes that we are not capable of mature, safe responses to 'immoral' material.

You will probably have found from your discussions with other students that most people's views on censorship depend on the context. There is a kind of continuum – at one end there is the view that media, including cinema, influence people and teach behaviour, like a hypodermic needle injecting 'effects' into passive viewers. At the other end, there is the anti-censorship view which feels that we are able to understand texts as works of fiction or art; if an individual commits an act of violence in response to a media experience, then the psychological condition of the perpetrator is the problem, not the film. In between are those of us who think that classification is needed and those who believe that some kinds of films might be 'harmful', but that others are not.

One famous advocate of censorship was Mary Whitehouse. For many years she lobbied for the banning of films and television programmes, on the grounds that media images of sex and violence are in part responsible for the decline of moral standards in society.

Whitehouse claimed that it is indisputable that young people are vulnerable to harmful screen images. She used accounts from psychologists and researchers to apparently prove the link between violent acts and exposure to violent images. In particular, Whitehouse decried films where violence is depicted without a moral context, or where violence is not punished. In this sense, those concerned about the effects of film images differentiate between the contexts for such images (i.e. the rationale for, or the justification for the violence).

Whitehouse believed that the burning issue is one of protection, arguing that it is a matter of getting filmmakers to accept a sense of their own responsibility for the health and welfare of the whole of society, especially for the welfare of children. She may be a rather extreme example of the pro-censorship lobby (and here we have dealt only with violence, remember there are at least six other criteria which have been used to scrutinise film content), but her views do resonate, in part at least, with those who believe that:

- Films are potentially influential
- Viewers of films receive messages which, in some cases, they need to be protected from
- There are certain people who are capable of judging what others should be able to see

Arguments against film censorship

There is a difference between an argument that disagrees with all of the three statements above (i.e. a view that suggests films are not influential) and an argument that asserts that films can influence, but that citizens should not be all treated as though they cannot interpret filmic images safely. What is really at stake is the assumed link between viewing and behaviour. This is referred to as the 'media effects debate'.

The effects debate

This debate rests on whether or not people agree with the 'effects model'. This way of understanding the relationship between film and viewer is grounded in **Behaviourist** Psychology which examines taught behaviour and 'stimulus-response'. In this framework, viewers of violent images take part in various tests. These determine the extent that people's likelihood to respond to certain situations violently is increased, as a result of exposure to violent images.

However, this approach has been refuted by those who think that this way of examining media and violence is 'topsy-turvy'. That is, looking first at film violence and then at the social problem of violence as an effect is less useful than to look at the social problem first and research the violent behaviour and the experiences and psychological profiles of violent people. David Gauntlett, a much published critic of the effects model suggested that this approach is like implying that the solution to the number of road traffic accidents in Britain would be to lock away one famously bad driver from Cornwall! In other words, the effects model tries to approach things the wrong way.

The many academics who have opposed the effects model have all argued against its central thesis – that we receive media messages passively, that violent films have a causal effect in the same way that cigarettes harm the lungs. While effects experiments and hypotheses have offered different 'spins' on this notion, they have all tended to assume this passivity.

Another outspoken critic of the effects model and the justification for censorship that it offers, is Mark Kermode. It is useful to look at two arguments he has put forward against censoring films. The first is his account of his own interest in horror movies. Kermode argues that, to the true horror fan, the pleasure of the genre lies in the ironic, excessive send-up nature of 'graphic' scenes. Hence, the horror fan is a sophisticated reader of filmic references. Horror can offer a post-modern approach to film (where horror films all relate to each other in what is essentially an intertextual game). This means that nobody is more aware that horror films are not real than the viewers who the censors are trying to 'protect'. To take this argument to its logical conclusion (and it is up to you to decide whether you agree), the only people truly qualified to judge how harmful a horror film might be, are people who have seen other horror films and have viewed them with the sophisticated engagement that only a fan is capable of. Kermode claims that the reason for the difference of opinion between censors and genre fans is not because horror fans have become hardened or insensitive to violence through years of exposure to sadistic material. Rather, the experienced horror fan understands the material through knowledge of a history of genre texts and this actually makes any sense of arousal, sadistic or otherwise, unlikely.

The BBFC today

Since the New Labour Government came to power in 1997, the BBFC has been seen to be mellower in its response to films, largely due to the appointment of Robin Duval as Director of the BBFC who took over from James Ferman. Duval continued Ferman's roadshows which travel around the country and where members of the public can take part in a 'Citizens' Jury' to give their views on classification issues. It might be possible to contact the BBFC to see if you can take part in one. In September 2000 the Board published new guidelines, relaxing the 18 category but becoming tougher at the younger levels. Most significantly, but least publicised, Duval's regime liberalised the R18 category, which essentially means that some forms of hardcore pornography are now legal in Britain.

Duval's main tactic was to increase the transparency of the Board's decision-making in order to reduce the misrepresentation of the Board's motives by the media. In 1999 the BBFC Annual Report stated that: 'harm will remain the abiding and central concern of the BBFC'.

This notion of harm and subsequently the importance of protection, remains at the heart of this debate. A famous recent example of this was the cutting of a few seconds from *Fight Club* (1999). The cut was criticised by many as merely 'tinkering' and unlikely to have made a tremendous amount of difference. BBFC News justified this: 'There were two scenes in *Fight Club* in which the violence was excessively sustained. In both scenes there was an indulgence in the excitement of beating a defenceless man's face into a pulp. The Board required that cuts be made.'

Duval's intention is to move towards a less mandatory, more advisory system and thus place more trust in the public. To this end, the BBFC have experimented with a 'PG-12' rating which allows the parent to decide whether a film suitable for 12 year olds might be suitable for their 10–11 year olds. Duval's desires revolve around a trust of the public to decide for themselves and a form of self-regulation as opposed to imposition from the censor.

ACTIVITIES

This section has introduced you to some of the arguments for and against censorship and/or classification. However, the most useful way to move towards a personal, informed response is to 'test' these perspectives on a case of your own. While you are working on this topic, there is sure to be a film released which is either banned or provokes calls for censorship. Investigate the reasons for the reactions to the film, noting the following:

- Provocative content
- Type of censorship/type of censorship called for
- Arguments in defence of the film
- Arguments against the film
- Notion of protection (who and from what)
- Your views

Exam practice question

Describe, through examples, how film censorship relates to notions of 'protection'. Explain your views on the issues.

ACTIVITIES

Through the internet, investigate an organisation who campaign for censorship. Summarise their views and offer opposing points of view.

PART SEVEN

Magazines and Gender

Synoptic links

In other units you could:

- *Design* a new magazine aimed at one gender or a website for the magazine, or simply a webzine for one gender
- *Produce* a documentary on the impact of the new 'lad mags' or on the responses of young females to women's magazines

● *Research* the launch of a new magazine from concept to product

The key concept for this topic is clearly representation. You need to tackle this on two levels.

1. How do magazines aimed at men and women specifically represent gender? (e.g. compare *Loaded* and *More*, or *Bella* and *Stuff*).
2. Do magazines like these reflect gender stereotypes, challenge them or actually construct them? In other words, are our ideas about men and women and their roles, interests and characteristics as a group natural or cultural? If they are cultural, what role do magazines play in this?

This section will establish a theoretical context for this debate, present differing points of view for you to evaluate and provide a specific case study on *Men's Health*. You can adopt the same approach for your own chosen magazines.

Magazines in general

Magazines in Britain are mainly published by a few dominant companies. Publishing, like all media industries is a phenomenon of convergence, cross-media ownership and oligopoly (a small cluster of bodies controlling the large market).

Being purely descriptive, we can say that magazines have colour covers, are generally glossy, and publish weekly, fortnightly, monthly, quarterly or bi-annually. There are fiction and non-fiction varieties and they appeal to mass audiences or niche audiences. Most magazines have a specific target audience, often a particular age and gender group attached to a hobby, interest or lifestyle choice. In fact, if we believe that media audience groups present an accurate view of the demographics of our society, we could identify the kinds of people living at any one time by the magazines on offer. Although, by this stage in a media course you should be sceptical about such 'transparent' ideas about media representation!

To be analytical, rather than just descriptive about magazines, you need to understand the following:

● What the conventions of magazines are and whether these can be organised into genres/sub-genres. How is this related to target audience?
● Who owns magazines and publishes them?

● What is the relationship between editorial content and advertising in magazines?

ACTIVITIES

Choose a magazine that you read either regularly or occasionally and, using one edition for close reading, see what you can say in response to the three questions above.

Look at the range of magazines on offer (a trip to a large newsagent with a pen and paper may be the quickest way to do this) and list items under genre and sub-genre. Can you think of any group of people for whom there is a gap in the market? If so, identify the gap in editorial terms (what would the magazine offer in terms of articles, information and features) and then consider the kinds of products and services that might be usefully advertised in the magazine.

Funding

In the early days of magazines, the cover price raised enough money for a profit. But as more magazines emerged, competition meant less sales for individual titles. When the tax on advertising was removed in the 1850s, the cover prices were lowered so that the revenue from sales did not even cover the costs of production. The reason was simple – the majority of revenue could be accrued from advertisers.

Advertisers use figures from the **ABC** (Audit Bureau of Circulation) and the NRS (National Readership Survey) to gauge which magazines to use. In addition, the publisher's materials (most magazines have a pack for advertisers) break down the figures into groups of people and make bold claims for the importance of the title in the lives of the readers. It is essential to send off for one of these for a magazine you are studying or to download it from the magazine or publisher website – they are invaluable in encapsulating the identity the title wants to have, especially when it relates to a gender and age group.

The thousands of magazines that are available have different functions. Some are related to specific business areas, trades or work practices. Others are related to hobbies or interests. Some are, broadly speaking, consumer-focused and some are entertainment-based, although the latter usually relate closely to particular kinds of consumption, whether it is music, film or football.

As well as targeting age and gender groups, or occupation/interests, magazines also appeal to particular socio-economic groups. However, this is rather a blunt instrument when it comes to categorising people and the following section comes with that disclaimer!

The socio-economic groups are labelled A, B, C1, C2, D and E. They refer to people's occupations, economic status, education and background. While we all know that labelling people into 'types' in this way is hardly accurate because it misses people's individual tastes and interests, advertisers have used this system for years and it therefore has some validity.

As well as this blunt way of categorising people, magazine publishers and editors and the advertisers they rely on, also use segmentation to cluster us into seven groups: succeeders, aspirers, carers, achievers, radicals, traditionalists and underachievers. They also define us in terms of our opinions and values, whether we be traditionalist, materialist, hedonist, post-materialist or post-modernist.

A magazine might be launched to attract young female hedonist B and C1 aspirers! Or middle-aged male traditionalist achievers in A and B.

These notions of the audience depend on substantial research to test consumption, lifestyle habits, tastes and responses to issues. The media in general often seem preoccupied with trends, scrutinising what we think, eat, buy and worry about, then categorising us with new labels such as 'ladette', 'spice girl', 'new man' or 'new lad'. This does not only involve the young. Other labels coined in recent years have included 'the oldie' and 'middle youth'. Advertisers in particular are aware of the fact that, because we now live longer and remain healthier and more mobile into our senior years, there is a whole new sector of society emerging, the 'young-minded older person'.

The simple questions to consider are whether magazines show us the real world, reflect our interests and concerns and whether the people they feature represent us.

It is argued that magazines collectively form an encyclopaedia of insecurities about health, lifestyle, looks, body image, success, material wealth and relationships. Therefore, a well-balanced person has no need for magazines.

The fact is that hardly any of us look like the men and women we see in

Men's Health and *Elle*. The variety of shapes and colours that people come in are not represented by these titles. The rise of male grooming products reflects a new market of narcissistic men to whom advertisers can promote their cosmetic products, playing on the kinds of anxieties that have traditionally been women's property.

The focus of this topic is gender and the debate we are considering is the extent to which men's and women's magazines construct ideas about gender rather than just reflect them. Like all of the topics on the Issues and Debates paper, this is an area where strong feelings and disagreements should be common amongst your peers. Some of you may be of the mind that 'men are from Mars, women from Venus' and that magazines simply appeal to our different gendered ideas and tastes. While others may think that without the media's perpetuation of old-fashioned sexist ideas about women, females would have a stronger stake in society. Much of the discussion is concerned with the 'nature–nurture debate'.

The nature–nurture debate

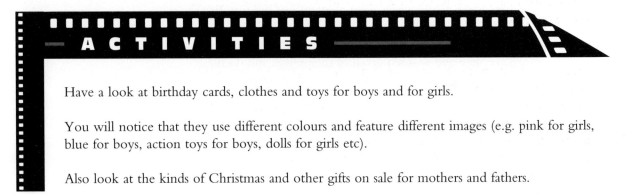

ACTIVITIES

Have a look at birthday cards, clothes and toys for boys and for girls.

You will notice that they use different colours and feature different images (e.g. pink for girls, blue for boys, action toys for boys, dolls for girls etc).

Also look at the kinds of Christmas and other gifts on sale for mothers and fathers.

From this activity you will notice the process of 'gendering' people. From the day a child is born, it is dressed in certain clothes, put in a nursery with certain wallpaper and given certain toys that relate to its gender. But gender is different to biological sex. We are born into a biological sex but the gender roles we are asked to take as men or women are cultural.

Some people argue that the reason men like cars and women like flowers is not cultural but natural. It's just the way it is, a natural instinct to form certain interests which relate to women's maternal and domestic programming. Others argue that culture dictates everything and the reason that men and women often have different gender-specific ideas and tastes is because of the way we are socialised. Recent novels and films like *High Fidelity* (2000) and *Bridget Jones' Diary* (2001) have dealt with these issues in new ways.

Women's magazines: a feminist reading

There has been something of a backlash against feminism in recent years. Many people (including many women) have argued that we are living in a post-feminist world where the battles for equality have been won and we can all relax about gender and move away from so-called 'political correctness'. However, it is important to remember that the essential feminist debate is concerned with equality for women so they can operate on a level playing-field with men and we can do away with sexism just as we want to do away with racism, for instance.

Women are still under-represented in parliament, in managerial posts in business and in much of industry and the professions and there is still inequality in pay and status. Worse, many women feel threatened by a media culture which constantly places great emphasis on the way that women look. The rise of eating disorders reflects this. Thus, when we are looking at women's and men's magazines, what we are asking is, what kinds of images are men and women given of themselves and do these different images challenge, reflect neutrally or actually construct inequality in society?

Contemporary women's magazines have moved on a great deal from their historical origins, offering visions of femininity that involve independence and confidence as well as beauty and domestic concerns. However, a feminist analysis of magazines like *More*, *Red* and *New Woman* will still find that women are encouraged to look good in order to attract men. On the other hand, it could be argued that the new crop of men's magazines, such as *Men's Health*, do exactly the same for men. However, the feminist response would be that two wrongs do not make a right; both of these genres are still perpetuating an obsession with appearance that discriminates against women, for instance, in the work place.

Men's magazines: a new market

Since the mid-1990s, a crop of very successful magazines aimed at young men has emerged, spearheaded by the controversial *Loaded*. Followed by a range of imitators and variants on the theme, *Loaded* was celebrated by some as a refreshing, post-politically correct opportunity for men to rediscover their masculinity. *Loaded* was condemned by others as a dumbed down 'year zero' in bad taste and analysed by yet others as an ironic post-modern text through which men can enjoy being 'new lads' without really being sexist.

As well as magazines in the *Loaded* mould, another range have emerged, magazines which are focused on the new acceptability of male narcissism, the most internationally successful is *Men's Health*.

Case Study

Men's Health

Men's Health, published by Rodale, features articles about working out, exercise in general, health tips, sports and action activities, work-related problems and solutions, relationship and sex issues and style and cosmetics.

It has the tone of a 'friend' and tries to emphasise a problem-sharing ethos amongst its readers, even to the point of men writing in with tips and solutions to common problems and anxieties. Its unique selling point is simple – this is an area in which men have never before been comfortable, but by mixing this advice with style and images of attractive, muscular, successful men in designer clothes, the magazine achieves the same blend of problem-solving and anxiety-creation as its female counterparts.

Men's Health has to be very careful to get the balance right. An example is the cover, which always features a topless man with an aspirational physique. The editors always use black and white for the cover image and there are three reasons for this. Firstly, black and white fits the identity and branding of the magazine, which is black, white and red throughout. Secondly, men's bodies look more angular and powerful because black and white emphasises muscle tone much better than colour. Thirdly, and perhaps most importantly, black and white creates a safe distance for the reader who needs to feel comfortable when buying the magazine. The editors believe that men feel less anxious about buying a magazine with a semi-naked male on the front if the image is in black and white.

An analytical reading of *Men's Health* shows that the overriding theme of the title is control and the quick-fix solution to common anxieties. Throughout the text, the theme of control over work, stress, style, relationships, diet and sex arises. Every edition offers a highly short-term (yet near impossible) solution to an image problem, such as a six week six-pack workout or a fortnight weight-loss programme.

Men's Health *content analysis*

The following is a set of notes that shows you how to produce a simple content analysis of a specific edition of a magazine, in this case the April 2001 edition of Men's Health.

Men's Health. *See figure 35.*

Price – £3

Frequency – monthly

Pages – A4, 192

Cover – always features perfect male specimen alongside 'quick-fix' pull-out

Design and layout – red, black and white dominate; consistent font, pagination and organisation; emphasis on bulletins, lists, surveys rather than text-laden features

Editorial approach – encourages 'sharing' atmosphere; balance of sensitivity and introspection with solutions/control, results and power

Advertising – main areas are cars, watches, clothing, fragrance/cosmetics (always at the more expensive end of the market), hair restoration products or treatment, dietary supplements for muscle development, sports wear, phones and other electronic 'toys', occasional financial services, occasional food and drink products

Promotional techniques – website, subscription with free T-shirt, free supplements on training or stress relief

Content – health advice, fitness advice (often 'solutions'), sex advice (usually about men in control), readers sharing advice and experiences, features on particular men in extreme or interesting situations, dietary advice, advice about dealing with stress and emotional problems, advice on fashion (often in the form of a manual on what to wear with what and for what occasion), advice about work, relationships, ageing (usually about taking control)

Content analysis from April 2001 edition

Cover

Summary of Pleasure – MOT your Life – Sex – Teach Her a Few Tricks – Model as Aspiration (always the same) – Key words: Fat, Cancer, Sex, Gym, MOT, Stress, Cancer – Consuming a Healthy Lifestyle through the magazine – taking control

Advert list

Polo/Ralph Lauren – clothing

Prada – clothing

Gap – clothing

Tag Heuer – watch

Clinique – skin cosmetics

Armani – clothing

AlfaRomeo – car

Chanel Homme – fragrance

Burberry – clothing

Versace Sport – clothing

Breitling – watch

Longines – watch

Hugo Boss – clothing

Jaguar – car

Nautica – clothing

Daks – clothing

Rotary – watch

Rover – car

Receptor – trainers

Peugeot – car

Tivo – TV recorder

Zegna Sport – clothing

Aquascutum – clothing

Oris – watch

Seiko – watch

Honda – car

Orange – phone

Siemens – phone

Circ – hair restoration

Suzuki – car

Renault – car

HMV/*Terminator* – DVD

Britannic – banking

Wellman – vitamins

Saab – car

Garnet Point – wines

Regaine – hair restoration

Nizorelle – dandruff shampoo

Safedoor – online shopping

Tesco/*Tomorrow Never Dies* – DVD

Whizz Kids/New York Marathon – charity

Bodi-Tek – electronic muscle stimulation

Tesco/*Goldeneye* – DVD

NTL – internet provision

Ford Mondeo – car

Hackett – rowing event

Stubbed out – quit smoking CD-Rom

Wellesbourne – hair restoration surgery

Thermobol – dietary supplement for muscle development

The London Men's Clinic – treatment for erection loss

Harley Medical Group – cosmetic surgery

Egg – ISA package

Million Dollar Body for Life Challenge

Tricho-Check – hair restoration treatment

Compeed – blister treatment for runners

London Smile Clinic – teeth treatment

Drink Fit – yoghurt drink

Creatine – dietary supplement for muscle development

Indirect advertising

Jeans feature, home gyms feature, health and diet advice that recommends particular products and ranges sometimes giving company details or retailer information.

Content examples

- Fat-burner's bible – achievable – ordinary bloke – diet and training – lifestyle and control
- Dating ... again – lifestyle – control, confidence
- Make her a better lover – poor sex life – responsibility on woman –

control and power – sensitivity and giving a route to pleasure and taking. Us and them discourse

- Stay in shape whatever your age – 30s man – control of ageing process – lifestyle
- Create a home gym that fits your budget – consumerism
- Why her breasts grab you – understanding desire (pseudo-psychological, reinforces excuses for women as objects) – control and deference of responsibility for sexism? Us and them discourse
- The busy man's fridge – consumerism, recognition, solution, control over lifestyle
- Sub-humans – reinforcement of 'bloke club' – hard, extreme, control
- Happy with the way you look? – closest to traditional female magazine discourse, for average blokes with average blokes' hang-ups – 'out of the closet' – very much a sign of its times. Contradicts the rest of the magazine with the reader encouraged to relax about body shape and appearance
- Cancer prevention – serious health advice – consumption
- In your jeans – consumption and vanity. Close to traditional female magazine – indirect advertising

ACTIVITIES

In groups of three or four, choose two other magazines aimed at men (ones where gender is the focus of the magazine's world) and two aimed at women. Taking one title each, produce content analysis notes following this approach.

This might work better if you work in a mixed gender group and each analyse a magazine that appeals to the other gender. It is essential that you get together to discuss your findings and to make sure that your assumptions about the other gender's interests and ideas can be challenged.

Having studied some 'gender magazines' in more detail, try to come up with an original idea for a new magazine aimed at one gender and age group. Produce a rough treatment, covering the following areas:

- Justification/gap in the market
- Audience
- Title
- Content
- Incentive to advertisers

Share your ideas with other members of your class and vote for:

- The most original/challenging/refreshing
- The most predictable
- The most offensive

Now decide which magazine would be the most successful.

Exam practice question

Do magazines aimed at one gender or another, help to solve problems, create them, or both?

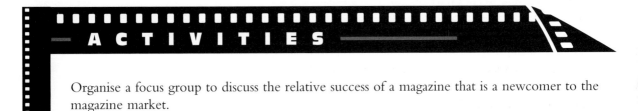

Organise a focus group to discuss the relative success of a magazine that is a newcomer to the magazine market.

PART EIGHT

Local Newspapers

Synoptic links

In other units you could:

- *Produce* a new local newspaper
- *Design* a website for a local newspaper
- *Research* the relationship between local politics and the local press

These days we are often told we are living in a global village where boundaries of time, space and culture are broken down by multinational corporations, brands and images which transcend national identities. The apparent trend shows that people shop at out-of-town supermarkets (rather than the local grocer), eat McDonalds when abroad, rather than the local cuisine and wear clothes that everyone else across the globe either wears or wants to wear. Children in Britain and across the world grow up supporting Manchester United, rather than their local team.

As a media student, you will be interested in how much of this globalisation is related to media imagery and advertising. It has been argued that the McDonalds yellow M and the Nike swoosh have become images as instantly powerful as the Christian cross in our consumer-media society. You will also be concerned with the relationship between globalisation and community. Local media, such as local papers and local radio, still play a hugely important role in maintaining community and their survival and enduring importance demonstrate a forgotten resistance to global trends.

By far the best way to get to grips with the conventions of local newspapers, the different types of papers, their audiences and what they provide, and the relationship between local papers and their national counterparts, is to work on a case study in your local area.

Here you are given an overview of the local press in Britain at the time of writing, a summary of the key issues relating to local news provision and an example of a case study, focusing on the local news provision available to the residents of Halesowen in the West Midlands. To get the most out of this topic area, use the case study as a 'template' for your own research and analysis on where you live.

Functions of local press

In terms of the amount of specific local information that any one medium can provide, the local press is by far and away the leading provider. Regional TV offers frequent bulletins and a half-hourly dedicated broadcast each day, although the regions are usually quite large. Local radio provides valuable time for discussion, but not the quantity that the local paper can offer. In this sense then, the local paper provides a public service. Most local areas have a paper that can be financed by advertising from the community.

Within the journalism profession it is assumed that the local paper serves as a nursery from which talented reporters graduate to the larger regional or metropolitan titles and then to the nationals. However, the local press has its own distinct role: being the first to uncover stories where they happen; enjoying large loyal readerships; and attracting large amounts of classified advertising. Even the internet and interactive TV do not seem to pose a significant threat to the cheap, regular 'local rag'.

Nevertheless, as with any media market, threats to established titles frequently arise. Free-sheets, depend entirely on advertising and achieve high levels of saturation in the area, up to 100 per cent in some cases. In 1970 free papers only accumulated 1 per cent of the regional press's advertising revenue, but 20 years on this had grown to 35 per cent. Recently, the launch of the free *Metro* titles, distributed in the mornings on public transport, has been another attempt to undermine the appeal of the paid-for paper in the local community.

Editors of the paid-for titles argued that the quality of journalism and the community ethos was undermined by free titles. However, readers voted with their wallets and the existence of free-sheets has inevitably heralded a partial decline of the paid-for paper. As both types of paper proved able to survive alongside each other, publishers began to realise that the relationship could be complementary. Now, both titles in one area are often owned by the same company.

Institutions and ownership

Over 50 per cent of local newspapers are owned by the 'big 5' companies (another media example of an oligopoly). These companies are:

● Trinity International
● Northcliffe
● Newsquest
● United Provincial
● Johnston Press

ACTIVITIES

Find out who owns your local papers, both free and paid for. Is it the same company? Is it a subsidiary of one of the five companies above? If so, which other titles does that company own?

Case Study

Halesowen

Halesowen is a small town in the area of the West Midlands referred to as the Black Country. Eleven kilometres from Birmingham, 5 km from Dudley and on the border of Worcestershire. Residents of Halesowen do not consider themselves to be from Birmingham. Because of this Halesowen offers an interesting example of the relationship between local and regional news.

Local papers on offer in Halesowen include:

- *The Black Country Evening Mail* (local version of the *Birmingham Evening Mail*) – daily
- *The Black Country Bugle* (a paper consisting of local history features) – weekly
- *The Sandwell Express and Star* (Sandwell version of a paper that covers the Black Country)
- *Halesowen News*
- *The Birmingham Evening Mail* (in many shops one can choose to buy the Birmingham or the Black Country edition) – daily
- *The Birmingham Post* (the only broadsheet of the bunch, a much larger paper with several separate sections) – daily

The best starting place for information about newspapers, ownership and circulation, as well as for contact numbers for the various publications, is the current edition of *The Guardian Media Guide*, produced by the newspaper annually. It is highly likely that the media department at your school or college will have at least one copy and it may be in the library.

Ownership
The Evening Mail is owned by the **Mirror Group** and with a circulation of almost 200,000 is one of the top five regional dailies. Also in the top five is the *Express and Star*, owned by **Midland News Association** (who also own *Halesowen News* and the *Halesowen Chronicle*), with an almost identical circulation to *The Evening Mail* (the circulation figures include all local editions).

Midland Independent newspapers own both the *Birmingham Post* and the *Sunday Mercury*. Other papers covering the same or nearby geographical area are the *Dudley Chronicle, Dudley News, Sandwell Chronicle, Stourbridge Chronicle, Wolverhampton Chronicle* and the *Kidderminster Chronicle* (all owned by Midland News Association).

There is a vast range of individual daily papers available to people in this region, but many of them are local versions of a larger regional title (i.e. *The Evening Mail*, the *Express and Star*). The Midland News Associaton dominates the Black Country provision, with the Mirror Group and Midland Independent Newspapers competing for the Birmingham titles.

Specifications
Both versions of *The Evening Mail* are tabloids, and on 7 November 2001 both consisted of 56 pages in one section. The centre spread and the front and back covers were colour, with the remainder red, black and white. The content for both was divided into approximately 34 pages of news, features and public announcements or information and 22 pages of advertising, including both display adverts and classifieds.

The Birmingham Post on the same date offered a main section of 13 broadsheet pages, a business and sport section (again, broadsheet) of 14 pages, and a style tabloid of 32 pages.

Taking the three parts as a whole, editorial content made up 33 pages and the remainder was either advertising or, more commonly, features that contained promotional content or advertorials.

The Express and Star consisted of one 40-page section sized between a tabloid and a broadsheet, 25 pages of which were editorial.

The Black Country Bugle, again a larger tabloid, offered 36 pages. This was harder to break down because each page contained a mixture of smaller ads and articles, but roughly 19 pages were editorial.

In all cases at least one-third of the publication's content was advertising or promotion and this rose to half for some titles.

Front cover designs (7 November 2001)

The Express and Star is the most text-based cover, with one image taking up 90 per cent of the page and another small picture used as an inset. There is one main story accompanied by a larger headline, surrounded by seven smaller stories and some news in brief in a left-hand column. The only colour on the front page was a blue text box for a smaller story and a red poppy symbol alongside the masthead.

The Birmingham Post, the only broadsheet, featured a large rectangular box using two colours to promote a car competition on the cover. The most dominant text on the page relates not to a story, but to the value of the car to be won. Four stories were featured on the front page, with one clearly dominant, taking up one-third of the cover, and the other three descending in size, with the smallest accounting for only 19 cm^2. The front page also used a logo for a campaign related to one of the stories.

The Black Country Bugle cover featured just two stories, a left-hand column listing the content within and one photo taking up one-sixth of the cover. Adverts accounted for over one-third of the page. Just below the title was a strapline – 'the voice of the Black Country'.

The two versions of *The Evening Mail* were interesting to compare. The Birmingham edition featured the most visually striking, tabloid-style cover of all, with a large emotive headline, an equally striking strapline and 11 photographs situated with clock graphics indicating the progression of time. However, the Black Country edition featured the same story and images, but the size was reduced so that a more local story could be situated alongside it. The number of images and graphics was reduced from 11 to five to allow for this.

Below the masthead in each paper was a blue banner featuring two content links. The first, a sports story, was different for each paper (focusing on the local team in each case) and the second, a promotional item, was the same for both versions.

Editorial material and news values

Space does not allow for anything more than a cursory glance at the main stories and the editorials of each publication here. A fuller case study would employ content analysis techniques to explore the full range of stories, the organisation of the paper (its narrative) and the ratio of each category of content. By doing so, comparative conclusions about the news agenda of each paper could be drawn. Nevertheless, by using the front pages and editorials alone, we can make the following points about the papers chosen for analysis.

The Evening Mail versions clearly indicate the differences in local focus. The Birmingham edition shouts 'You Idiots', referring to local people parking their cars in illegal places in the city centre, days after a real IRA bomb had exploded in a busy area. The use of clock graphics next to photos of people's cars indicates where the cars were parked and at what time. This method is clearly intended to accuse irresponsible members of the community and it has an inbuilt public/police information role.

The editorial ('The Mail Says') on page 10 moved away from this to deal with the success of an organ-donation scheme in nearby Walsall (calling for the rest of the country to follow its example) and there is a smaller statement urging shops not to open on Christmas day in order to preserve the tradition of one day free from commerce.

The Black Country edition reduced the size of the 'You Idiots' leader to devote equal space to a story about a glassworks factory closure in Stourbridge and the subsequent loss of 200 jobs, an all too common staple of local paper content. The editorial was the same as the Birmingham edition, as it always is.

The Express and Star also led with the glassworks factory story, alongside another main story featuring a local woman who had escaped with her children from a house fire. The cover photo is almost a classical stereotype of the local press, with the woman featured in her burnt-out home with one of her cats, rescued by firemen. Other smaller stories on the front page (unusually self-contained in the main, rather than leading to other pages) included the ex-Beatle George Harrison's cancer fight, a story about the murder of an ex-local politician and two more 'bad news' stories about a gun raid in a local shop and a local criminal being imprisoned. Finally, two stories which are headlined with almost a tone of parody with 'Tortoises taken from pet shop' and 'Cold spell on the way'.

The editorial 'Comment' on page 10, featured three statements in descending order of column space and importance. The main issue was the return of Concorde to the air, followed by the success of British beaches in passing EU regulations (and a call for Mediterranean beaches to follow suit) and lastly a jokey sentence or two about Oxford United FC blaming bad results on a gipsy curse. Unusually, none of the editorial related to local stories, people or events. It is important to analyse the ways in which local and regional newspapers react to stories of national and international significance.

The Birmingham Post led with an ongoing story of the bomb in Birmingham, this time updating the story with images from the police footage released that day, anchored by the headline 'Moment Hundreds Escaped Blast Death', offering positive elements to a negative story. To raise the emotive style and the impact on the local reader, a pull-out quote from the Assistant Chief Constable was used, saying, 'It is not unreasonable to think that virtually all of those people could have been casualties'. Many of the readers will have been in the area at the time of the blast.

Alongside this was a more positive story to offer balance, mocking Ken Livingstone's attempt to sabotage Birmingham's bid for the national stadium with his claim that water voles would cause problems for the project. This story clearly sets out to take a comical angle on what could be a serious aspect of the planning, in order to back the local project. The story is anchored by a 'Bring it to Birmingham campaign' logo. This is a common technique of the local paper – adopting a local issue or project in order to raise its community profile.

The *Post's* editorial, which is untitled, went with the Walsall organ donation story ('Walsall shows it is easy to save a life') and also a statement drawing attention to an increase in sales figures for locally manufactured cars.

Finally, **The Bugle** led with a photograph taken 90 years ago of local (Blackheath) Sunday School children winning a competition. The story informs the readers that the banner the children won is now on show in the local Black Country Museum. Here the paper serves as a promotional tool for the local tourist industry, all important in an area hard-hit by the collapse of industry.

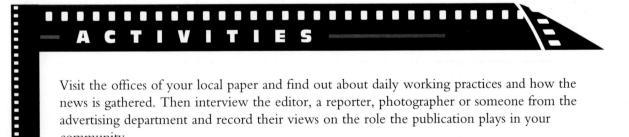

ACTIVITIES

Go back to the Radio and Television News Section (p. 153). Using the list of news values, find examples of them in the content listed above. In particular, focus on local human interest and local negativity, as opposed to more national-based stories.

When you carry out your own detailed case study, you are advised to focus in more depth on two publications, looking at content, news values and news agendas, layout and advertising, as well as institutional details to do with ownership and circulation. The information on the Black Country papers is only intended to get you started.

Your focus should be on:

- The ownership, circulation and funding context of local papers in your area
- The news values and news agenda of specific papers
- The representation of your community in the paper – to consider how fairly all groups are represented, you may need to do some demographic work on the range of people living in your area

You might be able to find a time when a local story is also a national story. The *Birmingham Post* and *Evening Mail*'s treatment of the real IRA bomb could be compared with coverage in the nationals. It would also be fruitful to compare local press coverage of specific items on local television and radio in order to test the claim that the local paper offers something more immediate and in-depth than local broadcast news.

Exam practice question

Do you think it is true that the local press will survive all developments arising from technological revolution and globalisation? Use specific examples to justify your response.

ACTIVITIES

Visit the offices of your local paper and find out about daily working practices and how the news is gathered. Then interview the editor, a reporter, photographer or someone from the advertising department and record their views on the role the publication plays in your community.

PART NINE

Freedom, Regulation and Control in the British Press

Synoptic links

In other units you could:

- *Design* a website campaigning for a free press in Britain
- *Produce* a documentary on recent cases that lead to differing views about the press and regulation
- *Research* the freedom of the British press to cover politics without constraint

You may feel that this topic lacks immediate interest. It sits alongside 'Broadcasting since 1990' as an area of study that demands a historical and political understanding. However, the vast majority of people consume the outpourings of the press, whether *Telegraph* or *Sun* readers, and as a media student your job is always to consider texts as constructions.

For much of the time the public display ambivalent attitudes towards the press, but events regularly occur that engender debates concerning how free the press should be and how they should be controlled and regulated. Events in recent years have included the death of Princess Diana, the political bias of *The Sun* newspaper and its shift of allegiance from Tory to New Labour and the collapse of the first assault trial of Leeds footballers because of articles published in *The Sunday Mirror*. These incidents bring up three different aspects of this topic.

1. **Princess Diana** – raises the issue of our obsession with celebrity and the intrusion of the press into public figures' privacy. Newspaper journalists and photographers usually defend this on the grounds that it is in the public interest, but others call for greater regulation.
2. *The Sun's* **political slant** brings up issues about the ownership of papers and concerns about the relationship between a successful newspaper entrepreneur and the political parties. These concerns strike at the heart of our notions of democracy and the freedom of the press to be neutral and truthful.
3. **The Leeds footballers** issue raises debates concerning regulations on the reporting of court cases in comparison to other countries, a type of control that some say should be removed.

The aftermath of the death of Princess Diana is a good place to start with this debate. Her brother, Earl Spencer, famously declared that the owners and editors of every newspaper that had paid for pictures of the Princess, infringing her rights to privacy, had 'blood on their hands'. This was an exceptionally emotional and hard-hitting condemnation of our press. The British nationals have always enjoyed a double-edged status internationally. On the one hand, we have a free press that can operate without government interference, reporting events in the public interest. On the other, we have some of the most infamous tabloid papers in the world, notorious for their stretching of the truth and their obsession with celebrity, royalty and the so-called 'build them up and knock them down' philosophy. Diana's death mobilised debate about tighter control of press intrusion.

Earl Spencer's harsh words also caused the British public to question their own contribution to the **paparazzi's** hounding of Diana (who died in a car crash while fleeing from photographers in Paris). After all, those photographers would not be paid to go to such lengths if there were not a readership at home hungry for the latest candid pictures of the royals and celebrities.

Press ownership

Newspapers in Britain, like other media industries, are today characterised by an oligopoly (a small cluster of powerful companies controlling a large market). The largest company is Rupert Murdoch's News International, enjoying a 35 per cent share of circulation through *The Sun*, *The Times*, *The Sunday Times* and the *News of the World*.

Murdoch's influence on the newspaper industry has been huge since the 1980s. He introduced the kind of tabloid journalism style we are now so used to when he took over *The Sun*. He then moved his operations to Wapping and with the support of Margaret Thatcher, the Prime Minister at the time, took on the previously strong print unions. Then, the Conservative Government wanted to reduce union power and introduce deregulation so that entrepreneurs such as Murdoch would have more freedom to run media organisations like his newspapers and BSkyB (see 'British Broadcasting since 1990', p. 161, for more background on this). Whether you see 'the Murdoch Effect' as increasing choice and offering the kind of **info-tainment** that the British public really want, or a 'dumbing down' of our national news provision depends on your point of view. There is a saying that 'the British people get the press they deserve'.

Another view, often expressed, is that newspaper owners exercise 'power without responsibility'. This phrase is really at the heart of this topic, for the British press enjoy a great deal more freedom than their broadcasting counterparts. Broadcasters are not allowed to express political bias whereas newspapers are merely controlled and regulated within the scope of their own self-regulation and statutory controls.

The Press Complaints Commission replaced The Press Council in the early 1990s. This body introduced a code of practice for journalists and photographers: a press complaints tribunal system and legislation relating to intrusion of privacy through hidden cameras, telephoto lenses and bugging devices. The code of practice was agreed to by editors and owners since it is essentially a form of self-regulation. They preferred this to direct censorship laws. However, as we have seen, the death of Diana brought the issue of tighter controls into the public domain. As a result, a revised code was introduced, covering issues of:

- Accuracy
- The right to reply for individuals that are written about
- The need to distinguish clearly between comment and fact (i.e. not to mislead)
- Privacy and harassment
- Misrepresentation
- Cheque book journalism
- Intrusion into grief or shock
- Identifying relatives and friends of convicted individuals
- The reporting of issues relating to children
- Dealing with victims of sexual assault
- Confidential sources
- The definition of the public interest

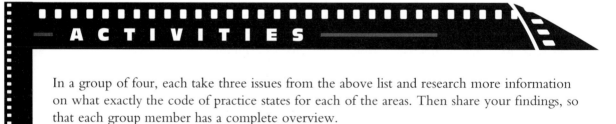

ACTIVITIES

In a group of four, each take three issues from the above list and research more information on what exactly the code of practice states for each of the areas. Then share your findings, so that each group member has a complete overview.

Despite the introduction of a more rigorous code of practice, we still have a free press in Britain which means that there is no censorship of news, government interference or controlled licences that can be removed. Anybody can publish a newspaper in Britain as long as they remain within the law. Nobody has the right to exclude the press from enquiries that are seen to serve the public interest. In practice this does not mean that our newspapers are free from bias, clearly the opposite is the case with different papers showing allegiance to political parties and offering distinct opinion and specific views in most major current affairs. However, what we do have is a variety of publications representing an array of political ideological positions. These positions are so well known that you may have heard people using stereotypes, such as 'liberal *Guardian* readers', '*Sun* reader' or '*Daily Mail* mentality'. In the case of *The Sun* it has been said that Tony Blair's greatest coup was *The Sun* switching sides, who turned its back on John Major's government after years of right-wing propaganda.

Although the press may be free from official state censorship, unlike film, broadcasting or advertising, there are forms of legislation which force impositions upon this freedom. These are referred to by the press as elements of 'the creeping censor'. These include the Official Secrets Act and the Libel and Defamation Laws.

The Official Secrets Act

Passed in 1911 and revised in 1989, this Act means that civil servants, soldiers, the police and various other people who officially work for 'the Crown' cannot speak on matters that are related to various forms of government activity. Editors of newspapers can be served with 'D-notices' which prevent information being published on matters of national security.

Libel and Defamation Laws

This much-used legislation gives members of the public the right to sue newspapers who print stories that damage their character and/or their livelihood. While newspapers are regularly threatened with libel action, very few of these threats become court cases because of the expense involved. However, this is a crucial form of 'creeping' or 'covert' censorship since the possible threat of libel action often makes editors withdraw stories. In this sense it is a form of self-regulation. Furthermore, people can take out injunctions by appealing to court and, if granted, this prevents a story being published until the court has considered evidence. On Sunday 11 November 2001, *The Sunday People* published a story about a footballer in a sex scandal without the names of those involved because the player had successfully applied for an injunction of this kind. This was an historical event because no similar judgement had previously been given. The press were outraged, arguing that many of the most important pieces of investigative journalism in history would never have made it to the pages had judges behaved in this way, and that the public interest was being undermined.

DISCUSSION

What do you consider to be the essential differences between newspaper stories that are 'of interest to the public' and 'in the public interest'?

Other restrictions on reporting

Contempt of Court is a broad restriction on any reporting that might impede the workings of the court. For example, the publication of a photograph of an accused person who has not yet been identified in court or providing comment on factual information which is before the court or criticising a judge while the case is being heard.

There are various other acts of law which journalists have to know inside out, such as the Sexual Offences Act and the Race Relations Act. The bible for journalists has always been *Essential Law for Journalists*, edited by Greenwood (The Old Book Company, 1995). This guidebook is highly recommended as a source of research.

Exam practice question

Britain has a free press, reflecting the democracy we live in, but editors enjoy this freedom only by imposing heavy self-regulation. Discuss.

ACTIVITIES

Interview a journalist or, ideally, an editor from your local paper about the restrictions they have to be aware of in their daily working practice.

Section 4
Writing Skills

Introduction

As you have discovered during your AS studies, a Media Studies course requires you to complete a number of different written tasks. Within your A2 studies you will also be asked to write essays, Production Logs and research projects. This section aims to help you create thorough, systematic and comprehensive written pieces. It will offer you guidance on using terminology appropriately, organising contents clearly and effectively and constructing critical debates. Some of the skills in this section are generic to all of your writing tasks and others are specific to particular parts of the OCR A2 course.

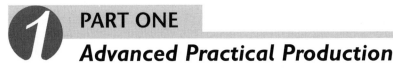

PART ONE

Advanced Practical Production

Written work

During your Advanced Practical Production project you will need to be able to create two types of written piece. One is assessed and one non-assessed, but they are both of equal importance to the overall success of the project. The first piece of written work will be a Production Log, in which you keep notes on the process of your project. The second piece is the Critical Evaluation which will be submitted as part of your assessment.

The Production Log

In order to be able to submit a Critical Evaluation that is comprehensive, it is essential to keep a record of your project while creating the practical work. Your Log will be a guide to your teacher for assessing how you have planned the project. It will also provide a template for you when referring to research, planning and process in your Critical Evaluation. The Log can be organised in a number of ways, but should include particular information. Try to keep updating your Log throughout the planning stages of the project. You could keep a separate folder for these notes, with divided sections for each of the areas below.

Initial ideas

In your first lesson of planning your project, you should brainstorm possible ideas. You will only develop one of these, but your initial responses to the task are an important indicator that all the process stages of your project are being gone through systematically. Try to elaborate and expand on these initial thoughts because you may need to go back to one of these ideas if your chosen one becomes unworkable. For each idea, make a note of the potential impact that your product would have on its target consumer and what its context would be in terms of already existing media products. You could present initial ideas in the form of a diagram or as a series of bullet points.

Group organisation

How is your group going to be organised? Is each member going to take on specific roles in the planning process or is the group going to tackle all parts collaboratively? You will need to keep careful notes on exactly what you did within the project and the roles of others.

Changes and developments

Within any media text production process, ideas will develop and change after the initial ideas have been noted. Changes are developmental and provide the person assessing your project with a clear indication of positive and focused process. If you have embarked on the production of a particular product and then continually scrap one idea for another, your project will appear disorganised. However, if you show modification and informed alteration to your product, this will indicate that you are continually researching and checking its many elements and its impact on the target audience.

Practical planning: storyboards/shooting schedules/drafts/mock-ups

The contents of this section will be defined by the particular type of media product you have chosen to create for your Advanced Practical Production. If you are producing a television programme, a video or a film then you will need to produce storyboards, shooting schedules, equipment lists and location reports and descriptions. If you are creating a piece of print-based media, then page mock-ups, sample photographs and article drafts would provide evidence for this section. Practical planning for an ICT/New Media product could be in the form of a paper draft for a new website (including linked pages). For a radio programme, recorded pilot shows, drawings for programme logos and detailed scripts (that include dialogue, any sound effects and technical direction) would provide good practical planning evidence.

Context research

Contextual research requires you to investigate other products that are similar to the one you are planning to produce and to analyse your potential target consumer's profile and preferences. When you have collected texts and products that are similar to your own, you will need to make comment concerning their context of consumption and their position within the market-place. How many possible consumption contexts do your researched products (and by extension your own product) have? What does this mean in terms of the potential target consumer? Are there specific conventions that you have identified in your researched products? How have you used these conventions within the production of your own product? Is the product you have chosen to create original within the market-place or is it placed within a tradition of such products? All of the notes that you produce regarding the context of your product will provide essential reference material when you come to write your Critical Evaluation.

Audience feedback

Your assessed written work requires you to comment on how an audience has responded to your product and it is extremely useful to ask for audience feedback in the planning stages of your work. Once you have defined your potential audience, you could begin by forming a focus group of target consumers with whom you discuss initial ideas and practical planning work. Make a note of what your focus group says about your ideas (both the positives and the negatives). You might alter certain features of the product in the light of the feedback you receive or you may have your ideas confirmed as successful. Within an industry context of production, audience expectations and feedback would be taken into account and your project and Critical Evaluation will also benefit from audience comment.

The Critical Evaluation

The Critical Evaluation is the written part of your Advanced Practical Production task and enables you to describe the process of your production and evaluate its success. You will have 3000 words in which to apply the key media concepts you have learnt throughout your A2 course (media forms and conventions, media institutions, media audiences and media representations) to the product you have produced. The most systematic way to organise your Critical Evaluation is to divide it into four sections: an introduction that does not count within the word limit and three other sections of roughly 1000 words.

Introduction

The introduction should explain the differences between the brief that was undertaken for your AS practical production project and the one you have completed for A2 Advanced Practical Production. Your medium will be different for the A2 project and you need to make clear in your introduction what the differences are within the briefs for the two pieces of work. Do remember, however, that you are able to work with moving image in both AS and A2. Film and television are counted as different media despite both being submitted on video.

Part one

In your Evaluation you should analyse the design process from its inception through planning to realisation. You should include reference to your research notes, clear indication about your chosen genre and your chosen approach. You may include selected deconstructions of similar texts that have influenced you. You should also include reference to your planning processes and highlight the creative decisions that you have made. You should also take care in this section to identify your particular role and responsibilities if you were working in a group, and to relate the production work closely to the genre and style, institution and audience that you are targeting.

Part two

The second part of your project asks you to step back and analyse your project as a finished product. This is where you will need to use your knowledge of key conceptual areas to comment on what you have created. How does your product use conventions? Have you followed conventions literally or subverted them in some way? How does the form of your product work to generate meaning for your target audience? For example, does it include some form of narrative and, if it does, what impact does this have on the target consumer? How does representation operate within your finished product? You can apply real media theories to your product when analysing in this section. Are there intertextual elements to your product and how do these impact on the target audience? Does the presence of intertextual elements place your product within a post-modern debate?

Part three

This section justifies your production in the wider context of media institutions and audiences by analysing the ways in which your product compares with other products of the same genre. You should include a detailed evaluation of the response of your target audience and also include evidence that you have tested your text and evaluated the feedback received. Use the research information that you gathered for your Log to discuss your product in relation to examples of real products. You could also include the focus group or audience feedback that you received during your planning to evaluate the effectiveness of your product in relation to real media examples. Where do you think your product would be placed in the media market-place? What would its potential context(s) of consumption be?

Do not forget that this section should also include the conclusion to your project and should offer summarised comment on the effectiveness of your product.

Finally

Remember that you have only 3000 words to include all of this information and analysis and so you should use supportive appendices and references effectively, but sparingly. Your text must be credible within a realisable context and you must be able to demonstrate competent and secure handling of the challenges and opportunities arising from this level of understanding and appreciation.

PART TWO
Critical Research Study

The Critical Research Study needs to be detailed and organised in a way which allows you to access relevant information easily. The Critical Research Study Section (p.81) goes into more detail concerning structure, content and methodology, but below is one possible way of organising your notes.

Generating the research title

Once you have chosen your topic, you should then brainstorm areas that may be of interest to research. Make sure that you choose an area that you will be able to explore fully, one in which you will be interested and one around which you can build an interesting thesis. It might be useful to create a more specific research area under one of the following general headings:

- Issues of representation, the relationship between product and audience
- The individual producer's relationship with the industry in which they are working
- Historical changes within the chosen area
- The role of the medium in which an individual producer is working
- Conflicts or controversial issues within the topic area

Finding references and materials

There are three main sources that you can access when searching for references and materials: the internet, print publications and visual materials. The internet can be used to find reviews, critical writing, popular criticism, surveys and institutional information. Make a note of the websites that you use and the authors behind the materials so that you can give correct references in the exam. Print publications may be books of media criticism, media-related magazines, biographies of particular individuals, newspapers or guides relating to specific texts. Note the author's name, the publication's title and the date of publication. Visual materials may include not only texts related to individual or institutional producers, but they could include TV programmes that discuss an issue concerning your chosen area.

Keeping organised notes and using reference materials effectively

You will need to organise your notes and materials in such a way that allows information to be easily accessible to you. You should use sectioned folders to store your findings but you will also need to break these down into particular areas. Below are some headings that might help you to organise your Critical Research Study.

Original research

Once you have chosen a topic, you should look at all of the sources you have located and create your own means of finding appropriate information. You could create questionnaires for target audiences and consumers, try to contact people within the industry connected to your area, post questions on websites for people to comment on/answer and note your own responses to texts associated with your chosen topic area.

Secondary textual analysis

Notes on academic and popular criticism that have been written on texts related to your chosen area.

Biographical information

Information concerning particular individuals who are significant within your chosen area.

Contextual information

Information on the social, political and ideological context relevant to your area. You may have looked at, for example, the impact of political shifts on your chosen topic area, the role and perception of producers or texts in a particular period or controversial issues which may be relevant to institutions or textual production.

Institutional detail

Your notes will include detail of the companies and organisations which are significant within your research area. You may have information concerning their attitudes to and intentions behind the media texts produced, their role within new developments (either technical or ideological) or their attitudes to certain groups of people who work within them.

Audience related research

You should have information concerning the audience for the texts related to your particular area in terms of their profile, expectations, consumption modes and contexts. This section should include any academic research that you think is relevant concerning audience reception, as well as details of audience research that you have carried out.

Finding and applying critical frameworks

Remember that this unit has been designed to enable you to use the materials you have created during your research to develop an independent critical response. Whatever ideas and frameworks you use from established critical work should be incorporated into your own arguments. You should remember, however, that established theorists can be challenged and your study should include discussion of the relevancy and pros and cons of using certain critical frameworks. The case studies section (p.88) will give you specific ideas concerning critics and critiques that may be appropriate to the set topics.

Creating your own critical response

Your own ideas and responses should always be fully substantiated, using examples from your primary research, and systematically argued. Your ideas may challenge much of the existing criticism you have read and this can provide a thought-provoking study if your argument is backed up by specific examples. Remember to refer directly to your area of research when you are creating your own response and not to formulate ideas that are irrelevant to your title.

Presenting your findings

We have already looked at how to organise your notes effectively. When you come to the exam you will need to select the notes which are specifically required for Questions One and Two. Always present your notes clearly, writing in full sentences and offering well-substantiated points. The examiner will want to understand a number of things:

- Your reasons for identifying your topic of study
- That the topic has been thoroughly and appropriately researched
- That you have made relevant use of existing criticism
- That you have considered the profile, expectations and text reception of your identified audience
- That you have understood the nature and impact of institutional questions
- That you have analysed historical and social context as factors which influence your topic area
- The way in which your research has formed conclusions concerning your topic

You will need to make sure, therefore, that your research notes include information that will be able to satisfy all of the requirements listed above.

PART THREE

Media Issues and Debates

Exam essay writing skills

There are many factors to consider when you are sitting an exam: question choice, your approach to the question and, the element that is often forgotten when you are under pressure, the structure and style of your writing. Below are some guidance points for you to remember when you are approaching any exam essay question.

Planning

It is extremely useful to make a plan before you commence writing. This can be a list of bullet points that indicate to you the areas to be covered in the exam. It is also worth making a brief note of any references or examples you are going to include in your essay. You should aim to spend up to 5 minutes making your plan.

Overall structure

The most obvious point to remember is that your essay needs a clear introduction and conclusion. Your introduction should address the essay question specifically and describe the particular approach to the question that you are offering. Your conclusion should offer a summation of your argument and not introduce new points.

What lies in between the introduction and conclusion should be a systematic and relevant development of your ideas. One paragraph should feed into the next. The examiner will not want to read a disjointed piece of writing. Avoid repetitious points and make sure that whatever you do write is fully substantiated by references to textual detail or theory.

Clear organisation is essential if you want your argument to have clarity. The organisation of the piece is up to you, but certain systems of organisation are particularly effective:

- If you are closely analysing a text it is much more useful to structure your paragraphs by 'area' (genre, mise-en-scène, editing, sound) than to work through the text chronologically
- If you are comparing texts then the same kinds of headings can be used
- With a question concerning genre conventions a systematic 'journey' through each of the relevant conventions and how they have been used is most effective
- If you have chosen a question that asks you to discuss an issue, then paragraphs that explore the key areas of the debate and include within them the different arguments offer a more systematic and comprehensive approach
- If you are creating an essay which offers a personal thesis (idea) then you do not need to give the alternative arguments, but you do need to set out your ideas logically and avoid too many personalised statements such as 'I think ...' or 'My opinion is ...'. The examiner will be able to recognise original approaches and will be happy provided your statements are fully substantiated.

For all of these possible essay styles, it is essential that you refer back to the title of your essay and connect your content and movement of argument to the original task. Try not to move off into tangents of the topic area which may be interesting, but have little connection to the essay title.

Paragraphs

The first thing to remember concerning paragraphs, is that you must use them! Clarity of argument is always lost when you adopt a 'stream of consciousness' style of writing. Try to make sure that each of your paragraphs follows the structure below:

- Open with a 'topic statement', a sentence that identifies the point you are trying to make
- Follow this with a clear (textual) example
- Next you should elaborate on your original 'topic sentence'
- To close the paragraph, try to refer to the viewer/audience's response to the issue you have raised

Language

In an exam you are expected to produce a piece of writing which has suitably academic form, tone and content. This does not mean that you have to adopt a cold, overly aesthetic, style but it does mean that you need to write formally and clearly. You should avoid the following.

Slang or imprecise terms

You are creating an academic piece of writing and slang terms that you may use in your everyday descriptions are not appropriate. By the same token, your essay will lose fluency and 'weight' if the terms you use are either imprecise or wrongly attributed. You should use specific media terms where appropriate. The examiner will not want you to clutter your essay with too much terminology, but you should use it where applicable. Use words such as narrative, genre, mise-en-scène and iconography. They will give clear indication that you know exactly what you are talking about. You should, however, only use terminology if you know exactly what it means. The glossary section of this book should provide a means of constantly checking your knowledge of specific terms.

Informality of tone or language

The tone of your piece is an important factor in how it is received by your examiner. You will have spent time revising subject matter and considering possible lines of argument appropriate to your essay topic. It would, therefore, be a shame to spoil all of this hard work by 'framing' your ideas within language that undermines them. Try not to offer too many anecdotal references to your own experiences (these are usually found within sentences which begin, 'I think ... ', 'In my opinion ...', 'When I watch/read/listen to ...') because your essay will begin to read as unsubstantiated opinion. Obviously, reference to yourself as a particular type of media consumer (with a particular profile) can be relevant, but only if you then move on to discuss the wider issues connected to viewing practices or consumption modes. You are, nevertheless, encouraged to show personal engagement with texts that you have studied and present your views.

Humorous asides!

No matter how tempting it may seem during the exam, a humorous quip or comical aside will never make your answer more palatable or impressive to an examiner!

Direct addresses to the examiner

Again, this is a question of keeping in mind what is appropriate within an exam context. Your essay should be clear, concise and well substantiated. If it is all of these things, you will not need to solicit the examiner's agreement or approval by using phrases such as, 'I am sure that we both agree that ...' or 'You know what I mean when ...'.

Over-long or meandering sentences

Syntax (the way sentences are organised) is an important factor in retaining clarity and sense in an essay. It is, therefore, very important that your sentences are not too complex or lengthy. Try to follow the paragraph model described earlier in this chapter and include no more than one relevant point in any one sentence.

Vague or absent substantiation

Appropriate and clear examples will provide clear evidence that you have understood the essay title, constructed an informed debate and identified an accurate frame of reference for your essay. Do not be vague when giving textual or institutional examples. If you are referring to a scene from a film, for example, then provide a precise reference for it: 'The final Coliseum confrontation, in which Maximus ...' is a much more precise introduction to an example from the film *Gladiator* than, 'The last fight scene in the film . . .'.

Once you have completed the writing for your essay, the final stage during any exam should be close checking for grammar, punctuation, spelling, appropriate reference and relevant argument.

The Media Issues and Debates exam

Questions, plans and essay examples

The Media Issues and Debates Section of this book (pp 141–215) will give you clear guidance on how to approach each of the set topic areas. For the purposes of this section, we will look at a few examples of essay questions and discuss how they might be approached. The focus will not be on detailed content but on planning, structure and fluency of writing. The examples below are created from one topic from each of the main section headings of Broadcasting, Film and Print. They include sample essay plans, as well as practice questions that you could use as timed essays to revise.

Broadcasting

To what extent do British television soap operas hold a 'mirror up to society'?

Essay plan example

Your plan for this essay should include notes on the following:

- Statements that outline your understanding of and response to the question. What does the phrase 'mirror up to society' mean and to what extent do you think it applies to the function of British TV soaps?
- Notes on the soap operas you are going to use as examples and to what extent you think they mirror social concerns
- Comments on audience expectations of British TV soaps and whether social realism is one of the criteria for viewing
- Details of soap functions other than as social documents

Your response to the title could include the following:

Introduction

Mirrors reflect the literal image which is placed in front of them. The image may be reversed, but is accurate in detail and not interpretative. British TV soap operas can be said to have a partially reflective quality. They mirror some social rituals, issues and dynamics, but deliver these within a package that includes the kind of dramatically unrealistic and melodramatic elements which will keep audiences engaged and watching.

Paragraph 1

In order for a soap opera to hold its viewing audience, there are a number of factors which need to be present. A degree of engagement with contemporary social issues is important, because it not only generates a sense of realism, but also gives the viewer a sense of familiarity with the world of the soap. If the storylines and issues of the soap opera do not, to some degree, approximate those of the potential audience, distance, detachment and non-engagement can ensue. However, an over-burdening of TV soap with reality effects can also have a negative effect because it will not allow for the escapism and entertainment which is necessary within the viewing experience. Melodramatic elements can hint at an issue or situation which is recognisable, but at the same time offer entertainment and positive distance. The voyeurism inherent in our viewing expectations requires that we, at times, feel pity or empathy for the characters, but distance from them and their plight. The episode structure of a soap also dictates the extent to which it can be realistic. The need for cliff-hangers to provoke continued viewing often means that a story is sequenced around a dramatic, but often unrealistic, episode ending.

Paragraphs 2 and 3

Example soap 1: *EastEnders*

How realistic are the storylines within *EastEnders*? You could discuss two or three recent storylines and consider how far they potentially mirror the real events that may go on in a community like this. To what extent do 'Albert Square' and its inhabitants reflect a real community? You could consider whether or not the characters within *EastEnders* represent a realistic cross-section of a typical East End community. Is it realistic to encounter so much drama within such a small community? How would you define the profile of the target audience for *EastEnders* and what would their expectations of the soap be?

Paragraphs 3 and 4

Example soap 2: *Coronation Street*

If some of the drama of *EastEnders* revolves around stereotypes concerning the inhabitants of London's East End, then does a small street in greater Manchester offer itself up as a context for the same kind of events? What have been some of the recent storylines of *Coronation Street* and are the same kind offered in *EastEnders*? Do the issues discussed mirror social concerns? You may consider whether the issues discussed in this soap reflect the general debates within British society or whether they are class specific. Do the groups represented in *Coronation Street* adequately reflect British society or are they specific to region? Because of the longevity of this soap, you could discuss the changes in storylines that have occurred in its lifetime and analyse whether they have become more realistic or melodramatic. Is melodrama predictable within the ratings war of the soaps?

Paragraphs 5 and 6

Example soap 3: *Brookside*

Part of the 'mission statement' of *Brookside* was to deliver a grittier and less sanitised soap. Do you think it has achieved this? Are the issues that *Brookside* deals with more or less controversial than the other soaps? If they are more controversial does this mean that the soap is rendered less realistic? One question that you could ask yourself (which would also be relevant to *Coronation Street* and *EastEnders*) is whether or not messages and discussions surrounding social issues are lost within heightened drama or do the issues necessitate a dramatic context? Who watches *Brookside* and are their viewing expectations met?

Paragraphs 7 and 8

Example soap 4: *Hollyoaks*

Part of your discussion concerning the issue of whether or not soaps 'mirror' social concerns, has dealt with the profile and attendant expectations of the target viewer. *Hollyoaks* provides a useful example in this debate because its target audience is much younger than that of the soaps we have already mentioned. It also comes in two forms: the pre-watershed show and the later *Hollyoaks: Moving on* version. A comparison of the types of issues included in both of these versions would help to address questions of content and audience. Do both versions of the show have the same audience? Do expectations shift pre and post-watershed? Do you think one 'mirrors' concerns in a more realistic or explicit way than the other?

Conclusion

Your conclusion should summarise your response to the essay question and evaluate the capacity of British TV soap operas to 'hold a mirror up to society'. Is it the intention of soaps to offer social comment? Are they an appropriate context in which social issues can be discussed? Do you watch British TV soaps in order to engage in social debate or are there other factors involved in your viewing?

Questions for your own practice

How do conventions of television news presentation affect the audiences for news programmes?

How has government legislation affected British broadcasting since 1990?

Film

'A knowledge of a genre's conventions can enhance an audience's appreciation and understanding.' Discuss.

Essay plan example

Taking the slasher horror genre as a case study, your plan for this essay should include notes on the following:

- Your response to the question, i.e. whether or not you think it is true
- Comments on how an understanding of genre conventions can affect/enhance the viewing of a film
- Details of the conventions of the slasher genre
- Details of how each convention might aid understanding and enhance appreciation

Your response to the title could follow the structure below.

Introduction

The horror genre has many subdivisions and this essay will concentrate on slasher films to discuss the importance of a knowledge of generic conventions. Conventions act as basic ingredients within a particular genre, but how they appear in different films can vary significantly. A writer or director may decide to subvert a convention or use it ironically to make a particular point. What may enhance an audience member's appreciation and understanding of a particular film is the recognition of conventions and the debates which their use may indicate. If we recognise a set of elements within a film, it can make the film seem less alienating and more accessible. The particular way a convention is used may help the viewer to understand the messages and values of the film and may even indicate its ideological context.

Paragraph 1

Convention: The frightening place. Details of how this convention has developed and what constitutes 'the frightening place' in different films. For example, *Psycho* (1960) (the Bates Motel/Bates' House), *Halloween* (1971) (the suburban domestic space), *Nightmare on Elm Street* (1984) (dreams).

Paragraph 2

Convention: The final girl. Details of the characteristics of the final girl. Links, for example, Laurie in *Halloween* and Sidney in *Scream* (1996).

Paragraph 3

Convention: The monster. Differences in representation from 'the internalised monstrous' (Norman Bates), to 'the masked, unstoppable inhuman' (Michael Myers), to 'the supernatural assailant' (Freddy Krugger).

Paragraph 4

Convention: Camera work.

a) The floating camera. Details of the disorientating effect, the positioning of the audience, use in film examples (e.g. *Halloween*).

b) Fragmented killer shots. You will need to discuss examples of slasher films in which the killer is only gradually revealed and is shot for the majority of the film in fragments. However, this is not consistent across all of the films you have studied and Norman Bates is an example of a killer who is 'seen' from the outset. It would be worth discussing the differing ways in which slasher films gradually reveal their monsters.

Paragraph 5

Convention: Iconography. Analysis of the use (actual and symbolic) of masks, knives and so forth. This paragraph should also discuss iconographic or emblematic images for example, 'the screaming face' and iconography which sharpens our understanding of character (e.g. the stuffed birds in Norman Bates' parlour).

Paragraph 6

Convention: Obscuring mise-en-scène. Discuss the ways in which mists, fogs and shadows are used to create tension and disorientate the viewer.

Paragraph 7

Convention: Narrative movement from disequilibrium to disturbance to a new equilibrium. Why is it that slasher films have a tendency to offer closure and resolution, only to offer a shock finale?

Paragraph 8

Convention: Atmospheric use of diegetic and non-diegetic sound. You will need to discuss the similarities between various 'monster' character themes, the use of soundtrack to build tension, the use of diegetic sound to signal danger and the use of soundtrack to express the interior workings or motivations of the killer.

Paragraph 9

Convention: Representations. There are certain groups who are often depicted within the slasher genre, for instance, the family, teenagers, the church and the police. Try to examine any differences in the ways that these groups are represented. What does the film intend to indicate by representing these groups in particular ways?

Paragraph 10

Convention: Discussion of certain themes. Slasher films often discuss themes such as death, sex, religion and the effectiveness of institutions of protection. Try to examine what the individual films you have chosen offer in terms of their discussions around these areas. For example, the equation of sex with death is quite common in slasher films. Does this mean that slasher films are intrinsically conservative?

Paragraph 11

You should have been discussing the implied ideology and historical context of each of your films as you discussed them in this essay. It may be useful at this point to summarise some of your thoughts on this subject. Do you think viewers of slasher films would interpret the use of conventions as a statement challenging dominant ideas and opinions or do you think they might see a reinforcement of traditional values in these films? Does the time in which the various films were made have any bearing on their treatment of the conventions you have identified?

Conclusion

Having explored your ideas, the conclusion is where you summarise your thoughts about the essay title. Does a knowledge of conventions aid understanding and increase appreciation or does it create a different kind of viewing process, i.e. one in which the viewer is self-consciously looking for recognisable conventions rather than suspending their disbelief?

Filmography

Referenced films:
Psycho (1960)
Halloween (1971)
Nightmare on Elm Street (1984)
Friday 13th (1980)
The Texas Chainsaw Massacre (1974)
Scream (1996)

Questions for your own practice

Are the British cinema products since 1990 recognisably different from those produced by Hollywood during the same period?

To what extent do shifts in legislation related to censorship reflect changing social ideologies?

Print

To what extent do women's lifestyle magazines accurately represent the lives of their target readers?

Essay plan example

Your plan for this essay should include notes on the following:

- The varying styles of representation presented in the women's lifestyle magazines you are going to analyse in your essay
- The target readers for each of these magazines, their expectations and lifestyles
- The relationship these varying representations have to dominant contemporary ideologies concerning women

Introduction

Women's lifestyle magazines are multifunctional. They can provide advice, escapism, discussion of familiar issues and a visual depiction of certain lifestyle aspirations. The women's magazine publishing market is an extremely lucrative one and there are product examples to suit most target readers. This essay will argue that the purpose and consumption of women's magazines is not wholly concerned with accurate representation, but involves the 'marketing' of lifestyles and attitudes that are escapist and sometimes problematic.

Paragraphs 1 and 2

Example text 1: *Vogue*

Vogue is a fashion magazine unapologetic in its depiction of a world of designer fashion and unaffordable lifestyles (unaffordable to the vast majority of British women). The magazine's adverts, articles and editorials all collude to promote exclusivity and luxury. Your study of this magazine should begin with an analysis of its readership. Are women who subscribe to or buy *Vogue* able to afford the lifestyle represented or are the reasons for buying such a magazine aspirational and escapist? You would also need to evaluate the purpose and intent of the magazine. Do you think *Vogue* begins fashion trends or merely describes them? Does it present a picture of a world which in reality does not exist? In terms of the ideological arguments around women's magazines, does *Vogue* represent women in a positive light or objectify them through its insistence on a particular 'look'?

Paragraphs 3 and 4

Example text 2: *Woman's Weekly*

Your essay should include contrasting women's lifestyle magazines, in order to discuss the different types of female representation that are available. *Woman's Weekly*, which has substantial circulation figures, is a publication aimed at a very different market to *Vogue*. Who are the target readers for this publication and what are their expectations? The magazine includes articles, rather than fashion spreads, that cover topics like dieting, knitting and health advice. Do the articles in this magazine represent the concerns of the target female reader? You will need to consider whether *Woman's Weekly* is more representative of its readers and whether it contributes to or challenges any stereotypes connected with them.

Paragraphs 5 and 6

Example text 3: *Marie Claire*

Marie Claire is often marketed as an issues driven women's magazine. It includes fashion and celebrity interviews, but also contains articles on the position of women in other countries and on the problematic and controversial issues which women face. An analysis of the readership profile of *Marie Claire* could consider how these types of articles inform purchasing. To what extent do you think that the women who read this magazine are represented as more socially aware? A more cynical question might be, 'to what extent are potential *Marie Claire* readers flattered into considering themselves as more serious than the readers of publications such as *Vogue*, *Cosmopolitan* or *Elle*?'

Conclusion

In your conclusion you will need to summarise your comments in response to the essay question. Consider whether or not you think the function of women's magazines is to represent the lifestyle of the target reader. If your analysis leads you to conclude that reflecting target consumer lifestyles is one of the ways in which these magazines retain readership, you could debate whether the representations offered confirm or challenge stereotypes. Your conclusion may make a distinction between various lifestyle magazines in terms of intent and function and draw attention to some of the debates surrounding the problems of certain types of representation.

Questions for your own practice

How do local newspapers represent the communities in which they are circulated?

How influential are regulatory bodies on the British press?

Glossary

The following glossary offers brief definitions of key words and should be used in conjunction with the index and more detailed definitions of key terms within the book as a whole. Some of the terms have not been used in the book but you may come across them in your further reading.

ABC – Audit Bureau of Circulation is an independent organisation that provides circulation figures for magazines and newspapers.

Aberrant readings – when a reading of a text is entirely different from the intended meaning. Such a reading may be mistaken or deliberate.

Advertorial – in a magazine or newspaper this is an advertisement that has the appearance of an article.

Aerial shot/bird's eye view – shots filmed from aircraft or helicopter, from an extreme high angle.

Ambient sound – natural background noise on television, film or radio. In the same manner **ambient light** refers to natural, available light that is not enhanced in any way.

American Dream – the belief that anyone in America can succeed and achieve their dreams, regardless of their social background.

Anchorage – Roland Barthes suggested that all images are open to a variety of interpretations or meanings. He referred to this as **polysemy**. However, if an image is anchored by written text or sound, then this restricts the possible meanings.

Art-house cinema – a cinema that shows films of acknowledged artistic merit, typically low to medium-budget films that address the aesthetics of film and are produced mainly, although not exclusively, outside the **mainstream**.

Artificial lighting – any lighting that is used to light a film or television programme that is not available from a natural source light.

Aspect ratio – refers to the size of the image on the screen and the ratio between width and height. The most familiar is the Academy ratio of

1.33:1 or 4:3 that was established from the outset of filmmaking. It was also the original standard for television images. Wide-screen ratios were developed in the 1950s and began at 2.55:1 but were adapted to 2.35:1 to accept optical soundtracks.

Audience – all those who receive or interact with any media product. A **target audience** is the group of people at whom a product is particularly aimed. It may be identified as either **mass** (or **mainstream**) if it is targeted at a very large number of people or **niche** if it is targeted at a smaller, more specific group of people.

Auteur – a French term meaning 'author'. It is used to refer to a film director who may be said to direct his or her films with distinctive personal style.

Avant-garde – innovative or experimental work made outside the **mainstream**.

Badged – a product is badged when given a specific style that makes it readily identifiable to its target audience. A product may be **re-badged** to target it at a new and different audience.

BARB – The Broadcasters' Audience Research Board is an independent organisation that is used to measure audiences for television companies. BARB is owned jointly by the BBC and the ITCA (the Independent TV Companies Association).

BBFC – The British Board of Film Classification. This organisation, established in 1913, was originally named the British Board of Film Censors. It was founded in response to chaotic and inconsistent practices of censorship in different Local Authorities. In 1982 the word 'Censors' was replaced by 'Classification' and in 1985 the Video Recording Act brought video into the Board's remit. The BBFC gives a film a specific classification, either U, PG, 12, 15 or 18. The Motion Picture Association of America is the organisation that produces a similar set of classifications for the US.

Behaviourism – a philosophy of social science that emphasises the experimental analysis of behaviour, concentrating on observable actions and reactions as opposed to mental processes that can only be inferred.

Binary opposition – where texts are organised around sets of opposite values such as good and evil, light and dark.

Bollywood – a colloquial term given to the Indian film industry which is the largest in the world as it continues to produce 600–700 films a year. The term was created by combining the names Bombay (home to India's most prolific studios) and Hollywood. Film production does, however, take place in other parts of India, notably Madras, Hyderabad and Calcutta.

British New Wave – the name given to the films of a small group of British directors (Lindsay Anderson, Karel Reisz and Tony Richardson) produced from the late 1950s to the mid-1960s. Many of the films were also referred to as **Kitchen Sink Dramas** or **social realist** films, offering progressive treatments of the working class and of gender and sexuality.

Broadsheet – the term strictly refers to the size or format of the newspaper although the term is frequently used as a synonym for the 'quality' press.

Camera angle – this refers to the position of the camera in relation to the main subject. It could be a high angle, low angle, worm's eye view or aerial view.

Character – the Russian critic and folklorist Vladimir Propp examined hundreds of folk tales and presented an analysis of characters and their specific roles in narratives.

Chiaroscuro lighting – a term originally applied to painting and drawing, it comes from the Italian for 'clear' and 'dark'. It applies to high-contrast lighting that gives deep shadows and bright highlights.

Chromakey – this technique enables a secondary image or set of images to be superimposed over part of the original camera shots. The original action must be filmed against a background of a single colour. Chromakey is used to superimpose a weather map behind the weather forecaster and was also used to make Superman appear to fly. Although green and yellow are sometimes used, the most commonly used colour is blue (hence blue-screen). It is important that any subject filmed is not wearing the same shade as the background. A substantial amount of action in *The Lord of the Rings* (2001) was filmed using blue-screen.

Cinematographer – the person in film who is responsible for cameras and lighting. Often referred to as the director of photography.

Connotation – Roland Barthes refers this to the meanings that words, images and sounds suggest beyond the literal description or **denotation**.

Continuity editing – sometimes referred to as invisible or academic editing, this is the unobtrusive style of editing developed by Hollywood and still employed in most commercial productions. The basis of continuity editing is to cut on action so that the whole sequence looks natural.

Convergence – the coming together of different communication devices and processes. With the aid of a modem the telephone and computer converge to enable us to access the internet, that is the 'new' means of communication. Convergence is often made possible by alliances between or mergers of different companies but the terms are not synonymous. Alliances are when separate individual companies work together in a business venture and mergers/takeovers are when separate companies become one larger organisation (e.g. the merger of AOL and Time-Warner).

Cover lines – information about major articles given on the front page of a magazine.

Crane shot – a shot filmed quite literally from a high angle and from a crane.

Cross-media ownership – when corporations own different businesses in several types of media, for example, News Corporation which has interests in other areas of the media, television film and the press.

Demographics – demographic data refers to the social characteristics of the population studied, according to groupings such as social class, gender and age.

Denotation – the simple description of what can be seen or heard (see **connotation**).

Depth of field – the distance between the furthest and the nearest points that are in focus. A wide-angle lens will have a much greater depth of field than a telephoto lens.

Diegetic/non-diegetic sound – diegetic sound appears to come from a recognisable source within the narrative of a film, radio or television text. Non-diegetic sound would include a film musical score.

Digital – the conversion of sound and visual to transmit information in a code using the numbers zero and one.

Discourse – a discourse offers a set of statements about a particular area for discussion and organises these statements, giving specific structure to the way that the subject is discussed. Discourses, therefore, give expression to the meanings and values of institutions or social groups. This can refer to the way in which a particular social group may construct discussion, for example, 'feminist' discourse.

Disequilibrium – see **Equilibrium**.

Dissolve – a form of **transition** in editing when one image gradually begins to fade and the second image begins to appear. For a brief time the two images can be seen simultaneously. This is not to be confused with **fades** or **wipes** which are different forms of transition.

Dubbing – a process whereby sound is added to film. This may take the form of adding music or additional sound to dialogue or it may refer to the addition of an entire soundtrack including dialogue.

Dystopia – a society that reflects the view that much has gone wrong, as opposed to Utopia which is a representation of a perfect society.

Editing – is the selection of material to make a coherent whole. It may refer to the editing of copy and still images for a print product or sound for radio, or images and sound for television or film. In film and television an editor will use a variety of methods of moving from one sequence to another, this is referred to as a **transition**.

Editorial – this may refer to a statement by the editor in any publication or it may also refer to any feature material, that is, not advertising.

Enigma – a question or puzzle that may be posed at the beginning of and throughout a text. It refers to one of Roland Barthes' codes of narrative that he called the 'Voice of Truth', also called the **hermaneutic** code. These puzzles work to maintain the interest of the audience; they are there to be solved or to delay the pleasure of reaching the end of the story.

Equilibrium, disequilibrium, restoration of equilibrium – tensions within a narrative. A secure and balanced state is often used to begin a narrative but this is soon disrupted by tensions or events that cause disequilibrium. A typical happy ending will result in a restoration of balance and restoration of equilibrium. The Bulgarian theorist Tzvetan Todorov is most frequently referred to in relation to this narrative theory.

Establishing shot – a **long shot** or **extreme long shot** that establishes the location, general mood and the relative placement of main subjects within a scene.

Fade – when the image gradually grows dim or faint and then disappears. This form of editing **transition** is not to be confused with a **dissolve**. A fade is usually to a blank black screen, hence 'fade to black'. This is the most common fade, although fades to white or red are used for special effects. If an image gradually appears from a blank screen this is called a 'fade up' or 'fade from'. Fade to and from black is commonly found as a standard feature in camcorders.

Fish-eye lens – is an extreme wide-angle lens covering 180°. This gives a high level of distortion (see also **lenses**).

Form – this term means the structure or skeleton of a text and the narrative framework around it. For example, a feature film commonly has a three-act structure. Some structures are determined by a genre and its corresponding codes and conventions.

Frame – as a noun this refers to the single area on a strip of film that holds a single image (or a single still image on video). As a verb it means to adjust the position of the camera or to adjust the camera lens in order to compose the required image. You would frame your image to construct a close up, long shot or medium shot. If the framing of a shot is at an angle this is referred to as a **canted frame** or **Dutch angle**.

Gatekeeping – the process by which news stories are selected or rejected. A **gatekeeper** is a journalist, usually the editor, who filters the news stories in order to present them in the most successful way possible to the audience. The term is also applied to other major decision-makers in the media industries.

Gaze – at its most basic this refers to the act of looking that takes place as part of the experience of watching films and the process of looking between the actors on the screen and the audience. Since the 1970s the term has been a key term for film theorists. Much feminist film theory takes the starting point that cinema was constructed around male

scopophilia and that the camera operated through a male gaze, looking at women as objects.

Genre – this is the classification of any media text into a category or type, e.g. news, horror, documentary, soap opera, docu-soap, science fiction, lifestyle, etc. Genres tend to have identifiable codes and **conventions** that have developed over time and for which audiences may have developed particular expectations. Media texts that are a mixture of more than one genre are called generic **hybrids**.

Hegemony – the process by which **dominant ideology** is maintained is called hegemony. This concept owes much to the work of the Italian political theorist Antonio Gramsci. It is a form of consensus that is initially constructed by institutions that wield social and political power, such as government organisations, the mass media, the family, the education system and religious groups. It is a form of consensus that is frequently renegotiated between the powerful and the dominated.

High/low key lighting – high key lighting is an even lighting scheme that emphasises bright colours giving a cheerful effect often used in comedies and musicals. Low-key lighting is where the scene appears under or dimly lit. The overall appearance is of darkness and shadow. This style of lighting is characteristic of thrillers, horror movies and film noir.

Hooks – refers to any device used in the construction of a media product to attract or hold onto the attention of the audience. For instance these devices are most frequently used at the beginning of a film to make sure the audience is enthralled.

Horizontal integration – when an organisation owns different companies of the same type, for instance Rupert Murdoch owns several newspapers. This occurs when a company takes over a competitor at the same level of production within the same market sector. (See **vertical integration**.)

Iconography – familiar symbols in works of art have a cultural meaning that has a resonance beyond the individual work. In film, iconography may refer to particular objects, stars, archetypal characters, actors or even specifics of lighting, sets and props.

Ident – in broadcasting this refers to a jingle or logo that identifies the channel, station or programme.

243

Ideology – often referred to as the system of ideas, values and beliefs which an individual, group or society holds to be true or important. These are shared by a culture or society about how that society should function. Ideas and values that are seen to be shared, or perpetuated, by the most influential social agents (the churches, the law, education, government, the media etc.) may be described as **dominant ideologies**.

Info-tainment – a colloquial term used to identify the trend towards increasing the entertainment value of factual programmes in order to increase their popularity with audiences, despite accusations of trivialisation.

Intertextuality – often related to **post-modernism** and its culture and criticism. The notion being that we now understand texts by their relationship or reference to another text, or that a text is successful principally because of its intertextual references (e.g. *The Simpsons, Scream*). One of the effects on the audience of recognising intertextuality is that it flatters their ability to recognise references and feel superior, or to feel part of a group who share the same 'joke'.

Jump cut – a break in the continuity of editing. The cut goes from one shot to another in such a way as to disorientate the viewer. This may break the continuity of time by leaping immediately forward from one part of the action to another even though it is clear that they are separated by an interval of time leap. Jump cuts can also break the continuity of space in the same way.

Kitchen Sink Drama – a term that became popular in the middle and late 1950s. Often used derogatorily, it was applied to plays that, in a realistic manner, showed aspects of working-class life at the time. It was so-called because the plays centred, metaphorically, psychologically and in some cases, literally, on the kitchen sink. The term was also used by some critics to refer to the British social realist films of the late 1950s and the early 1960s. Tony Richardson's film versions of John Osborne's play *Look Back in Anger* and Shelagh Delaney's play *A Taste of Honey* bridge the theatrical and cinematic products.

Lenses (telephoto, wide angle) – a telephoto lens enables objects to appear closer to the camera without moving the camera itself. It is the camera's equivalent to a telescope. A short telephoto is flattering for faces in close up. A long telephoto can also give crowded streets the appearance of being even more congested. A wide-angle lens offers a range of more than 60°. It offers a certain amount of distortion, magnifying the foreground and reducing the size of images in the background. Used for close ups, this lens will distort the image.

Mainstream – a term that refers to a commercially orientated media product that appeals to a wide audience demographic (or refers to the people who consume them). The term is sometimes used derogatorily to suggest products lacking in flair, imagination or innovation.

Manga – a distinctive genre of Japanese comics that mix reality and fantasy. **Anime** is the animated version of manga.

Masala – a term used to describe films made in the popular Hindi style of Indian cinema. Masala films are characterised by mixing very different genres within one film, such as comedy, action, melodrama and song and dance. Masala is Hindi for spices or flavours, and the analogy is that you would blend masalas in the right proportions to create a single dish.

Masthead – the title of a magazine or newspaper, usually placed at the top of the front cover.

Mise-en-scène – literally everything that is 'put in the scene', or frame, to be photographed (appropriate to the time or era portrayed). This usually includes production design, set, location, actors, costumes, make-up, gesture, proxemics/blocking, extras, props, use of colour, contrast and filter. Lighting is often included within mise-en-scène. Camera shot composition, framing, angle and movement is sometimes referred to as mise-en-shot.

Montage – taken from the French, 'to assemble'. It has several meanings in the context of film and is not exclusively used to refer to **Soviet montage**. (1) As a synonym for editing. (2) In Hollywood cinema to edit a concentrated sequence by a series of brief cuts that use a series of transitions to create the effect of the passage of time or movement over large distances or for expressionistic moods. (3) **Thematic** or **Soviet montage** was developed by Sergei Eisenstein by arranging striking juxtapositions of individual shots to suggest an idea that goes beyond meanings within the individual shots. He called this 'collision' montage. (4) Any sequence that creates a particularly significant effect mainly through its editing. The shower scene in *Psycho* (1960) would be such an example.

Moral panics – individuals, social groups, or even patterns of behaviour can be presented by the mass media as a threat to society's status quo. Moral panics reflect the fear of society that the dominant culture might be subverted and are often presented by the mass media in an hysterical or stereotypical manner.

Narrative – the way in which a plot or story is told, by whom and in what order. Flash backs or forwards and ellipsis may be used as narrative devices. Tsvetan Todorov, Richard Branigan, David Bordwell and Kristin Thompson and Robert McKee all have interesting points about narrative development.

Narrowcasting – contrasted with broadcasting, where product makers aim their programmes and advertisements at a specialist interest audience.

Naturalism – this term is frequently used synonymously with **realism**. However, realism means something much broader, using more generalised methods of trying to represent the 'real'. Naturalism is a narrower and more focused strategy that involves trying to recreate faithfully the exact conditions of location and exact representations of character through performance. With naturalism the audience is offered the opportunity to observe as if viewing through a one-way mirror. We see a copy of life based upon very close observation.

Newsgathering – the process by which news is collected from its source in order to be treated or packaged for presentation.

News values – the process by which news stories or features are selected and their priority and style of presentation, also referred to as gatekeeping. These are sometimes categorised as 'hard' or 'soft'. Galtung and Ruge's definitions (recency, currency, negativity etc.) are commonly used to categorise news values in greater detail. The news values are usually determined by the producers and editors, to reflect the values of the target audience and what they are interested in reading about or looking at. However, it could be asserted that they also influence and determine the agenda of the readers.

NRS – National Readership Survey is an organisation that sets out to provide information on the number and nature of readership of magazines and newspapers.

Occupational soaps – television series that reflect the conventions of soap opera but are based around a single occupation such as *The Bill*, *Emergency Ward 10* and *The Dream Team*.

Oscar – the popular name for an Academy Award, but actually refers to the trophy itself. The gold-plated statuette is awarded by the **Academy of Motion Picture Arts and Sciences** and it is so-called, it is claimed, because an early librarian of the Academy, Margaret Herrick, thought that it looked like her Uncle Oscar.

Pan and tilt – a pan is to turn the camera from a fixed position horizontally on the axis of its mount. **Tilt** is to move the camera from a fixed position vertically on the axis of the mount. A **whip** or **zip pan** is the movement done rapidly rather than the usual slow and smooth movement.

Paparazzo – this term is usually seen in the plural form as **paparazzi**. It refers to an aggressive and unscrupulous freelance photographer who specialises in taking pictures of celebrities. The word is an Italian surname and was originally suggested for the name of a character in Fellini's *La Dolce Vita* (1960). The term is often incorrectly used to refer to any group of persistent or aggressive journalists.

Parody – a media text that ridicules another more serious product by humorous imitation. Mel Brook's *Blazing Saddles* (1974) is a perfect example of a parody. A parody is frequently referred to colloquially as a **spoof.** A parody is not the same as a **pastiche.** A parody deliberately sets out to ridicule the original whereas a pastiche is a text composed in the recognisable style of another maker. If you were to make a film in the style of Alfred Hitchcock then this would be a pastiche.

Plugs – information about the contents of a magazine or newspaper given on the front cover.

Pluralist – a view that modern societies comprise populations that are increasingly different in kind (i.e. heterogeneous) divided by such factors as ethnic, religious, regional and class differences.

Point of view shot (POV) – a shot that shows the point of view of a character. This will often be shown as an over the shoulder shot. A **subjective point of view** is when the camera functions as if it were the eyes of the character.

Polysemy – the possibility of a sign to have several meanings. (See also **anchorage**.)

Post-modernism – a movement or phase in twentieth-century thought. The term is complex and difficult to define in simple terms. It is applied to all the arts and at its most basic refers to the way that new products can be constructed by making reference to already existing ones.

Post-production – the period and the processes that come between the completion of principal photography and the completed film or programme. This involves the editing of a film or programme including titles, graphics special effects, etc.

Preferred reading – this term describes the way in which a media text offers a reading or meaning that follows the intentions, either conscious or unconscious, of the maker or the reading 'preferred' by the dominant forces in society. (See **ideology**.)

Pre-production – the entire range of preparations that take place before a film or television programme can begin shooting.

Primary research – research information or data that you collect yourself. Sources for this may include interviews, questionnaires, analysis of original photographs or other media texts that you undertake yourself. (See also **secondary research**.)

Production – is either the product itself or the actual process of filming.

Properties – more commonly referred to by the abbreviation **props**. The terms refer to any object that can be carried and used by the actors, as opposed to the larger items of furniture that are considered to be part of the décor of the set itself. In the singular, **property** is also used to refer to any copyrighted text – anything from a complete novel to a song title or synopsis of a plot.

Proxemics – the study of the way people approach others, or keep their distance from others. What we do with the space between us is seen to be a form of non-verbal communication. It also refers to the way we inhabit our own space, including 'extensions of ourselves' such as our rooms, houses, towns and cities.

Public Service Broadcasting – broadcasting that is intended to 'entertain, educate and inform' but does not have a primary commercial intent.

Puff – words or phrases on the cover of a magazine used to boost its status.

Pyrotechnics – are all explosive devices used in films, television or in theatrical stage productions. They are commonly referred to by the abbreviation 'pyros'. In common usage pyrotechnics is a term more narrowly applied to fireworks.

Qualitative research – research undertaken through observation, analysing texts and documents, interviews, open-ended questionnaires and case studies. It is reasoned argument that is not based upon simple statistical information. Overall qualitative research enables researchers to study psychological, cultural and social phenomena.

Quantitative research – primarily statistical data most frequently obtained from closed questions in questionnaires or structured interviews. Qualitative research may estimate how many 15-25 year old males watch *EastEnders* but quantitative research is necessary to determine why they watch it.

RAJAR – Radio Joint Audience Research is an organisation involving the BBC and commercial radio, similar to BARB, that is responsible for controlling the system of calculating audience figures for radio.

Ratings – the estimated numbers of people who watch or listen to broadcast programmes and seen to be a guide to the relative success of broadcast material. (See also **BARB** and **RAJAR**.)

Readership – this does not simply refer to those who buy a newspaper or magazine, but the total number of people who are likely to read the publication: usually considered to be three or four times the number of copies actually sold.

Realism – the dominant mode of representation in television, mainstream films and print. The term usually implies that the media text attempts to represent an external reality: a film or television programme is 'realistic' because it accurately reproduces that part of the real world to which it is referring. The concept is, however, much more complex than this brief definition.

Reithian – defines attitudes to broadcasting typified by the views of the first Director General of the BBC, Sir John Reith. His philosophy was that broadcasting was an ideal opportunity to educate and enlighten the public with high quality broadcasting and he rejected the view that the public should be given what they wanted. He also believed that broadcasting should be free of all commercial imperatives.

Re-badged – see **badged**.

Representation – the process of making meaning in still or moving images and words/sounds. In its simplest form, it means to present or show someone or something. However, as a concept for debate, it is used to describe the process by which an image or similar may be used to represent or stand for someone or something. For example, a place or an idea. Inherent in this second definition is the notion that there may be a responsibility on the part of the producer for any representation, with regard to accuracy, 'truth' and the viewpoints and opinions that such a representation may perpetuate.

Saturated colour – colours that are extremely rich and vivid. **De-saturated** colours are pale and watery.

Scheduling – the process by which programmes are broadcast at particular times and in particular sequences to maximise their potential audiences.

Scopophilia – means literally 'the pleasure of looking' and is often discussed in conjunction with the term **voyeurism**, meaning to observe people without their permission or their knowledge. Many theorists have considered the whole basis of cinema through scopophilia and voyeurism with the audiences sitting in the dark watching the action unfold. Many films have used the act of voyeurism as an integral part of the action such as Alfred Hitchcock's *Rear Window* (1954) and Michael Powell's *Peeping Tom* (1960).

Secondary research – research into information or opinions already in existence, including material from books, study guides and other resources such as newspapers, magazines, journals, videos, DVDs and television documentaries. (See also **primary research**.)

Semiology/semiotics – the study of sign systems and their function in society.

Shot-reverse shot – a standard technique for filming a conversation in which shots from one character's point of view are intercut with those of the second speaker.

Signifier – the Swiss linguist Ferdinand de Saussure established a division of signs into two constituent parts: the signifier (the physical form that we perceive through our senses) and the signified (the mental concept of what it refers to, or means). Barthes gave the example of the rose – we perceive it as a flower (the signifier) but if given to a girlfriend by a young man it becomes a sign (the signified) and signifies his romantic passion.

Social realism – a form of realism that attempts to capture in a 'true to life' manner, the lives of urban working-class communities. (See also **Kitchen sink drama** and **British New Wave**.)

Stereotype – an over-simplified representation of people, places or issues giving a narrow set of attributes. Stereotypes are frequently thought to be entirely negative but this is not necessarily the case.

Stop-motion – this technique may be used as a simple special effect, initially used by George Melies. By stopping the camera during a shot, adding or removing something from view and continuing to shoot, the impression is given of objects appearing or disappearing from the frame. When used with a series of single frames this creates the illusion of animation and is called **pixillation**.

Storyboard – the planning of a moving image text by using a series of drawings with written instructions for the methods of filming.

Stripping – (also occasionally referred to as **stranding**) the form of scheduling on television whereby the same strand or genre of programming (e.g. sport, soap opera, consumer programmes) is offered at the same time every day, every week.

Style – this refers to the 'look' of a media text, its surface appearance. It can be recognised (according to the medium), by the use of colour, **typography**, graphic design and layout, vocabulary, photography or illustration, mise-en-scène, lighting, music, camera angle, movement, framing, dialogue, editing and so on.

Suture – a common term in medicine for stitching a wound. In film studies it refers to the way in which a spectator is 'stitched' into or becomes fully involved with the film text and is drawn into the illusion of the 'whole reality' of the film.

Synchronous/asynchronous sound – synchronous sound is where the sound matches the action or speech in film or television. Asynchronous sound is when there is a mismatch – the most obvious example is when **lip-synch** is out, in other words, when the words spoken and the lip movements of the actor on screen do not match.

Synergy – the establishment of the relationship between different areas of the media for mutual benefit. This may or not be within the same organisation, although conglomerates such as AOL/Time Warner and News Corporation are in enviable positions to make the most of such opportunities. An example might be when the launching of a new film is accompanied by the promotion of a wide range of merchandise, or just a CD of the music. Synergy between films and music is quite common. A more rare example occurred in 2000 between a novel and music. The success of the best selling novel by Vikram Seth, set in the world of classical music, *An Equal Music* led to the production of a CD featuring all the music referred to in detail within the novel.

Tabloid – a 'half-sized' newspaper. The term is, strictly speaking, related to the size only but is frequently used critically referring to newspapers such as *The Sun* and *The Mirror* (these are also referred to as **red-top tabloids**). *The Daily Mail* and *The Daily Express* are referred to as mid-market tabloids. It should be pointed out that several broadsheet newspapers have tabloid supplements.

Take – a take is a single run of film (or video) as it records a shot. In commercial filmmaking several takes of the same shot would be filmed until a satisfactory one has been achieved. A **long take** is a single uninterrupted shot that lasts longer than the usual few seconds to half a minute or so.

Teasers – short phrases on the front cover of a newspaper or magazine to tempt a reader to buy the publication. **Teaser trailers** are short film or television trailers shown before a full-length trailer is released.

Terrestrial – transmissions of radio and television that are from land-based transmitters.

Tone – the overall impression that is given by a media text such as serious, comic, romantic, sensationalist etc.

Tracking shot – (also referred to as a **dolly shot**) originally used when a camera was moved along on rails or tracks to follow the action. When the camera was removed from the rails and placed on a platform with wheels or castors the platform was referred to as a dolly, hence a dolly shot. These shots are also referred to as **trucking** or **travelling shots**.

Two-shot – literally a shot with two people in the same frame.

Bibliography

Books

Abercombie N, *Television and Society*, Polity Press, 1996.

Andrew G, [Ed.] and Bertolucci B, *Film: The Critics' Choice*, Aurum Press, 2001.

Ang I, *Watching Dallas*, Routledge, 1985.

Bordwell D and Thompson K, *Film Art: An Introduction*, McGraw-Hill Publishing Company, 2000.

Brewster B and Broughton F, *Last Night a DJ Saved My Life*, Headline, 2000.

Buckingham D, *Public Secrets Eastenders and Its Audience*, Routledge, 1987.

Buckland Warren, *Teach Yourself Film Studies*, Teach Yourself, 1998.

Cantor M, *Prime Time Television,* London, 1994.

Cartwright M, Hague A and Lavery D, *Deny All Knowledge: Reading the X-Files*, Syracuse University Press, 1996.

Cashmore E, *And then there was television*, London, 1994.

Chambers C, *Behind the media: Newspapers*, Heinemann, 2001.
   A fairly straightforward account of how a newspaper is produced. Some good tips along the way and a lot of useful institutional information.

Christiansen H-C and Magnussen A, [Eds], *Comics and Culture: 13 Analytical and Theoretical Approaches to Comics*, Museum Tusculanum Press, 2000.
   A useful reader containing a range of writing from academics interested in the comic genre and its contribution to the cultural landscape. Some are very readable, others quite obscure but this is a good introduction to a range of academic thinkers.

Coleman J and Rollet B, *Television in Europe*, Intellect Books, 1997.

Cook David A, *A History of Narrative Film*, W.W. Norton, 1996.

Cook P, and Bernink M. [Eds], *The Cinema Book*, BFI (British Film Institute) Publishing, 1999.

Corner J, [Ed.], *Popular Television in Britain: Studies in Cultural History*, BFI (British Film Institute) Publishing, 2001.

Crafton D, *Before Mickey: The Animated Film 1898–1928*, University of Chicago Press, 1982.

Creeber G, Miller T and Tulloch J [Eds], *The Television Genre Book*, BFI (British Film Institute) Publishing, 2001.

Crisell A, *An Introductory History of British Broadcasting*, Routledge, 1997.

Eisenstein S M, *Eisenstein on Disney*, Seagull Books, 1993.

Fiske J, *Television Culture*, Routledge, 1987.

Frith S, Goodwin A and Grossberg L [Ed.], *Sound and Vision; The Music Video Reader*, Routledge, 1993.
A detailed academic study of the music video.

Frith S and Straw W [Eds], *The Cambridge Companion to Pop and Rock*, Cambridge University Press, 2000.
Not directly focused on music video but a good primer and reference work.

Goldman Rohm W, *The Murdoch Mission*, J Wiley & Sons Inc, 2001.
A very detailed analysis of the NewsCorp institution and Murdoch's role in shaping its future.

Hall P, Codrington A, Hirshfeld J [Ed.] and Barth [Ed.], *Pause: 59 Minutes of Motion Graphics*, Laurence King Publishing, 2000.
Lots of pictures and some helpful information.

Hayward S, *Cinema Studies: The Key Concepts*, Routledge, 2000.

Hill J and Church Gibson P, [Eds], *The Oxford Guide to Film Studies*, Oxford University Press, 1998.

Hollows J, and Jancovich M, [Eds], *Approaches to Popular Film*, Manchester University Press, 1995.

Horstmann R, *Writing for Radio*, A&C Black, 1997.

Keeble R, *The Newspapers Handbook*, Routledge, 2001.
Reprinted several times, this is probably the best book to start with, it is almost a definitive work about newspapers.

Kelly R, *The Name of This Book is Dogma 95*, Faber and Faber, 2000.

Laybourne K, *The Animation Book*, Random, 1998.

Le Grice M and Cubitt S, [Preface] *Experimental Cinema in the Digital Age*, BFI (British Film Institute) Publishing, 2001.

Lord P and Sibley B, *Creating 3-D Animation, The Aardman Book of Filmmaking:* Harry N Abrams Inc, 1998.

Luckhurst T, *This Is 'Today'*, Aurum Press, 2001.

McCloud S, *Understanding Comics*, Harper Collins, 1994.
Highly recommended as an introduction to theoretical study of comics this is a detailed history of the form with plenty of examples and detailed deconstruction. It is presented as a comic but the level of the discussion makes it an important book.

McCloud S, *Reinventing Comics*, Harper Collins, 2000.
Sequel to *Understanding Comics* bringing digital and electronic media into the discussion – a useful overview of the ways the medium is changing.

McKee R, *Story*, Methuen Publishing Ltd, 1999.

McLeish R, *Radio Production*, Focal Press, 1999.

MacLoughlin S, *Writing for Radio*, How To Books, 2001.

Maltin L, *Mice and Magic*, New American Library, 1987.

Masterman L, [Ed.], *Television Mythologies*, Routledge, 1984.

Monaco J, *How to Read a Film*, Oxford University Press Inc, USA, 2000.

Nelmes J, [Ed.], *An Introduction to Film Studies*, Routledge, 1999.

Newton J, *The Burden of Visual Truth: The Role of Photojournalism in Mediating Reality* (Lea's Communication Series), Lawrence Erlbaum Associates, 2000.
A perceptive and detailed study of the role and function of photojournalism within newspapers and society as a whole.

Nowell-Smith G, [Ed.], *The Oxford History of World Cinema*, Oxford University Press, 1997.

Proctor W, *The Gospel According to the New York Times: How the world's most powerful news organisation shapes your mind and values*, Broadman and Holman Publishers, 2000.
Heavy-going in places but a very detailed study of the relationship between institution and audience.

Reah D, *The Language of Newspapers*, Routledge, 1998.
A detailed study of the ideologies operating within newspapers and society with a good range of examples.

Reiss S, Feineman N, Harry N Abrams Inc, *Thirty Frames Per Second: The Visionary Art of the Music Video*, 2000.
Lots of pictures and some good inspiration.

Romanek M, *Mark Romanek: Music Video Stills*, Arena, 1999.
Lots of inspiration. Very useful for research about some of the major exponents of the genre, but mostly pictures again

Sabin R, *Comics, Comix and Graphic Novels*, Phaidon Press, 2001.
A well-researched study of the entire genre with valuable examples and exploration of the relationship between theory and practice. Stronger than *Understanding Comics* on British comics.

Salisbury M, *Writers on Comics Scriptwriting*, Titan Books, 1999.
A series of interviews with comic artists. There is a lot to be gleaned from this in terms of the understanding of production practice although there is a lot of less relevant stuff as well.

Swann P, *TV Dot Com: The Future of Interactive Television*, TV Books, 2000.

Taylor J, *Body Horror: Photojournalism, Catastrophe and War (Critical Image)*, New York University press, 1998.
A thought-provoking study reflecting on the use of disturbing news images in newspapers and on television and the impact these images have on an audience.

Thomas and Johnson, *The Illusion of Life: Disney Animation*, Hyperion, 1997.

Thompson K and Bordwell D, *Film History: An Introduction*, McGraw-Hill Publishing Company, 1994.

Tulloch J, *Television Drama*, London, 1990.
Vineyard J, *Setting Up Your Shots*, Focal, 2000.
Wells P, *Understanding Animation*, Routledge, 1998.
Whitaker H and Halas J, *Timing for Animation*, Focal Press, 1981.
Wilby and Conroy, *The Radio Handbook*, Routledge, 1999.
Wright N, *The Classic Era of American Comics*, Prion Books Ltd, 2000.
  A useful history of the beginnings of the genre as we know it today.

Websites and e-zines

http://www.imdb.com
  Probably the most useful film archive on the web. Contains information for almost every film produced globally, with a fully searchable archive and links to useful institutional and textual information

Film

http://www.absoluteauthority.com/Film_Studies/
  A useful site with links to some informative theory sections
http://www.aber.ac.uk/media/Sections/film.html
  Media and Communications site index for film section – a good starting point for many links, articles and information
http://www.ualberta.ca/~slis/guides/films/film.htm
  Substantial and informative list of academic and professional film links
http://www.film.com/
  Trailers, clips, photos and other useful information about (mostly) big studio releases
http://www.movieflix.com
  Source of clips, information and free viewing material for a range of films – useful supporting research but some obscure films
http://www.darkhorizons.com
  Another good site for access to streaming films and downloadable trailers
http://www.apple.com/trailers/
  The official Apple site for trailers

TV

http://www.bbc.co.uk/TV
  Homepage for all BBC TV channels
http://www.aber.ac.uk/media/Documents/short/usegrat.html
  Useful article by Daniel Chandler about uses and gratifications

http://www.cybercollege.com/tvp_ind.htm
  A very detailed on-line practical site about TV production
http://www.popcultures.com/articles/tv.htm
  A diverse range of theoretical articles about television and popular
  culture
http://www.granadamedia.com
  Granada television site – access to all Granada channels and television-
  related pages
http://www.itv.com/
  ITV portal site
http://www.nbc.com
  NBC television (United States)
http://www.ibb.gov/worldnet/AfricaJournal.html
  Homepage for Africa journal – television about Africa for Africa
  (includes link for live and archive broadcasts)

Comics

http://www.dccomics.com/
  Home site for many comic heroes
http://www.marvel.com/
  Home site for some of the most well-known comics and comic
  heroes
http://lcg-www.uia.ac.be/~erikt/comics/welcome.html
  Valuable links for various sites with a focus on European comedy.
  Some links are more valuable than others.
http://www.webcomics.com/
  A hive of comic activity and a good place to see many different types
  of comic and animation
http://www.comicscontinuum.com:8080/
  News and reviews about comic heroes, creators and the institutions –
  new links usually added daily
http://www.scottmccloud.com/
  Homepage for Scott McCloud who wrote *Understanding Comics* and
  Reinventing Comics – some useful information and links

Newspapers

http://www.newscorp.com/operations/newspapers.html
  Launch site for the corporation's newspapers
http://www.thesun.co.uk/
http://www.express.co.uk
http://www.mirror.co.uk
http://www.people.co.uk

Site for the *Sunday People*
http://www.megastar.co.uk
Site for the *Daily Star*
http://www.ronreason.com/dallas/guide/index.html
An interesting site with detailed information about the design decisions involved in the relaunch of the *Dallas Morning News* weekly entertainment guide – sample designs shown and detailed justification given for the final design choice

Radio

http://www.bbc.co.uk/radio
Homepage for all BBC radio stations
http://www.virginradio.co.uk
Homepage for a major commercial station
http://www.classicfm.com
Homepage for Classic FM
http://www.radio-locator.com/cgi-bin/home
Good programme for finding a wide variety of (primarily) US-based programmes which broadcast live across the internet
http://www.radio-now.co.uk/
UK-based programme giving information about streaming programmes in the UK, information about local radio stations, live football commentaries, press releases and much more information relating to UK local radio
http://www.vtuner.com
Gives a range of radio stations from around the world which can be accessed easily. The search engine is very good and the information about the quality of each programme helpful. Good for checking out the lists of the most and least popular/successful radio stations!

Video

http://www.mtv.com/music/video/
A good range of videos, good for dipping in and researching themes and trends. Reasonably strong on British bands and a fair contemporary coverage
http://www.rollingstone.com/videos/default.asp
This has a really good archive of videos for many recording artists and interviews with many as well, although there is a slight US bias at times
http://www.geocities.com/SunsetStrip/Stage/2484/thesis.html
An academic article about visual images in music videos with reference primarily to *Duran Duran*

http://www.arts.uwaterloo.ca/FINE/juhde/stonm931.htm
  An article considering the impact and control of MTV on the
  development of the music video
http://broadcast.yahoo.com/music/Music_Videos/
  Quite a range of videos, quick to download
http://www.musicvideoinsider.com/archive/issue5.html
  A music video e-zine and community intended to link and support
  music video directors. Some useful pages

Animation

http://www.awn.com
  Animation world network
http://www.pixar.com/
  Homepage for Pixar
http://www.animationartist.com
  Site with useful links/articles about animation
http://looneytunes.warnerbros.co.uk
  Warner brothers cartoon homepage
http://animation.about.com/mbody.htm
  Useful articles
http://www.animationmagazine.net/
  An academic site
http://www.animationjournal.com/
  Peer reviewed academic journal
http://www.animationartgallery.com/
  Site where you can buy original Disney cels etc.
http://www.aardman.com/
  Homepage for Aardman
http://memory.loc.gov/ammem/oahtml/oahome.html
  Library of Congress site with downloadable (large!) examples of early
  American animations including Krazy Kat

Index

Page numbers in *italics* refer to illustrations.